Prime-Time Television

Prime-Time Television

A Concise History

Barbara Moore, Marvin R. Bensman,
and Jim Van Dyke

Westport, Connecticut
London

Library of Congress Cataloging-in-Publication Data

Moore, Barbara, 1956–
   Prime-time television : a concise history / by Barbara Moore, Marvin R. Bensman,
and Jim Van Dyke.
        p. cm.
   Includes bibliographical references and index.
   ISBN 0–275–98142–8
   1. Television broadcasting—United States—History. I. Bensman, Marvin R., 1937–
II. Van Dyke, Jim, 1947– III. Title.
PN1992.3.U5M623 2006
384.550973—dc22   2005034612

British Library Cataloguing in Publication Data is available.

Library of Congress Catalog Card Number: 2005034612
ISBN: 0–275–98142–8

First published in 2006

Praeger Publishers, 88 Post Road West, Westport, CT 06881
An imprint of Greenwood Publishing Group, Inc.
www.praeger.com

Printed in the United States of America

The paper used in this book complies with the
Permanent Paper Standard issued by the National
Information Standards Organization (Z39.48–1984).

10 9 8 7 6 5 4 3 2 1

Contents

Introduction

This book examines trends in the prime-time programming of the broadcast networks. Because television is a direct descendant of radio, we begin back in the 1920s to understand the foundations of the medium. Then we examine programs by genre until press time for this book, 2005.

The obvious question is: How did the authors decide on which programs to include and which to emphasize? The answer is that we chose the programs on a fairly idiosyncratic basis. Which shows had an impact on the industry or on the audience? Which were interesting to the historian, perhaps because they were innovative or influential? We chose some because they were typical of a genre in an era. We apologize if we overlooked one of your favorites.

As for our commentary, we are academics who have studied the history of TV programming, but we confess that our opinions are more reflective of the viewpoints of fans. (But like sports fans, we reserve the right to be critical and make fun of what we love.)

Underlying our analysis are some assumptions about the major influences on programming:

- Law and regulation—The radio and television industry is regulated by the Federal Communications Commission (FCC). Sometimes, the impact is direct. For example, the FCC has said that broadcasters can't use indecent language or images during the hours when children are likely to be listening. (This rule doesn't apply to cable networks and pay channels.) Sometimes, the impact is indirect. When the FCC eliminated the restrictions on the amount of programming a network could produce, networks began to schedule more of their own productions in order to increase profits. Underlying the power of the FCC is that station affiliates always know that they can lose their licenses if they have serious violations of FCC rules. No other medium faces as heavy a burden of regulation.

- Technology—This consideration is sometimes obvious. When radio programming moved to television, stars who were physically wrong for a show had to be replaced. When television went from black and white to color, the western, *Bonanza*, with its colorful scenery, was introduced. Production techniques, acting styles, and content changed as the medium went from live broadcasts to film, and then to videotape. And the crisp, clear pictures of digital will have an impact soon, as well.

- The Industry—Radio and television have been dominated by the networks, CBS, NBC, and ABC. Later, Fox, WB, UPN, and others were added. Some production companies and talent agencies had a major influence on the shape of programming. As owners changed and these companies entered the age of the conglomerate, budgets and priorities for programming changed. But the purpose of the television business has always been to make a profit, and all decisions about content must reflect that goal.

- Culture—Some genres have come and gone, whereas others remain forever popular—at least so far. Variety shows disappeared as America's taste in music became more divergent. Those who wanted to hear Broadway show tunes didn't want to hear rap, and vice versa. Crime-solvers have gone from the smooth, suave private eye to the team of forensic specialists. And the vanishing of the western from the small screen could reflect several trends: (1) The lone hero was replaced by the team; (2) The change in attitude toward the treatment of Native Americans meant that it was hard to root against them as the bad guys; (3) The urban and the present were considered more interesting than the vast countryside of the past; or (4) The western's morality, with its clear-cut difference between right and wrong, may have started to seem old-fashioned and simplistic in a time of moral ambiguities.

- Leaders—Many people have imposed their personal imprint on TV programming. David Sarnoff of RCA/NBC and William Paley of CBS basically created the network business and set the model, for good or bad, on how the industry worked. Some producers have put their own creative twist to the genres of broadcasting. And many other people in a variety of positions have influenced the direction of TV programming.

- Advertising—The revenues from advertising drive the business. In the early days of radio and TV, programming was created and supervised by agencies that represented advertisers. The quiz show scandal and other problems of the era have been blamed on the timidity and interference of the agency men. The fear of displeasing the advertiser led the agency representatives to "improve" programs to suit their clients. (It is rumored that Westinghouse agreed reluctantly to a drama about the holocaust, but only if gas ovens weren't mentioned.) By 1960, the networks had taken direct control of their schedules, but pleasing the companies that spent millions of dollars purchasing time within the programs is still the purpose of the business.
- Research—Advertisers buy time in programs in order to gain an audience for the commercial message. To ascertain if sufficient people have been reached to justify the cost, research is necessary. No perfect method of measuring viewers has been found, and if it were possible, it is doubtful anyone could afford to use it. Therefore, stations, networks, and advertisers have had to settle for a variety of unsatisfactory techniques. Programmers know their success is judged by the ratings and are always eager to get an edge somehow. Now, for example, advertisers want to reach women 18 to 49 years old; therefore, many of the shows on TV are aimed at that target. If the goal changes or if the method of measuring changes, then programs will change to meet the new challenges.

In the book, we use some terms that may be familiar, but the exact meaning of which may be uncertain. Here we define them:

- *Broadcasting*—sending out a signal via airwaves to a large number of receiving sets simultaneously. This technology is in contrast to cable, where signals reach the TV set via a coaxial cable or fiber optic wire.
- *Networks*—the organizations that send programs simultaneously to stations in cities and towns around the United States. These stations are called *affiliates*, and they broadcast the signal to the home, where it's received on your antenna, or they can deliver the signal to the cable system, which brings it into your home via wire. We talk only about ABC, CBS, NBC, Fox, WB, UPN, and Pax, but there are other networks: for example, PBS for noncommercial broadcasting and Telemundo and Univision for Spanish-language programming.

- *Syndication*—Stations basically have three sources for programming: (1) They can produce it themselves—for example, local news; (2) they can get it from their network; or (3) they can buy it from outside suppliers—in other words, syndicators. These syndication companies sell reruns of network shows, movies, talk shows like *Oprah* and *Dr. Phil*, game shows like *Jeopardy* and *Wheel of Fortune*, entertainment news shows like *ET*, courtroom shows like *Judge Judy*, and fiction like *Xena* and *Star Trek: The Next Generation*.
- *Prime-Time*—Originally, 7:00 to 11:00 P.M. Eastern Standard Time was considered the time period when the number of viewers was at its height and, therefore, when the potential for ad revenue was the greatest. Later an FCC rule said that network affiliates could schedule network programs only from 8:00 to 11:00 P.M., except Sundays when it remained 7:00 to 10:00 P.M. Now ABC, CBS, and NBC still consider 8:00 to 11:00 P.M. Monday–Saturday and 7:00 p.m. to 11:00 P.M. Sunday as prime-time, while Fox goes from 8:00 to 10:00 P.M. Monday–Saturday and 7:00 to 10:00 P.M. Sunday and WB from 7:00 to 10:00 P.M. Sunday and 8:00 to 10:00 P.M. Monday–Friday and UPN 8:00 to 10:00 P.M. Monday–Friday.

Our source of information for television programs about correct titles, names, dates, cast members, and character names was *The Complete Directory to Prime Time Network and Cable TV Shows* by Tim Brooks and Earle Marsh, now in its eighth edition; but again, the judgments of the programs are our own.

CHAPTER 1

The Heritage of Radio Programming (1927–1947)

When the technical age burst upon the world at the beginning of the twentieth century, the average person was living very much like the generations before them. Communities were isolated from each other. Transportation was primarily horse-drawn in the country, and the most prevalent means of travel in the city was the bicycle. Most people still depended upon gas or kerosene for heating, cooking, and lighting. Electricity was a novelty, and devices like the telephone were scarce and only used by businesses and the wealthy. Poverty was the norm in the urban setting. People were compelled to work 60- to 70-hour weeks to earn a minimal living. New occupations and trades were springing up: day-laborer, street-car conductor, mechanic, factory worker, teamster, clerk, grocer, restaurant worker, garment worker, salesperson, typist, and telephone operator, to name a few—and a number of these occupations were opening to women. The United States was transforming from a rural to an urban nation.

Many outdoor activities in urban areas became difficult because of limitations of time and space, and people developed the habit of watching others in the field of sports. Baseball grew into a fan-driven pastime. Boxing was no longer a gentlemen's sport, but gained mass male appeal. Theaters multiplied, providing traveling troupes of vaudeville performers with trained animal acts, acrobats, sentimental ballads and comic songs, jugglers and magicians, comedians, and dancing acts. On a less family-oriented level there were dancehalls, shooting galleries, beer gardens, bowling alleys, and billiard parlors. The well-to-do could spend their time with music, either as participants or part of an audience. The phonograph was seen as something for those who had no time to learn to play a musical instrument or who were untalented and could not carry a tune. The casting of moving light on a screen in a darkened room became a phenomenal success; the silent movie shows in "nickelodeons" evolved into multireel films with recognizable stars performing in a story.

People became used to the increasing pace of technology. They expected to be entertained even if they were illiterate and poor. They participated as audiences in mass appeal presentations that collected vast sums of money by charging small amounts to a lot of people. The structure for film, vaudeville, and the recorded music became the industry model for radio, and the technical, financial, and programming structure developed for commercial radio broadcasting became the basis for commercial television. For the most part, the same people and the same companies that had pioneered the construction of a national radio industry developed television.

In 1920 there were some five thousand amateur radio fans in the United States. Their chief amusement was picking up and listening to wireless-telephony messages, principally from ships at sea, on crude, homemade receiving sets. A number of these amateurs even experimented with transmitting their own content. But there was no entertainment or news programming. The radio existed only for communication from point to point, person to person.

BROADCASTING

Apart from a few limited demonstrations, it was not until 1920 that broadcasting in its modern sense became an actuality. (By *broadcasting*, we mean sending out a message meant to be received by a large group of people simultaneously, rather than sending a message from one person to another with a chance of outsiders listening in.) In that year enthusiasts who lived near Pittsburgh were surprised to hear music being "broadcast," though the word was hardly known. The sounds originated from the garage of Westinghouse's Dr. Frank Conrad, who was testing equipment. A number of listeners wrote to him suggesting a regular program and requesting certain songs be played. He put on the air baseball scores and popular music every Wednesday and Saturday night. Soon afterward, a Pittsburgh department store began advertising in the daily newspaper "improved radio receiving sets for listening to Dr. Conrad's concerts." Westinghouse officials suddenly realized that they had stumbled on something. Here was a way to increase sales of equipment by providing entertainment, news reports, and educational features for a mass audience.

Arrangements were promptly made to establish KDKA as a regularly scheduled broadcasting station. It formally opened on November 2, 1920, to broadcast to a few listeners the results of the Harding–Cox election for president. There were other stations on the air elsewhere, such as WWJ, Detroit, which also operated on election night. But Westinghouse's efficient promotion department got the most public attention. With the published success of the experiment, KDKA's activities expanded, and within a year other pioneer stations were established.

Radio stations grew slowly in number in 1920–1921, but then burgeoned in 1922, expanding to more than 600 stations. Programming during this early period was experimental, noncommercial and sporadic in scheduling, and subject to a great deal of interference among the growing numbers of stations that operated on one wavelength by sharing time. There were those owned by major electronics manufacturers—General Electric, Westinghouse, Stromberg, and so on. Other groups interested in broadcasting were large newspapers, department stores, and insurance companies, and the remainder were owned by churches, schools, radio repair concerns, and amateurs who operated stations "just for fun." A large number of people and companies soon seized the opportunity to operate noncommercial stations for various reasons, including the desire to get their names before the public in a favorable light. They were not always sure what to do once they were on the air, but it didn't really matter. The novelty of any broadcast made it a success.

Many went off the air when the expense of operation became too much, but others took their place. Practically all major experimentation in the development of new and improved transmitters and receivers was carried on by the manufacturers of radios. They were the "leaders" in broadcasting. There was no full-time operation by any station. In part, the manufacturers of radios broadcast to supply a reason for people to buy their products. No one yet had figured out any way to create financially self-sustaining programming.

By the mid-1920s, people were beginning to listen to radio for content as much as for the novelty of hearing voices and music from a box. The main concern of the stations was to take the few hours they were initially on the air and fill the time at no cost. This was an opportunity for the ambitious amateur, but there were some stations experimenting with broadcasting on a commercial basis. WEAF, a New York station owned by AT&T, is credited with airing the first commercial in 1923. Chiefly, it was a period in which some persons at least saw in broadcasting a possible source of revenue—from sale of time, rather than the sale of receiving sets. Others considered radio a fad that would not last.

These stations, like all other stations that followed and, later the networks, depended on live programming to fill most of their hours. There was no method of recording audio programs except by creating records, a difficult and expensive process. The announcer, the talent, the musicians—everyone was live, even the commercials. If mistakes were made, they were heard by the audience. There was no chance to redo the program or edit out anything. For fans, the live quality added to the enjoyment of radio. There was an excitement that flowed when actors and crew walked nervously on a tightrope without a net.

Station programming was still intermittent and shows would last as long as talent was available. Music was the most prevalent programming content followed by shows with a variety of performers. Traveling vaudeville performers could be enticed to appear to promote their stage appearances. Amateur talent was used less as more accomplished talent became available. But there was little or no money to pay performers. Station staff varied from station to station with the announcers becoming more recognizable and important. Part of their job was to fill in for the volunteer talent who failed to show up.

The rapid expansion of broadcasting outlets and growth of the great invisible audience constituted one of the most amazing phenomena of the decade. In 1924, the news of President Coolidge's election was sent out over a hookup of stations that reached some five million homes. Twelve years later the number of household receiving sets had more than quadrupled, and the great majority of people throughout the country learned of President Franklin Roosevelt's second election over the air.

With the rapid multiplication of broadcasting stations in those first years after 1920, the airwaves were soon featuring music, stock-market reports, accounts of sporting events, and even bedtime stories. A new entertainment industry had burst upon the scene: the first broadcast of a church service; a few months later an appeal for funds to support European relief work; the Dempsey–Carpentier fight. A growing army of radio enthusiasts realized that something important was taking place.

There was radio music in the air every night, everywhere. Anybody could hear it at home on a receiving set, which any child could assemble. Hundreds of thousands made that discovery and rushed to buy parts or complete radio sets. President Harding had a radio installed in his study at the White House. This new device annihilated the distance between people and places. The rapidity with which the radio spread cannot be easily understood today unless you compare it to the World Wide Web or iPod adoption.

There was a great deal more on the air than what might normally fall under the heading of entertainment, but radio made a spectacular advance because it was such a novel amusement. Programs covering the entire day—from fitness exercises at 6:45 A.M. to jazz at midnight—were inaugurated as early as 1923 by a few stations in major cities. Music predominated, with soprano solos proving most popular, but there were also informative talks on every conceivable subject and the beginning of radio dramas. It was radio's awkward age. Critics were concerned about its influence and became vocally worried. But the new industry seemed to be filling its primary function in providing amusement for the American people and satisfying public taste.

Legal Considerations

The increase in the popularity of radio created a technical problem. If two stations broadcast on the same frequency at the same time in the same area, they interfered with each other. The resulting static made both stations hard to hear. The obvious solution was to find a traffic cop, a government agency that could limit the number of stations, their locations, and their power. Radio had been regulated by the Department of Commerce under the Radio Act of 1912 in the days when the communication among ships was the concern. For nearly 15 years, radio operators and radio stations were licensed under this law. Stations could take any frequency, use any power, and operate any time. A system of voluntary compliance collapsed in 1926. The listening public put pressure on Congress to do something to remedy the increasing interference problems as they bought more expensive sets. New laws were necessary. Finally, the Radio Act of 1927 was passed. Network broadcasting and advertising were still relatively new concepts, and the law ignored them. Instead, the law focused on making sure stations had the equipment and personnel to follow technical guidelines to prevent interference. All stations were required to get a license from the federal regulatory agency, called the Federal Radio Commission initially, and it could be renewed only with the agency's permission. This level of control meant that broadcasting was the most regulated medium in the United States.

Could the federal government use this power to influence or control programming? The commissioners were forbidden by the law from censorship. And broadcasting was protected somewhat by the First Amendment. But when the Commission refused to renew the licenses of stations owned by a quack who prescribed his medications over the air based on listeners' letters, and by a rabble-rouser who used the airwaves to criticize religious and political groups, the Supreme Court agreed with the agency's decisions. It did have the power to make sure programming was in the public interest.

THE NETWORKS

In 1924, nationwide, stations hooked up together to share coverage of the national political conventions. A few years later, in 1926, NBC, created by a partnership of RCA, Westinghouse, and General Electric, began network broadcasting, linking stations over the entire country and enabling listeners everywhere to hear the same programs. The inaugural broadcast featured the bands of Vincent Lopez, Ben Bernie, Fred Waring, and others, plus lots of speeches. By the end of the year, NBC started up a second network, NBC Blue, with stations obtained from AT&T. The first coast-to-coast broadcast was the Rose Bowl in 1927. The programs were delivered to affiliates throughout the United States by land lines owned by AT&T. (In 1932, at the urging of the Justice Department, General Electric and Westinghouse withdrew, leaving an independent RCA and its NBC Red and Blue networks.)

The network was highly successful at providing programs to stations around the country. People in small towns could hear music, comedy, and drama from New York City. National advertisers were attracted to this widespread audience. The result was that everybody seemed to prosper.

Within a year of NBC's inauguration, a competitor appeared. CBS (named after Columbia Phonograph Co. and later purchased by William Paley, who had been in the cigar business) also offered programs to radio stations. The three networks—NBC Red, NBC Blue, and CBS—each contracted with one station in a market. The station agreed to affiliate exclusively with that network and carry its national commercials, and in return received hours of smoothly produced, highly popular programming. The station could even sell some of its local time within the shows. When the network wasn't available, the station could produce its own local programming or later buy syndicated shows. (This same deal is still the accepted way of doing business between networks and affiliates in television.)

Sensing the potentialities of a medium reaching an audience now numbering many millions, national advertisers ushered in a new era in broadcasting with sponsored programs over these networks. At first the sales effort was indirect. The A&P Gypsies played music, brought to you by A&P Grocery Stores. There was a feeling that coming into your home with a heavy-handed spiel for a product might be improper or even illegal. Leading manufacturers sought merely to associate in the mass mind the excellence of the entertainment they provided with the excellent qualities of their toothpastes, automobiles, cigarettes, mattresses, ginger ales, deodorants, watches, or cough drops.

MUSIC

It was no longer the minstrel show, the vaudeville team, or the circus that introduced new songs throughout the country. It was the radio that gave popular songs an almost instantaneous nationwide attention. There were well-developed musical shows built around specialty orchestras. Bands such as the Coon-Sanders Nighthawks became nationally known from their late evening remote broadcasts. Guy Lombardo, Paul Whiteman, Kay Kyser, Clyde McCoy, Ted Lewis, and many other dance orchestras obtained a large following and went on to do prime-time music-variety programs.

As receivers improved, they cost more and radio stations began aiming musical programs at discriminating listeners. Concert studio broadcasts introduced many to classical and semiclassical music. A large number of symphony orchestras and, later, renowned solo artists performed. The first network broadcast of a symphony orchestra was in 1926; the first sponsored one came in 1929. The Metropolitan Opera was put on the air in 1931, and Arturo Toscanini was hired as conductor of the NBC Symphony Orchestra in 1937. By 1938, it was estimated that *The Music Appreciation Hour* (NBC, 1927–1942), hosted by Walter Damrosch, was heard each week by seven million children in some 70,000 schools and that *The Ford Sunday Evening Hour* (CBS, 1934–1942), featuring the Detroit Symphony, was fifth among all radio programs in popularity. The same phenomenon took place when early TV sets were very expensive, and ballet, opera, and classical material was prevalent. The radio networks programmed primarily music and talks.

Grand Ole Opry from Nashville, Tennessee, began broadcasting a country variety format in 1925 and is still on the air. Like many other programs, it started out as a local show but became a Saturday night staple on NBC in the 1940s and 1950s. But more importantly, "hillbilly" music was elevated and introduced to people who had never heard it. Swing and jazz were popularized over radio. There was general agreement that radio was definitely changing popular taste. Many whose musical knowledge and interest would have been limited in an earlier period were now able to identify new styles and forms.

An interesting influence was exerted on the phonograph. Record playing had become one of the most popular of all home diversions. The American

Maestro Arturo Toscanini led the NBC Orchestra for radio listeners. In the early days of the medium, NBC believed the prestige of classical music enhanced the network's image and attracted wealthy consumers. Courtesy of Photofest.

people in 1919 were spending more money on phonographs and records than they were on all musical instruments, on all books and periodicals, or on all sporting goods. The radio caused an almost immediate collapse in these sales. But the networks bought up the record companies, primarily to obtain their contracts with musical talent. More expensive phonograph players, combined with radios, slowly began to make up some of this lost ground. Music in general (popular and classical in equal amounts) made up some three-fourths of radio's programs in its early years.

Unions had an influence on programming. The American Federation of Musicians (AFM) required major stations and the networks to employ staff musicians even if recordings were used. So house orchestras replaced any use of phonograph records. In 1946, Congress forbid stations from hiring unneeded personnel merely to satisfy union demands, banned unions from preventing transcriptions (a form of records), and prohibited them from preventing amateur musicians and students from broadcasts. Networks were also concerned about transcribed programs. Stations could preempt their live programs for recorded programs, and their revenues would decline. Networks were compensated for the number of stations they could promise to an advertiser for any particular program. In part, network contracts optioning affiliates' time was to prevent independent program producers (syndicators) from getting airtime. This would be a problem in TV as well.

COMEDY

By 1930, radio was well established in the United States. It had become a mass medium; well over 50 percent of the population had radios. The next 10 years saw radio undergo a great expansion—an expansion in size of audiences, of programs, and of revenue, even though the country was in the Great Depression. The forms and quality of programs greatly improved, and the Depression had relatively little effect on broadcast revenues. It was also a period of greatest "idea" development in the history of American radio—with respect to network programs in particular. By this time musical programs, situation comedies, children's programs, adventure and action shows, daytime soap operas, crime shows, adventure stories, westerns, quiz shows, prestige dramas, and news had become the familiar staples of programming.

Radio, called "the theater of the mind," had developed new art forms. "Music variety" shows were hosted by singers and bandleaders, but with plenty of comedy acts every week. For example, *The Rudy Vallee Show* (NBC, 1929–1939) starred the popular crooner and his band, but included funny interludes with regulars and guest stars. Also, an early form of "comedy variety" appeared, consisting of a series of four or five comedy "single" acts in a half-hour period. Perhaps the best example of the audience's use of imagination was the hit, *The Charlie McCarthy Show* (originally entitled *The Chase and Sanborn Hour*, NBC, 1937–1948). Edgar Bergen was a ventriloquist and Charlie his wooden companion, but to the audience the dummy was a smart-aleck character who won their hearts. Each week they would do comedy routines and bring on musical guests. The most famous show featured Mae West, the movie star. She used her sexy delivery to serve up some double entendres, and controversy ensued.

Very popular throughout the period, both on networks and locally, were two-person "acts" appearing for either 15 or 30 minutes. One of the earliest was *The Amos and Andy Show*. This was perhaps the most popular radio show of all time. Water companies attributed the lack of demand followed by a huge rush immediately following the show to the fact that the sizable audience waited until the program was finished to relieve themselves. (TV's *I Love Lucy* was credited with the same phenomenon.) Freeman Gosden and Charles Correll, both white men, performed on a five-evenings-a-week basis for a 15-minute period from 1929 to 1943. A half-hour version of *The Amos and Andy Show* lasted until 1956 when they hosted a variety show, which in turn lasted until 1960. The show was the first significant serial. It utilized cliffhanger endings to bring an audience back for the next week. The stars' success enticed vaudeville stars to seriously consider radio.

Another groundbreaking ethnic dramatic comedy serial was *The Goldbergs* (NBC, 1929–1950). The Jewish comedy was one of the first programs to

Freeman Gosden and Charles Correll captivated a nation with their performances as Amos and Andy. People bought radio sets just to hear their program. Courtesy of Photofest.

focus on the family. Its immediate success led to other shows that featured domestic situations with recurring characters and continuing story lines. The show was owned and written by Gertrude Berg, who played the lead character. She was considered one of the most important pioneer women in radio.

Some vaudeville acts made a successful transition to radio and then TV. A married team, George Burns and Gracie Allen (*Burns and Allen*, NBC, 1933–1950), had the combination of Gracie's voice and scatter-brained view of the world with George's deadpan delivery of straight lines to captivate the audience. Jack Benny's (*The Jack Benny Program*, NBC, CBS, NBC, 1932–1958) radio career became legendary. He introduced many bits that ran on and on and became a part of his show business persona, such as a mock feud with comic Fred Allen, which made great copy and boosted his ratings.

A satirist and friend of George Burns and Jack Benny, Fred Allen (*The Fred Allen Show*, NBC, 1932–1949) focused on topical humor. He developed

Major Bowes sat behind his desk for his *Original Amateur Hour*. Aspiring talent tried to win the applause of the live audience and the hearts of the radio audience, while avoiding the sound of the gong. Courtesy of Photofest.

a format revolving around a different occupation each week. Half of the show consisted of low-budget amateur talent. Frank Sinatra was one discovery by Allen. The amateur segment was so popular that it led to the *Major Bowes' Original Amateur Hour* (NBC, CBS, 1934–1952), another successful transplant to TV. (It can be considered an ancestor of *American Idol*.) Fred Allen did not succeed on TV, and he bitterly said, "They call it a medium because nothing on it is ever well done."

Chicago became a broadcast center for the networks as the point of origin of nearly 120 programs each week when the new NBC studios opened on top of the Merchandise Mart in Chicago in 1931. Among the better-known radio programs originating in Chicago was the long-running *Fibber McGee And Molly* (NBC, 1935–1959), a situation comedy about a wise-cracking, long-suffering wife and her charming but annoying husband. Sound familiar? Other comedy/variety shows that went on to TV after success on radio were *The Bob Hope Show* (NBC, 1935–1955) and *The Red Skelton Show* (NBC,1939–1953).

DETECTIVES

By 1930, most large stations were broadcasting a full evening schedule and two to four daytime hours. Sponsored network programs were at least 30 minutes in length; at least half of all sponsored evening programs were full-hour broadcasts. An early type of variety program was carried on networks from their beginnings—*variety* in the sense of "using a different type of material each week"—one week a musical program, another week a debate, a third week a dramatization, and so on. Dramatic programs, using materials adapted for radio from short stories or original materials appeared as early as 1927. Dramatic forms included hour-long serious dramas, 30-minute "thrillers," both 30-minute and 15-minute "light" or "homey" drama, and 30-minute informative programs mostly about historical events. The first westerns and thriller dramas began in this period.[1]

Program production companies originated in the early days of radio to supply programs. One of the earliest was owned by Phillips Lord, who created and produced such thrillers on network radio as *Gang Busters, Mr. District Attorney*, and *Counterspy*. Other important radio programmers included Carleton B. Morse, who produced *One Man's Family* and *I Love a Mystery*, among others. Frank and Anne Hummert packaged at least a dozen different daytime "soaps," so called because they were sponsored by laundry detergents. Ralph Edwards was responsible for the quiz show *Truth or Consequences* and produced the reality show *This is Your Life*.

Crime drama was a popular feature. *Gang Busters* (NBC, 1935–1957) had one of the most recognized openings, using sound effects, rather than music. A police whistle. Shuffling feet like in a chain gang or prison yard. Gunshots. A breaking window. The sharpness of a burglar alarm. A police siren. Machine gun firing. Tires screeching as if in a getaway.

Big Town (CBS, 1937–1952) was one of the most famous shows about crime reporters. The first cast had Edward G. Robinson as Steve Wilson. The show attempted to deal with current societal problems. It opened with a stirring echoing voice: "Freedom of the Press is a flaming sword! Use it justly; hold it high; guard it well!"

Covering crime from the prosecutor's position was *Mr. District Attorney* (NBC, 1939–1953). It was supposedly inspired by Thomas E. Dewey, New York's district attorney, who parlayed fighting racketeers into becoming state governor and then two unsuccessful runs as a Republican for President.

The cast of *Gang Busters*, a popular radio crime show, is shown gathered around the microphone. The sound effects technicians on the right added gunshots and other noises to make the program seem real to listeners. Courtesy of Photofest.

"Mr. District Attorney! Champion of the people! Guardian of our fundamental rights to life, liberty and the pursuit of happiness! (Music swells-Echo)...and it shall be my duty as district attorney not only to prosecute to the limit of the law all persons accused of crimes perpetrated within this county but to defend with equal vigor the rights and privileges of all its citizens."

OTHER GENRES

A number of serials and soap operas made the cut in the 1930s. Once considered to be classic but forgotten by everyone except aficionados is *Vic & Sade* (NBC, 1932–1945). The five-day-a-week comedy serial from Chicago was about the Gooks, a middle-class Midwest family, doing mundane things. It was placed between tear-jerking soap operas. The show consisted of only three, and later, four voices. *The Andy Griffith Show* has been called the nearest thing to *Vic & Sade*. *One Man's Family* (NBC, 1932–1959) had the distinction of being a prime-time soap opera with lasting power—3,276 episodes; the longest uninterrupted narrative on radio. It appeared to be literature as it was divided into books and chapters. The final program was Chapter 30 of Book 134.

Other formats became popular in the mid-1930s. The quiz show began to become popular in prime time during the late 1930s. *Dr. I.Q.* and *Information Please!* were examples.

Suspense and *Inner Sanctum* were programs designed to give the audience an entertaining scare. The listeners—using the dialogue, the plot, the music, and the sound effects—could conjure up a world of thrills and chills limited only by their imagination. The villains and the heroes looked exactly the way the audience wanted them to look. The listeners could create the most frightening monsters and the most spectacular visual effects in the theater of their own mind. To true fans of radio, the visual element of television was a limitation, not an addition.

Children came home from school and listened to animal adventure dramas like *Rin-Tin-Tin* (NBC, CBS, 1930–1955), about a heroic dog. Other early children's adventure shows, such as *Captain Midnight* (Mutual, 1939–1949) grew out of the flying craze of the decade. *Terry and the Pirates* (NBC, 1937–1948), from a comic strip, was one of the most action-packed adventure stories and was noted for its strong anti-fascism storyline. The comics also gave us *The Adventures of Superman* (Mutual, 1940–1951). The radio and then TV thrilling opening still brings memories alive: "It's a bird! It's a plane! It's *Superman*." (It was never quite the same on TV with George Reeves wearing long johns.) There were also teenage situation comedies; the most popular was *The Aldrich Family* (NBC, 1939–1952), in which, thanks to the magic of radio, Henry Aldrich could remain 16 years old forever.

As indicated by the previously mentioned shows, a fourth network, the Mutual Broadcasting System, was organized in 1934 and originally consisted of only four stations, but during 1935 from 50 to 60 additional stations were

MERCHANDISING

An example of the merchandising of toys and premiums in connection with TV programs was Ralston Purina's sponsorship of *Space Patrol*. Sponsorship of a program was not just to sell a product but to profitably tie in with the show. In 1952, the company had been one of the most prolific sources of premiums on radio with Tom Mix and his Ralston Straight Shooters, and it made the crossover from radio to television with its merchandising. With small change and a box top from the sponsor's product, children could get cardboard mock-ups of the spaceport Terra City, Rocket Ships, Toy Space-a-phones, Ray Guns, magnifying goggles, and official belts with buckles that had decoders built in. There was an official "Top Secret Space Patrol United Planets Treasury Dept. Diplomatic Pouch" filled with paper goods, and the Cosmic Smoke Gun.

Buck Rogers also spawned toys throughout its tenure. In about 1952, the Zooka Pop Pistol, a gun identical to a 1930s Rocket Pistol, except for its bright, multi-colored finish, was put into toy stores. A short while after the Zooka Pop Pistol, the Rocket Dart Pistol, a toy that shot darts instead of simply making a popping noise was produced. The last two Buck Rogers ray guns of the mid-1950s were flashlight guns. The Sonic Ray flashlight became so popular that it served as a model for subsequent flashlight guns made by other companies. Later, the Super Sonic Ray was even more successful. With its fluted, trumpet-like barrel, and rakishly exaggerated rear site, it had an imposing visual presence—perfect for scaring off unfriendly space aliens.

The merchandising produced by the ad agencies behind *Tom Corbett, Space Cadet* was also a factor in its success. Children could get books, comics, comic strips, toys, premiums, records, games, and other items about their favorite hero.

The FCC now forbids broadcasters from selling a product directly tied to a children's program within the show, but all producers hope their animated characters will attract a loyal audience of kids who will buy anything connected to their favorite characters. Of course, children's programming has now almost disappeared from prime-time broadcasting; it's been banished to afternoons, weekend mornings, and cable.

added because of the success of *The Lone Ranger* (1933–1956). In terms of programs, however, Mutual was not a serious rival to the older networks.

NEWS

News reports—not only sports and market prices but foreign and domestic news—grew as World War II approached in the late 1930s. The radio commentator became a new figure on the air. CBS's president, William Paley, hired knowledgeable men to comment on the daily news. In December 1930, Paul White, from the United Press wire service, was hired by Paley as CBS's news editor. To get White, Paley gave him the responsibility for three five-minute newscasts a day and the power to interrupt programs for breaking news stories. NBC employed A. A. Schechter, who had reported for the Associated Press and International Press services. The first sponsored network newscast was *Lowell Thomas and the News* on NBC in 1931, sponsored by Sun Oil, who also sponsored the first TV network newscast. Other commentators who obtained star status were H. V. Kaltenborn, Gabriel Heatter, and Fulton Lewis, Jr.

The American Newspaper Publishers Association applied pressure to the wire services to limit radio's use so that no breaking news could be used until newspapers had been distributed. They dictated that newspapers should not print program schedules on their entertainment pages. The so-called Press–Radio War had started. CBS hired part-time reporters and opened bureaus around the world, while NBC ran up huge bills using the telephone to contact newsmakers and officials to put them directly on the air.

After a year, the newspapers opened a Press-Radio Bureau to feed bulletins to the networks for two brief unsponsored newscasts daily, timed to be broadcast after newspapers had hit the streets. Among other restrictions, all newscasts had to end with the following disclaimer: "Details can be found in your daily newspaper." But it was too little too late. The networks' own efforts at news had already proven successful. By 1935, United Press and International News Service agreed to sell news to radio stations and networks.

The networks had developed technology to get the news via short wave. They created a staff of "commentators" who were really news reporters. Edward R. Murrow was hired by William Paley in 1935 and in 1937 was sent to London as Director of Talks. He set up a group of reporters who on March 13, 1938, began a "World News Roundup" from capitols around Europe. In 1939, with England and Germany at war, Murrow broadcast live from a bombarded London. News reports grew in number daily. The voices of these radio reporters were soon familiar to everyone in the United States.

Graham McNamee was one of the first sportscasters. He called football and baseball games and interviewed the greats like Babe Ruth. Sports played an important role in attracting listeners to radio. Courtesy of Photofest.

WAR OF THE WORLDS

In this climate of pending war, Orson Welles caused a sensation. CBS had hired Welles's and John Houseman's Mercury Theatre group for weekly radio dramatic adaptations of literary works. The show was moved from Monday to Sunday opposite the very popular *The Charlie McCarthy Show* (NBC, 1937–1956). For Halloween 1938, Welles had Howard Koch write his first professional script. He adapted H.G. Wells's classic, *War of the Worlds*, to radio. It was set in the present and took place in New Jersey, near Princeton. Koch utilized Welles's idea of having the sound of radio news bulletins in the first half of the show. Listeners heard what appeared to be interruptions of an ongoing network music broadcast. The program was sustaining (non-sponsored). Apparently, few listeners heard the opening of the Mercury Theatre program. When the McCarthy show broke for their first commercial some people tuned over to CBS, like today's channel surfers. A number of people came upon the first bulletins about gas eruptions being seen on the planet Mars. Some were hooked and continued to listen as the story unfolded; others believed they were hearing news of a real invasion and panicked. The half-hour came with the standard station break, and the second half of the show was almost a soliloquy about how the Martians came to their end. When police entered the studio at the end of the show, confiscating scripts and questioning actors, there was a great deal of concern about the panic caused by the program. The press had a fantastic story and Orson Welles's reputation was made. A number of lawsuits were filed against CBS; all settled out of court. The FCC investigated and banned interruptions of programs for fake announcements.

Orson Welles, on the left, performed in *War of the Worlds*, a production of his Mercury Theatre. The result was panic and fear across the country, as the radio audience began to believe the story was really a newscast. Courtesy of Photofest.

The Office of Radio Research at Princeton University received a grant the day after the program and immediately surveyed people who said they had listened to the broadcast. Hadley Cantril's "Invasion from Mars" is a classic study of the effects of propaganda. No other radio program in the history of broadcasting has had such a long-lasting and profound effect. A recreation in Spanish in 1949 led to rioting and several lives lost in Quito, Ecuador. Orson Welles went on to Hollywood to make his first film, *Citizen Kane*, which is considered one of the best films ever made.

THE AUDIENCE

Throughout the day, housewives, half listening to the radio as they went about their work, were regaled with health talks, fashion hints, recipes, and general household advice, much as happens today with those at home during the day who half listen to and watch TV. The introduction of daytime drama produced the practice of five-day-a-week daytime "across-the-board" programming. Prior to 1932, daytime programming had been scheduled like evening hours, on a one-time-a-week basis. The thought that housewives would be of value to advertisers was new, and the difficulties of providing serious drama in continuous segments was daunting. But the story lines developed by writers like Irna Phillips and Frank and Annie Hummert gave women hope in the economic hard times of the Depression that common people could overcome difficulties. The longest-running soap opera in broadcast history, *The Guiding Light* (CBS 1937–1956) continues to this day on TV. The last seven daytime serials ended on CBS radio in 1960.

The invisible audience continued to grow. The 12 million sets in use in 1930 increased to some 40 million by 1940. More than four-fifths of the entire population could listen in, and sometimes did on special occasions. There were not only radios in more than 26 million private homes, but they could be found in countless clubs, taverns, hotels, schools, hospitals, and other institutions, and also a greater number of them in automobiles. The radio became one of the most commonplace features of American life. Here was something for all the family. In planning any social function, one had to allow for the program schedule.

ADVERTISING

From an economic as well as social point of view, radio had become immensely important. Its advertising potential grew as manufacturers and retail merchants increasingly geared their selling campaigns to radio programs. Never before had entertainment become not only such a big business in itself, but also an integral part of the country's basic economic system. Radio reached more people than any other medium. Every study of how people spent their leisure time in these years before World War II placed listening highest on the list of popular amusements.

There were important changes in the broadcast advertising picture. As a result of the Depression, networks let down the bars with respect to commercials. No longer was the message buried subtly in the program. For the first time, advertisers were allowed to sell directly with clear calls for the consumer to buy.

The radio advertisers bought time on networks and owned the programs. Their advertising agencies became creators and producers. Advertisers and their agencies owned and controlled their own programs, and the networks and stations just provided the broadcast facilities and technicians. The agency representing the advertiser could choose a program, its stars, and its writers, and oversee all of the creative elements. For the hours when sponsors didn't offer programs, the networks filled in with their own creations, always hoping for a success that would attract an advertiser willing to pay the costs of producing the show, including the talent's salaries, and to run commercials within it.

RATINGS

Advertisers had a growing interest in getting information about the radio audience. This need for information was answered by the Cooperative Analysis of Broadcasting (CAB), the first radio rating service, 1929–1946. It used the telephone recall method, in which the researcher would call the home and ask the person who answered to list programs that they had heard recently. It was bought by the American Association of Advertisers (AAA), consisting of national advertisers and agencies and cofinanced by the networks and the National Association of Broadcasters (NAB), the broadcast trade organization. It researched all advertising media. The radio data primarily showed the size of the audience per program. Since audience characteristics could not be broken down, the mass audience became the yardstick of success.

Then, C. E. Hooper (1934–1950) provided competition. Magazine publishers felt that CAB overstated radio's audience. HooperRatings methodology weighted those surveyed to make them representative of the total population. Hooper was also able to produce numbers the day following a program and achieved name recognition by providing a constant stream of publicity material to newspapers. When the CAB changed its methodology to match that of Hooper, the expense and redundancy ended its operation.

From 1941 through 1980, the A.C. Nielsen Company became the primary radio rating service. Nielsen started in the 1920s to survey a sample of retail stores and track the inflow and outflow of specific product categories. Clients requested information to help them make advertising decisions. Nielsen bought the rights to a mechanical device he named the "Audimeter" from two Massachusetts Institute of Technology professors. The device attached within a radio made a tape of when the radio was on and to what stations it was tuned. The tapes had to be retrieved each month to be read. He produced a report called the Nielsen Radio Index. One of its advantages was that it did not depend on the telephone for information. Some one-third of U.S. homes did not have a telephone, even in the 1940s. In 1946, the tape could be mailed in by the survey participant, and reports were generated every two weeks. The service expanded to include multiple sets in the home, including FM and subsequently TV.

A NEW LAW

Congress passed the Communications Act of 1934, which was almost identical to the Radio Act of 1927, except for an expansion of duties over all wired and wireless communication and a new name for the old Federal Radio Commission. There was also controversy over whether the new Federal Communications Commission (FCC) should have the same jurisdiction over networks that it did over stations. To this day, networks are not licensed, but they are vulnerable through the stations they own and operate and their affiliated stations. Some rules are written: "No station may belong to any network that . . . [fill in the blank]."

In 1940, the FCC made changes in the status of networks. It issued the "Report on Chain Broadcasting." The major effect of the report was to force NBC to sell one of its radio networks. The "duopoly" order of the FCC, effective in 1941, prohibited stations from belonging to any network that owned more than one. NBC in 1941 sold its "Blue Network" to Edward Noble of Lifesaver fame. The name of the network changed to the American Broadcasting Company.

But there were other important issues. Paley of CBS had supplied hours of sustaining (nonsponsored) programming at no cost to the affiliates to get stations to carry his network. However, the network contract specified that only CBS programming could be carried by that station. NBC, under David Sarnoff, also resorted to optioning affiliates' time, arguing that that was the only way the network could guarantee coverage to advertisers. This also had the effect of keeping stations from using syndicated (recorded or transcribed) programs and from producing more of their own programs in those lucrative time periods. And, of course, NBC and CBS had affiliated with the stations that reached the most people with the best signals. A new competitor would have to settle for leftovers.

The FCC in its report ruled that network contracts could not prevent stations from preempting network programming at will. This decision was likely the result of Gillette buying exclusive rights to the World Series for 1939 and 1940. Prior to this all the networks broadcast the Series. Gillette then contracted with the Mutual network to exclusively broadcast the Series. Mutual had to sign up NBC and CBS affiliates to carry the games to obtain the needed coverage. NBC and CBS informed their affiliates that they were under contract to take only their network's programming and pressured stations to drop the Mutual World Series coverage. This infuriated the public and, therefore, Congress.

The second change concerned artist bureaus. Sarnoff had been averse to paying talent agents and started NBC's own agency. CBS followed and performers had to sign up with the in-house talent agencies before they could be employed by the network. Thus, the network was able to get 10 percent off the price of the artist. The FCC found that serving as both agents and employers of artists was a conflict of interest. (In other words, negotiating with yourself brings the temptation to cut a deal that may harm the represented artist.)

WORLD WAR II

Before the U.S. entrance into World War II, NBC remained the leading network both in program popularity and in income; CBS was a strong second; ABC a weak third; Mutual a much weaker fourth. On December 7, 1941, CBS's John Daly was the first to report the Japanese attack on Pearl Harbor and the U.S. entrance in the war.

Radio made more money than ever before during the war for a number of reasons. Newsprint was rationed, but radio could provide air time for programs and commercials. War industries with rationed products that were buying evening network time were interested in prestige programming; ratings were of secondary importance as they had little product to sell to the public. Therefore, many war industries presented informative dramatic programs—in some cases, virtually documentaries—dealing with their contribution to the war effort. Another factor that had some effect was the Congressional enactment of a law imposing a 90 percent tax on the excess profits of war contractors, allowing them only a reasonable return. A company whose income was subject to the tax was allowed to deduct advertising as a legitimate business expense; thus, advertising had a net cost of 10 cents on the dollar. Even industries engaged entirely in war production with no goods to sell to the consumer advertised heavily to keep their competitive position so when the war came to an end, they would have retained the goodwill of consumers.

Broadcasting could have been censored in a time of war by the government, as it was everywhere else in the world. NBC, CBS, and Mutual issued a joint declaration of news policy that no news analyst "is to be allowed to say anything in an effort to influence action or opinion." With the urging of CBS commentator Elmer Davis, an Office of War Information (OWI) was created five months after Pearl Harbor to bring together various disparate agencies of government that had been disseminating information to journalists. Davis was named director, and OWI expanded into the policy arena, as well as information dissemination. Davis got the networks, in voluntary cooperation, to integrate information into regular programming. Networks and stations gave copious amounts of free airtime to government programming and bond drives. Scripts were rewritten to encourage enlistment and support the war effort.

The Voice of America became a part of OWI with John Houseman appointed as its first director. Broadcasters also voluntarily went along with an Office of Censorship that presented guidelines of prohibited topics and programs (i.e., weather reports, troop movements, man-on-the-street interviews, and the downplaying of racial incidents). CBS did a dramatized documentary-style program "An Open Letter on Race Hatred" in 1943 in an effort to defuse resulting racial tension surrounding a race riot in Detroit.

There was a decrease in prime-time quiz shows and other types of human interest programs—a decrease somewhat difficult to understand, since at the same time, daytime use of such programs had increased substantially, and virtually all types of audience participation made use of those in the armed services.

The two years following the war were a highly important period in the history of American radio and television. There was an enormous increase in the total number of radio stations, the building of 108 TV stations—and the beginnings of a shift in importance from radio to television, especially on the network level.

CONCLUSION

Radio had changed society. Many people who half a century ago would not have had any idea on how to comport themselves in various social situations learned from radio. The social distance between the extremes in American life was shrunk by common experiences heard on the radio. Radio was essentially a middle-class medium and helped create a culture of the middle class with an emphasis on consumption and home-centered recreation. What had developed was an all-American standard of living.

Radio, like most new media, drew inspiration for its content from its predecessors and competition—vaudeville, Broadway, record industry, books, newspapers, movies, magazines, and so on. The audience knew the performers and the formats from these other media and felt comfortable with them. Television, in turn, borrowed heavily from radio—not only for content, but also for every element of the structure of the industry.

For example, radio stations were in towns and cities across the United States, but the stations with the best signals and the largest audiences affiliated with the networks NBC, CBS, (later) ABC, and, to a far lesser extent, Mutual. The major networks, headquartered in New York City, provided programming to stations. The programs were live, not recorded. They were overseen by advertising agencies for their clients with the networks providing technical facilities and filling in the unsponsored hours with their own productions. Because the industry was driven by revenues from advertising, measuring the size of the audience became highly important. The criterion for success was attracting the largest number of listeners.

The FCC licensed a limited number of stations to be on the air and renewed the privilege only if the station was perceived to have acted in the public interest. Unacceptable content of programs was one reason for losing a license. First Amendment protection for media kept the FCC from too much heavy-handed meddling.

This framework remained in place for television. Although the structure may sound inevitable, there were other paths that television could have followed. In many countries, radio and then TV were controlled and programmed by the federal government or its representatives; funding came from taxes. Or suppose that television had risen from the film industry. What would programming have looked like: movies without commercials? Funding could have come from a subscription charged to viewers.

Not only did the patterns of ownership and economics come from radio, but also many of the program formats and even the actual shows made the switch. Radio had provided sports, news, drama, mystery, comedy, detective shows, variety, situation comedies, quiz shows, reality programs, westerns, music, soap operas, and so on. Television borrowed all of these concepts and added very few new ones. Some stars made the transition from radio to television effortlessly: Jack Benny, George Burns and Gracie Allen, Ozzie and Harriet Nelson, and so on. Some programs worked well in both media: *Father Knows Best; The Life of Riley; My Little Margie; Our Miss Brooks; Topper; You Bet Your Life; Dr. Kildare; Gunsmoke; Have Gun, Will Travel; Your Hit Parade;* and so on. Television offered very little that was new or different to its audience in the early years. The radio listeners who became TV viewers were offered the familiar and the comfortable. The content of radio had been mainly derived from its predecessors and reflected the needs of its owners; television inherited that legacy.

CHAPTER 2

The Experimental Days of TV Programming (1939–1947)

The development of television technology depended on finding a way of converting light energy into electrical energy and then electrical energy back into light. The first successful method of scanning a scene was achieved by a mechanical, spinning disc perforated with a spiral of holes. The receiver reversed the process with its own synchronous spinning disc. During the 1920s most experimental mechanical TV stations had the audio broadcast separately over a radio station. The Federal Radio Commission (FRC) granted the first TV license to Jenkins Laboratories, Washington, D.C., which ceased to operate on October 31, 1932.

The first regular schedule of TV programming was begun by General Electric in Schenectady, New York, May 11, 1928. Programs were transmitted three afternoons a week for a total of six hours. The picture achieved was only 24 lines. (TV pictures now in the United States use 525 lines, and high definition has up to 1,080 lines.) But there are a number of other firsts for mechanical television that portended what programming would be like when electronic commercial TV was authorized.

The purpose of TV programming in those early years was purely experimental. Companies that hoped to develop television into a commercial product put on shows just to see how well they could be transmitted and received. There was no audience, except for the scientists and their employers. For example, in 1928 the first televised tennis match was presented. Al Smith accepting the Democratic presidential nomination was televised.

These were the first over-the-air remote pickup and the first TV news event. The first play, "The Queen's Messenger," was broadcast on W2XAD (owned by GE). The audio was broadcast over WGY radio. *The New York Times* gave the event page-one status the next day.

Simultaneously broadcasting both the TV and the radio version of a show, or *simulcasting*, as it came to be called, began as early as 1928, when W1XAY (C.F. Jenkins and Smith-Dodge) in Lexington, Massachusetts, simulcast one hour of WLEX radio daily. W1XAV (Shortwave and Television Laboratory) Boston broadcast a video portion of the CBS commercial radio program *The Fox Trappers Orchestra*, sponsored by I. J. Fox Furriers, although commercials were prohibited by the FRC for experimental broadcasting. W1XAV also tried on a few occasions in 1930–1931 to telecast a Boston radio station's programming. However, the FRC took a dim view of their attempts to telecast a network program and advised them not to try it.

In 1929, RCA's station began two-hour daily broadcasts, and the first public demonstration of mechanical color TV by H. E. Ives and his colleagues at Bell Telephone Laboratories in New York was offered. The first images were a bouquet of roses and an American flag using a 50-line color television image.

In 1931, W2XAB (CBS) New York began broadcasting the first regular seven-day-per-week schedule in the United States, 28 hours per week with live pickups and a wide variety of programs. The first broadcast included New York Mayor James J. Walker, singer Kate Smith, and composer George Gershwin. In that same year, NBC put the first TV transmitter atop the Empire State Building and began experimental broadcasts.

ELECTRONIC TV

But even with these firsts and considerable publicity, mechanical television was on its way out. The experimenters started working with electronic means of broadcasting signals. Vladimir K. Zworykin developed the iconoscope tube, a storage-type camera tube patented in 1923 and demonstrated publicly in 1928. At about the same time, Philo T. Farnsworth developed an electronic image-dissector tube that allowed the photoelectric current to be measured one point at a time, the output signal directly proportional to the amount of light falling on a cathode-ray tube. It was an instantaneous, or non-storage-type, tube that would be useful for scanning motion picture film but required a great deal of light for practical use in live situations.

By combining Zworykin's iconoscope and Farnsworth's image dissector, the Radio Corporation of America (RCA) laboratories, joined by

Westinghouse and General Electric engineers, worked for better picture definition and more flexibility with the equipment. RCA developed the image iconoscope camera and then the orthicon tube. Then came improved methods of producing an acceptable picture by interlaced scanning, scanning first the odd lines then the even lines. The number of lines making up the picture definition increased each year.

In 1932, RCA demonstrated an all-electronic television system with 120 lines, and its network, NBC, made a first attempt at actual programming on July 7, 1936, after six years of tests of its electronic system. The program was a 30-minute variety show strictly for RCA licensees, with speeches, a dance ensemble, a monologue, vocal numbers, and film clips.

The Federal Communications Commission (FCC), as the FRC was now known, licensed some 21 stations in 1935 and two years later adopted new television allocations. Seven new TV channels were added. Higher frequency channels were reserved for a time when workable tubes were devised that could use them.

In 1938, W2XBS (NBC) telecast the movie *The Return of the Scarlet Pimpernel*, starring Leslie Howard. The projectionist played the last reel out of order, ending the film 20 minutes early. After this incident, NBC did not obtain first-run movies for many years. The first telecast of an unscheduled event, a fire, took place from NBC's portable transmitter W2XBT, November 15, 1938. The mobile unit was in a park in Queens when a fire broke out on Ward's Island, across the river.

WORLD'S FAIR

President Franklin D. Roosevelt was the first American president to appear on television. On April 30, 1939, he gave a speech opening the New York World's Fair on W2XBS (NBC). Ten days prior to President Roosevelt's speech, David Sarnoff of RCA opened his company's exhibit to ensure that RCA would capture its share of the newspaper headlines. The ceremony was televised and watched by several hundred viewers on TV receivers at the RCA Pavilion on the fairgrounds as well as on receivers installed at Radio City, as he announced the launch of electronic television and the NBC TV network.

Television sets were available for sale at the RCA Pavilion with prices ranging from $200 to $600. These prices were considered very expensive; therefore, advertising was initially aimed at the wealthy, depicting viewers dressed in evening gowns and suits watching TV. The sets received channels 1 to 5. (The frequency for channel 1 had not yet been taken over for other uses.) Screen sizes on the four models ranged from 5 inches to 12 inches diagonally. The picture tubes were mounted in the larger-sized models vertically because of their length. A hinge-mounted mirror at the top of the receiver cabinet permitted viewing. Although people were curious, television sales right up until the beginning of World War II were disappointing.

There was one thing needed to sell more TV sets—more and better programs. The NBC station at the World's Fair offered operas, cartoons, cooking demonstrations, travelogues, fashion shows, and skaters at Rockefeller Center. There were also numerous live telecasts relayed from within the fair transmitted from the NBC mobile camera trucks to the main transmitter. The first professional football game was televised over NBC's station to some 500 or so people. But many others saw the telecast on monitors at the RCA Pavilion, where it was scheduled as a special event.

PRODUCING CONTENT

One constant of new entertainment technologies is the chicken-and-egg dilemma. For example, people won't buy an expensive TV set unless they can get a plentiful supply of desirable programming. The cost of sets won't go down until they can be mass marketed. Therefore, someone has to offer content, but how can a business afford to make the costly investment in programming that goes only to a few people? Who would advertise to such a small audience?

RCA, a TV set manufacturer and owner of patents, had hoped its network, NBC, would lure an audience and advertisers with its programming, but the public seemed reluctant to buy an expensive piece of furniture to see amateurish programming, when they had the alternative of radio, which seemed to offer so much more.

To attract new viewers, sports were an early feature of TV programming starting in 1939. The first sports telecast was likely a Princeton–Columbia baseball game. Then the first heavyweight boxing match was televised, Max Baer versus Lou Nova. The NBC station continued to bring sport firsts, such as a double-header major league baseball game between the Cincinnati Reds and the Brooklyn Dodgers. Following was the first televised college football game, Fordham versus Waynesburg, at Randall's Island, New York. In 1940, the first hockey game, Rangers versus Canadians, and the first basketball game, Fordham versus the University of Pittsburgh, were televised.

To understand the difficulty of shooting these events, imagine how awkward it was to move those big, bulky cameras (the size of refrigerators) on rollers. Sometimes only one or two cameras were used. There were no telephoto lenses that would allow a zoom in to a hockey puck or a player's face. Instead, everything was seen at a distance, as though the viewer had front-row seats but was allowed to wander up and down the sidelines. And, of course, everything was live. The audience got to view every single mishap of the TV crew.

A Tentative Start

At the beginning of 1940, the FCC held public hearings about television, and a month later announced "limited" commercial television service would be authorized on September 1. In other words, television began the slow move from experiment to a commercial reality. The technical standards were not set, pending further research on the best system possible. Until the FCC could definitely make up its mind as to the channels to be used for television, most manufacturers did not dare to attempt to produce sets. The people most likely to make the investment were the owners of radio stations. Their networks encouraged them to make the change to a new medium. Although many broadcasters believed in the future of television, the construction of a television station cost from $750,000 to $1.5 million—and that was a great deal of money to risk, when commercial television had not yet had the opportunity to prove itself.

At this point, RCA's David Sarnoff announced RCA was cutting the price of television sets and started a sales drive to put a minimum of 25,000 TV sets in homes in New York. His idea was to let the public decide what they thought of TV. The FCC chairman, James L. Fly, became extremely angry as he believed Sarnoff was attempting to freeze TV standards from any further improvement. He called a new hearing. Within two days he had the commission suspend its authorization for limited commercial service, declaring that the marketing campaign of RCA disregarded the commission's findings and recommendations.

Technical Developments

Programming continued on the still experimental stations. Then, in 1940, Peter Goldmark of CBS made an announcement that complicated the issue of what technical standards to use for TV: He introduced his invention of a color TV system, catching RCA by surprise. Within a month CBS presented the first showing of color TV on W2XAB transmitting from the Chrysler Building, using 343 lines. This was the first telecast of any kind from CBS since the closing of their mechanical TV station in 1933.

In 1941, the National Television System Committee, composed of industry engineers, set the standards for television transmission that would remain virtually the same for more than 50 years: the pictures would consist of 525 lines, 30 frames per second, or 60 fields per second, each scan covering only 262.5 lines, on channels 6 megahertz (MHz) wide. The audio signal was to be frequency modulated (FM). The two signals were joined together and transmitted from an antenna 30 to 65 miles, depending on channel placement, power, and geographic factors. Color was deemed not ready.

The FCC intended to have a system of local community stations producing their own programming, but that had been the intent for radio as well. The broadcast industry could see that interconnection among stations from the very start would likely follow the radio example. After all, the stations profited from carrying network programs. The advertisers were willing to pay the networks and stations big money for the right to sell their wares. And the audience was happy with the quality of the radio network shows. Why change a successful pattern?

In May, the first 10 stations were granted commercial TV licenses. They were required to broadcast a minimum of 15 hours per week. The first sponsors of the first commercial telecasts were the Bulova Watch Co., Sun Oil Co., Lever Bros. Co., and Procter & Gamble. WNBT New York broadcast the first day authorized for commercial television on July 1, 1941.

On that first day, the CBS station in New York went on the air with its first news telecast at 2:30 P.M. This was the station's first actual programming other than test patterns and a color demonstration. At 3:25 P.M., it broadcast *Jack and the Beanstalk*. The program ran each afternoon for the first several months of the station's operation.

WORLD WAR II

The United States entered World War II in 1941, which blunted the development of television. The equipment and expertise were needed for sonar and radar technology in the war effort. But experimentation in programming at those stations that were initially licensed continued, and they remained on the air. Four months later the FCC dropped the minimum number of required hours from 15 hours a week to 4 hours. Although there were no more TV sets to be had, the licensees of the earliest stations tried to maintain at least some programs, mainly reading the news and an experimental effort now and then. In 1943, for example, the first complete opera, *Hansel and Gretl*, was telecast by WRGB Schenectady.

CBS continued to develop a partially mechanical field-sequential color television system. The network proposed in 1944 that the start of postwar TV should be with full-color pictures and recommended broadcasting on 16 MHz channels as compared to the 6 MHz channels for black and white that had been approved before the war.

After delays and hearings the FCC surprised many by accepting CBS's proposal in 1950. But the FCC insisted that the color system had to be compatible with the millions of black-and-white television sets that used the standards set in 1941 and that had been sold for the past five-year postwar period. The delays gave RCA the time it needed to improve its all-electronic compatible color system, which was approved in 1953.

At the war's end in 1945, nine so-called commercial television stations were on the air serving about 7,500 sets distributed in New York City, Schenectady, and Chicago. As late as October 1947, there were only 7,514 television receivers operating in Chicago: 4,139 in private homes; 2,295 in bars and grills; and 1,080 in other public places. The average daily audience in Chicago in the fall of 1947 was estimated at fewer than 96,000 viewers.

A NEW BEGINNING

The two years following the war were a highly important period in the history of American radio and television. There was an enormous increase in the total number of radio stations, the building of 108 TV stations—and the beginnings, at least, of a shift in importance from radio to television, especially on the network level.

After the war, the newest status symbol became a TV in one's home. Sets were expensive, a big complicated piece of furniture. There were many vacuum tubes and transformers, requiring adjustments that had to be made often. The screen was a little five- or seven-inch diagonal picture tube. At first there was a waiting list to get one, just as there was for automobiles. Many had their first exposure to TV standing in front of a department store or a store window just to watch a test pattern, or at the local saloon. There were almost as many TV sets in bars as in homes. Just as at one time bars had signs in their windows, "We have Radio," they now promoted, "We have Television." In the 1950s they would announce, "We have Color Television" and later "Big Screen Television." (The bar audience perhaps explains why wrestling and roller derby were staples of TV in that period. Also, those sports were played indoors in small arenas, not requiring the heavy cameras to move about much. And some have said that both sports were sometimes scripted, making them easier to shoot.)

THE NETWORKS

Between 1945 and 1948 was definitely still a time of experimentation as there were so few TV sets available. Independent stations (without network affiliations) could survive only in the largest markets, where sufficient advertiser support existed. As with commercial radio, educational TV, minority entertainment, and much local programming were limited because of the emphasis on networks that were able to attract larger ratings and deliver them to advertisers.

Now that television was moving away from the laboratories and into the professional realm, most manufacturers quit producing programs. NBC (owned by the TV manufacturer RCA) and CBS dominated and were eventually joined by ABC, which had a much smaller budget and fewer affiliates. Their only competitor was DuMont, a network created by an inventor who hoped that the superior technical quality of his pictures would lead the audience to ignore the cheap budget for production.

In 1943, WABD (DuMont) installed a new transmitter and antenna at its studios on Madison Avenue in New York and commenced program service. By 1944 the DuMont station had enough advertisers to offer the first full schedule of commercial shows. This example applied pressure on CBS and NBC to match DuMont's efforts.

THE SCHEDULES

Stations scheduled programming mostly in the afternoons and/or evenings. In January 1945, WABD's (DuMont) schedule was as follows: Sunday 8 P.M.: *Sham*; 8:30: *The Queen Was in the Kitchen*; followed by the last program that day, an hour-long film at 9 P.M. The station did not go back on the air until Tuesday at 8 P.M. with *WOR Presents* and at 8:30 with *Television Producers Association Presents*. On Wednesday at 8 P.M., the broadcast evening started with an hour-long film, and at 9 P.M. *Wednesday at Nine*, followed at 9:30 by *Macy's Teleshopping*. Most of the programs were sponsored. The station ran a test pattern one-half hour before showtime to help viewers adjust their TV picture properly.

One of the reasons stations did not operate on a longer day and night schedule was that the vacuum tube equipment could not take protracted use. Studios were heavily air-conditioned to almost freezing, not for the benefit of the performers, but of necessity as the lighting caused a great deal of heat under which tubes could fail. Studio production required not only very hot lights, but also heavy makeup for the performers. The depth-of-field for the lenses was poor; therefore, scenes emphasized sideways movement, not back and front.

Prime-time in the evenings was the first to expand, then afternoon hours, and finally other day parts. The *Voice of Firestone Televue,* a documentary show, was one of the very first television series starting April 10, 1944, at a time when there were very few television sets capable of receiving it. The show was transmitted to the entire NBC television network, as the first network-wide program in April 1944. It ran until January 1947. The *Voice of Firestone,* a classical music show, began in 1949 and continued off and on until 1963.

On May 9, 1946, the first variety show, *Hour Glass,* premiered on NBC. The show ran 10 months. On June 22, 1946, television made a big impression

Meet the Press survived the early days of television and is still a fixture on Sundays. The original host was Lawrence Spivak, here with guest Sister Kenny, an expert on treatment for polio, and regular panelist, Martha Rountree. Courtesy of Photofest.

Howdy Doody played the piano for host Buffalo Bob Smith; his marionette neighbor, Mr. Bluster; and Clarabelle the Clown. A live audience of children, called the peanut gallery, and children at home delighted in their afternoon antics. Courtesy of Photofest.

when an audience estimated as high as 140,000 saw the first televised heavyweight title fight (Joe Louis vs. Billy Conn). One year later, the Louis–Walcott fight was viewed by 1 million people. On October 2, 1946, *Faraway Hill,* airing on the DuMont network, became the first TV network soap opera.

Only DuMont and NBC broadcast in the evening in 1946. DuMont was doing the same nights and hours as in 1945. NBC ran an hour of programming on Sunday, two hours on Thursday, and the *Gillette Cavalcade of Sports* on Monday and Friday nights, with an additional hour on Fridays for fans of boxing. On May 7, 1947, *Kraft Television Theatre* premiered on NBC, the first regularly scheduled drama series on a network.

Some of the early daytime programs became classics. On November 6, 1947, *Meet the Press* first appeared as a local program in Washington, D.C. By September 12, 1948, it was a weekly program on NBC and continues to this day. At the other end of the entertainment spectrum, on December 27,

1947, *Puppet Television Theater* (later called *Howdy Doody*) debuted on NBC-TV with Buffalo Bob Smith. It was carried by six stations.

By 1951, there were coast-to-coast hookups. Networks finally reached from New York to Los Angeles. Stations that had to rely on syndication and their own programming now had access to the network shows.

CONCLUSION

Television was influenced by the business structure of radio, so it came as no great surprise that a great deal of the early programming resembled that of radio. The previous chapter notes some of those programs that successfully made the transition to the new medium. Radio formats like situation comedies, comedy-variety, quiz shows, and radio personalities shaped the identity of television. There were 216 network programs that appeared in both media, mostly in the late 1940s and early 1950s, and usually they were series. Scripts already used on radio were recycled for their equivalent TV shows. Into the 1960s, a number of soap operas were using the same scripts on radio as on TV, among them *The Guiding Light* and *The Brighter Day*. And a number of programs, such as Arthur Godfrey's, were simulcast on both radio and TV.

The experimental nature of these early TV programs—low budget, unreliable equipment, untrained personnel, a handful of viewers—meant that they were not remembered for their quality. Few were recorded, and that's probably a blessing. But they achieved their purpose. Staff members were trained, new techniques were learned, and the equipment was improved. The audience was introduced to the poor quality pictures on expensive TV sets—and became interested. Programmers learned what formats would work and what the costs would be. By the end of this period, the industry was ready to offer shows that would attract a mass audience.

The basic lesson learned in this period was that the radio model would work. The same networks would continue to dominate. Many of their affiliates were owned by companies that had owned radio stations. Advertising would remain the primary source of income and would control the programming. Because the FCC had set up the allocation of stations across the country so that most midsized cities could have two or three TV stations, that meant two or three networks would be leaders. Most importantly, from a programming viewpoint, the industry learned that the most of the formats of radio could make the transition to TV cheaply and easily with an audience already comfortable with the content; therefore, the early days of the new medium looked a lot like televised radio.

CHAPTER 3

Finding an Audience
(1948–1952)

World War II's end coincided with a rise in birth rates and the growth of mass-produced suburbs. By 1948, wartime rationing was over and manufacturers got back to the steady production of TV sets. While 1948 to 1952 could still be considered experimental as far as technology and technique were concerned, it was also a time of discovery for a growing audience. The rate of increase of TV sets in the home paralleled closely the development of radio and sound movies. Print had taken 80 years to reach saturation, movies took about 40 years, radio about 20 years—TV took only 10 years. This rapid acceptance of television was based on programming and falling prices for TV sets.

On September 30, 1948, the Federal Communications Commission (FCC) announced it was discontinuing temporarily the granting of *new* television licenses. The FCC had already granted more than 100 licenses and was inundated with applications for hundreds more. Unable to resolve several important issues—interference, allocation, and other technical questions—the FCC believed that a "freeze" would allow it to hold hearings and to create something of a "master blueprint" for television. This freeze was originally intended to last only six months, but the outbreak of the Korean War as well as the difficult nature of some of the issues, extended the freeze to four years. More than 700 new applications were on hold. Only 24 cities had two or more stations; many had only one. Most smaller and even some major cities—Denver, Colorado, and Austin, Texas, for example—had none at all. Rural areas had none.

Applications for early stations had come from many of the first to become owners of radio stations, such as networks and broadcast equipment manufacturers. These companies had strong financial reserves to cover the high costs for construction and development. Profits were low or nonexistent for many years. Stations were also started by some newspapers, automobile dealers, and other local entrepreneurs, but they had to have enough money to withstand continuing financial losses. The FCC was more likely to give licenses to individuals or groups with experience in radio. The agency used the organization, financing, and regulation of the existing radio industry as a model for television broadcasting. Local TV stations—like local radio stations—were to serve as the basic infrastructure of the industry.

As with the beginning of radio, the FCC made channels so scarce that TV was dominated by the few corporations able to afford stations in the largest cities, provide attractive programs, and lure national advertising dollars. It would be almost impossible for a new competitor to quickly build a chain of affiliates and form a network to reach a mass audience. The FCC's decisions inhibited competition and made oligopoly inevitable. Those few stations to get on the air between 1948 and 1952 had been given a license to print money.

THE FIRST TV SETS

Initially, most people saw their first TV programs in bars, which were the first major buyers of sets. Because most bar patrons were men, the first popular television programming was primarily of a male orientation. Network coverage was demonstrated on September 30, 1947, with the first telecast by NBC of the World Series, featuring the New York Yankees and the Brooklyn Dodgers. Almost 4 million viewers watched this series on TV, with 3.5 million people watching mostly from bars. When NBC in 1947 carried heavyweight fights and the Army–Navy football game, the sales of TV sets spurted. Full-scale commercial television had begun. Stations presented baseball, boxing, wrestling, roller derby, and bowling. These events were cheap to produce, and especially in the case of boxing and wrestling, it was easy to schedule commercials between innings, rounds, or bouts.

When the first TV set was delivered to a home in the neighborhood, it was an event that quickly attracted friends and relatives the family had not seen for a long time. Although the number of channels was limited except in the big cities, the program schedule started to expand slowly, as did the audience. Television stations mainly carried local programs of events that were being staged anyway in their communities. They brought the show into the studio, rehearsed it (mainly how to move the cameras to get the right shots and not run over cables, scenery, or talent), and aired it. As the equipment improved, field cameras (actually the same as studio cameras on lighter pedestals) made broadcasting at remote locations possible.

All of the earliest television stations were necessarily programming locally because network connections were not fully developed. AT&T began to lay special cable and microwave towers to interconnect TV stations. To go as far west as Chicago and St. Louis and south to Charlotte, North Carolina, by 1950 was estimated to cost $76 million dollars. As stations were linked, network affiliations became vital for the stations. A few cities featured network owned-and-operated stations, but most independently owned stations affiliated with more than one network. The three cities that had more than four stations supported nonaffiliated channels.

TV moved into the home of the wealthy and then became part of the middle-class family. Most of the conventions of television that we accept today came about during this period. The parents of the baby boomers were ready to settle down, buy homes, and watch TV. It is no wonder that television was perceived as a family medium. The TV set was the center of the living room as there was only one set. (Multiset homes come later.) The sponsors and, later, the television networks developed prime-time fare that would appeal to the general family audience. Programming reflected a presumed typical family, with a similar workweek and school day pattern. Children's shows quickly became a late afternoon staple. Cooking and homemaking shows were popular around midday. Movies and sports programs dominated evening and weekend hours.

LOCAL TELEVISION

Local television was not then considered just a supplement to the networks. In fact, many original formats and regional distinctions emerged in local TV before being subsumed or displaced by network schedules and priorities. In Chicago, the pioneers who had developed a casual but intelligent style of programming found that when Chicago became connected to the East Coast in 1949, as time went on, many of the most popular shows were retooled according to standards in the New York offices or dropped entirely, and the regional style evaporated.

Within four months of NBC starting television operations in Chicago, the network premiered *Garroway at Large* in April 1949. Garroway's show epitomized what became known as the "Chicago School." Garroway wandered in and out of scenes or from behind sets, stopping to hold quiet conversations with occasional celebrities who would drop by or talking directly to the home viewing audience. The show's technicians and vocalists and orchestra leader were included. It was a wry, offbeat humor new to prime-time television. *Garroway at Large* broadcast its last show from Chicago on June 24, 1951. On January 14, 1952, NBC's *Today* show premiered in New York with Garroway as host. Garroway's low-key, friendly style influences morning television to this day.

The Chicago School created inventive programs in limited spaces with local talent and small budgets. Children's shows consisted of an extraordinary number of award-winning entries including *Quiz Kids* and *Watch Mr. Wizard* and the highly rated, low-budgeted cowboy film series, *Cactus Jim*. For comedy and drama there was Studs Terkel's *Studs' Place, Portrait of America,* and *The Crisis.* Actuality programming featured *Walt's Workshop, The Pet Shop,* and *R.F.D. America.*

THE NETWORKS

The first year of formal operation of TV networks—NBC, CBS, ABC (all from radio), and newcomer DuMont—was the 1948–1949 season. Some 43 new TV programs were introduced on the networks that season. With only 190,000 TV sets in use, the networks were attracted to sports originally not as a source of advertising dollars, but as a means of boosting demand for television as a medium. Because NBC, CBS, and DuMont manufactured and sold receivers, their more immediate goal was to sell more of them. Sports soon became a fixture on prime-time network programming, often accounting for one-third of the networks' total evening fare. But in the early 1950s, as TV's programs developed, the female audience reached 50 percent. Sports began to disappear from network prime-time, settling into a very profitable niche on weekends.

Unlike ABC, CBS, and NBC, DuMont had no connection to radio and as such had no network infrastructure in place, which forced its founder, Allen DuMont, a manufacturer of television sets, to construct his new network from the ground up. It went on the air during World War II in 1944 as a single station in New York City and became a network of sorts when DuMont opened a second station in Washington, D.C., in 1946. The two were linked by AT&T telephone lines, which carried audio and visual signals and permitted the simultaneous broadcast of programs in each city. DuMont's plan was to extend his network down the East Coast and then move inland, following the westward expansion of the AT&T coaxial cable that was slowly linking cities while carrying programs that originated in New York City, then the center of television production.

Economics worked against DuMont from the beginning. Without the radio network revenues that the other three networks enjoyed, DuMont had little money to subsidize its operations and no cadre of established stars on which to draw. Despite massive public demand for TV sets, the sale of DuMont TVs proved insufficient to fund the sort of high-budget programs with known stars that viewers were rapidly coming to expect from television, so DuMont relied on low-budget programs with largely unknown actors. For example, *Rocky King, Inside Detective* had a budget so small that a novel way to save money was invented: The now-obscure actress Grace Carney, who played the lead character's wife, was unseen. Viewers only heard her from off-camera, which allowed her to also play on-screen characters.[1]

And even when something close to a hit came to DuMont, the other networks would in effect steal it. The stars of its most popular programs were lured away by the promise of larger paychecks, bigger audiences, and a chance to work in programs with generous production budgets. For example, Jackie Gleason was the $1,600-a-week host of *The Cavalcade of Stars* variety program when in 1952 CBS waved an astronomical $8,000 a week and a larger production budget at him.[2] He accepted the offer, of course, as had *Cavalcade*'s two previous hosts, Jack Carter and Jerry Lester, both of whom left DuMont for NBC.[3]

Even the structure of the television industry worked against DuMont. A limited number of stations were on the air—only 108 by 1952—so many communities had just one television station, and operators in smaller markets would pick and choose the most popular programming from the other networks, ABC, CBS, and NBC. The network suffered from the circular reasoning that was a result: There was little national demand for DuMont programs because few people on a national basis had ever seen them, but it's not possible to grow a large national audience unless the programs are available to them.

Program quality was also a problem and was again related to budget constraints. For example, from 1951 to 1954, DuMont counterprogrammed the hugely popular *I Love Lucy* with boxing and *Guide Right*, a low-budget military-themed variety program designed to beef up enlistments during the Korean War in the armed services. The rest of the DuMont schedule was heavy on sporting events, discussion programs, and quiz shows, all of which could be produced for relatively small amounts of money.

This is not to say, though, that DuMont's programming was entirely second-rate. Religious programming, both Protestant and Catholic in orientation, played a more significant role on DuMont than it did on the other networks. *This Is the Life* was an unusual religious-themed drama produced by the Missouri Synod of the Lutheran Church, which bounced back and forth between DuMont and ABC in 1952 and 1953 and was produced in syndication through the 1980s. *Life Is Worth Living* was the famous half-hour sermon by Bishop Fulton Sheen. And *Youth on the March* offered a combination of preaching and music in a program that, as had a few others, began elsewhere, in this case on ABC, before moving to DuMont.

Other DuMont programs were innovative, if nothing else. Music programs that would today be celebrated for their "diversity"—*Delora Bueno, Flight to Rhythm* and *The Ilona Massey Show*—were built around the "exotic" and "sultry" personas of their stars: Delora Bueno had been raised in Brazil, while Ilona Massey was from Hungary. The tastes of children were catered to with the earliest children's science fiction program, *Captain Video and His Video Rangers*, and *Life Begins at Eighty* was a panel discussion program that targeted, and starred, senior citizens. The program was also seen at various times on NBC and ABC, both before and after its run on DuMont.

But the DuMont network simply couldn't compete with the greater resources of ABC, CBS, and NBC. Over the years programs fell away one by one, and the end of DuMont came at 8 P.M. on Friday, September 23, 1955 with the close of the final broadcast of its last regularly scheduled series, the quiz show *What's the Story?* The next night, "the big three" had prime-time to themselves.

For the first three years, television was all live since there existed no practicable way to record the television signal. Theoretically, the programs could have been filmed, just like the movies. But the networks had no contracts with film unions and no desire to abandon the "live" model from radio. If stations could get films of TV programs directly from the producers or the ad agencies, did they need a network?

Shows were confined to studios and rarely were produced on location. In the medium's first five years, from 1948 to 1953, the networks did not produce much of their own programming. As in radio days, sponsors hired advertising agencies to create, budget, and produce shows that would fit their marketing needs. The networks agreed to sponsor-controlled production as they could not afford to produce the quantity of programming they were promising affiliates, particularly in such an experimental and trouble-prone medium.

MUSICAL PROGRAMMING

James Petrillo, President of the American Federation of Musicians (AFM), banned "live" music on television until the spring of 1948. The union also ordered that all programs with music must be broadcast "live" before they were syndicated via kinescopes, and these kinescopes could only air on a station affiliated with the originating station. This arrangement favored network affiliates over independent stations. The union also prohibited its members from recording for television films until 1950, when the AFM negotiated a system of royalty payments from television producers to musicians. Television music also was hampered by disagreements between program producers and music publishers. Producers sought a broadened general license fee for music use, rather than a special license, whereas the major music publishing concern (the American Society of Composers, Authors, and Publishers, or ASCAP) demanded three times the rate it received for film music.

The networks at first had the idea that an audience that would buy expensive TV sets had to be most interested in upscale programs, and they sought a way to add cultural legitimacy to the new medium. The networks featured classical music and opera on a semiregular basis. The first telecast of a major American symphony orchestra took place in March 1948. By a coincidence, that same night brought together two noted orchestras on rival networks: At 5:30 P.M., CBS put the Philadelphia Symphony playing under Eugene Ormandy at the Academy of Music, Philadelphia, on the air by cable to New York through WCBS-TV; the NBC Symphony, in an all-Wagner program under the direction of 81-year old Arturo Toscanini, went on the air through WNBT an hour later. That same year opera was televised for the first time from the stage of the Metropolitan Opera House when NBC transmitted Verdi's *Othello,* performed on their opening night of the season. The *NBC Opera Theater* began in 1950 with four programs and continued to air opera specials until the 1960s. However, there was criticism that they were sung in English, often condensed into one hour, and had too much movement by the cameras.

The networks also showcased classical music in specials and short series. In 1951, ABC's Chicago affiliate (WENR-TV) became the first station to regularly televise an orchestra, and NBC aired *Meet the Masters*, a classical music series, that spring. The network continued to air occasional telecasts of the NBC Symphony Orchestra, and CBS countered with specials featuring the Philadelphia Orchestra. NBC's musical specials in 1951 showcased the works of Richard Rogers and Irving Berlin, and it continued to air musical specials throughout the decade.

The most well known of the relative handful of classical music programs was *The Voice of Firestone,* which ran for 11 years, on NBC from 1949 to 1954, on ABC from 1954 to 1959, and again on ABC from 1962 to 1963. The program had begun on NBC network radio in 1928, and during its long life, it presented classical and "semi-classical" music, as well as some of the "better" (i.e., not rock) popular music of the early 1950s. But as classical music on television fulfills the desires of only a minority of viewers, *The Voice of Firestone* drew only a "small" (by network standards) audience of between 2 million and 3 million people, and, after being shoved around the prime-time schedule, was eventually permanently cancelled.[4]

For those who preferred the popular music of the time, there was *The Fred Waring Show* (CBS, 1949–1954) with an orchestra and chorus who sang the standard tunes. Youth-oriented music programs were rather more difficult to find, and rock and roll was conspicuously absent for the most part. When it was heard, it was often as something reinterpreted by mainstream performers, the kind of people who sang standards or show tunes and who clearly didn't understand the changes in popular music then underway.

For example, the long-running *Your Hit Parade* (NBC and CBS, 1950–1959), which had begun on radio in 1935, interpreted the Elvis Presley hit "Hound Dog" as a child's novelty song. The show featured the most popular songs of the previous week, supposedly determined by a national survey of record and sheet music sales. The top seven tunes were counted down in reverse order, like the popular music countdowns currently on radio and music cable channels. The American Tobacco Company's Lucky Strike cigarettes sponsored the show through its entire run. The television *Hit Parade* attempted to dramatize each song, but devising new settings for long-running hit songs was more difficult in a visual medium. A much more serious problem was rock and roll displacing the love songs that had been the mainstay of popular music during the 1930s and 1940s. *Your Hit Parade* catered to a family audience. Rock targeted a younger audience.

In the days of live television, most television programs offered new shows each week. If a performer insisted, maybe the show would be replaced for a couple of weeks in summer. But the networks learned that even with fresh programming each week, the audience numbers went down in summer. People could find better activities to do than watching TV. As a result, summer became the season for trying out new acts and new programs. In 1950, Kate Smith and Sammy Kaye hosted replacement shows on NBC, while CBS countered with several summer series hosted by crooners Perry Como, Vaughn Monroe, and Frank Sinatra. Country singer Eddy Arnold, nicknamed the "Tennessee Plowboy," was tapped as a summer replacement for Perry Como in 1952, and his program was syndicated throughout the 1950s.

But other variety programs that were more focused on vaudeville as a theme appeared occasionally in programs that lasted for a few months. Before the 1952–1959 period, viewers could find *School House* (DuMont,

1949), which was based on a circa 1900 vaudeville act, and *The Gay Nineties Review* (ABC, 1948–1949).

A handful of vaudeville-themed sitcoms were scheduled over the years, but they met with varying degrees of success. At the top of the heap was *The George Burns and Gracie Allen Show* (CBS, 1950–1958), a combination of something that looked like a standard-issue 1950s happy-family-in-the-suburbs sitcom and the Burns and Allen vaudeville act that dated back to the 1920s. Oddly for the time, the married Burns and Allen played themselves in the program (or at least characters based on their famous stage personas), and in the show they were vaudevillians who were the stars of a network sitcom. During the program the action would stop as Burns did stand-up comedy bits and directly addressed the TV audience in an early example of the postmodern television technique of "breaking the fourth wall" that was regularly exploited by programs like *Malcolm in the Middle* a half-century later.

CBS's *Omnibus* debuted in 1952. The program aired as a weekly, 90-minute series in the "ghetto" of weekend programming, Sunday afternoon. As that day part became more valuable with the success of professional football, *Omnibus* shifted to other networks. Developed by the Television-Radio Workshop of the Ford Foundation, *Omnibus* was the most successful cultural magazine series on commercial television. The master of ceremonies was journalist Alistair Cooke, known for his literate commentary on *Letter from America*, a BBC radio series heard throughout Great Britain. *Omnibus* was a variety show for the intellect, a compendium of the arts, literature, science, history, and even some pure entertainment. Although it won numerous awards, because of poor ratings it was canceled in 1959. The Ford Foundation, citing *Omnibus*'s struggle for ratings, questioned whether commercial broadcasters were dedicated to "the development of mature, wise and responsible citizens," and began to fund educational television projects.

VARIETY

As more people bought TV sets, the audience was perceived to have changed, and Nielsen ratings became important. Television was ready for some major hits. On June 20, 1948, *Toast of the Town*, with Ed Sullivan, premiered on CBS, with guests Dean Martin and Jerry Lewis. In 1955, its name was changed to *The Ed Sullivan Show*. It was as much a ritual as a TV program, one of those shows that seemingly everyone watched on Sunday night. Over the years viewers saw Topo Gigio, the little mouse puppet who would say "Kiss me, Eddie" in his sweet (but no longer politically correct) faux-Italian accent; Elvis Presley, famously shown only from the waist up; The Beatles, who lip-synced songs that still couldn't be heard above the screaming of teenage girls in the audience; Marcel Marceau, the mime; and literally thousands of lesser-known performers. Half of the appeal of the program was simply watching Ed introduce the acts. He was the most awkward of TV hosts, which somehow made him seem more genuine and, therefore, more likable. His oddly enunciated promise of a "really big show"

Ed Sullivan was the awkward, but charming, master of ceremonies for his own variety show. A wide range of guests from Catskills comics to dog acts, from opera singers to rock and roll bands provided the entertainment. Courtesy of Photofest.

was easily mimicked by professional and living room impressionists. The program would last until 1971.

The Milton Berle Show, with its hammy host and improvised style, was at the opposite end of the spectrum from *The Ed Sullivan Show*, with its stilted host and sedate style, and as far removed philosophically as it could be from its chief competitor in the time slot, *Life Is Worth Living* with the stern Bishop Fulton J. Sheen. Most of it centered on Berle himself, who came to be called "Uncle Milty," a sort of national eccentric relative to all viewers, and, appropriately, "Mister Television," a title he deserved by dint of the program's massive rating of 61.6 during the 1950–1951 season, making him the biggest of the first generation of big stars in the new medium of TV.

In 1948, *Texaco Star Theater*, with Milton Berle as one of several revolving hosts, started on NBC. Soon he became the star of *The Milton Berle Show*. The program was a televised version of vaudeville with comedy skits and musical performances. Most of the jokes sounded as though they had been delivered many times on many previous stages. The show became popular, perhaps

Part of the routine on *The Milton Berle Show* was an appearance by the star in drag. The show was immensely popular in the early days of TV, perhaps because of its visual appeal. Courtesy of Photofest.

partly because of its reliance on visual gags—including Berle dressing up as a woman. So many other programs seemed to be designed for radio, with the visual aspect an afterthought.

But *The Milton Berle Show* was surprisingly short-lived given the size of its audience and its place in the collective memory of television scholars, and Berle became a victim of the times in which he lived. After allegedly bringing the country to almost a complete standstill on Tuesday nights in the late 1940s and early 1950s, the program ended its run in 1956 as dramatic series and anthology programs came to dominate the prime-time schedule. Many credit Milton Berle and Ed Sullivan for making the purchase of a TV set imperative.

Somewhere in between the order of *The Ed Sullivan Show* and the disorder of *The Milton Berle Show* was *The Red Skelton Show*, which ran for 20 years on NBC (1951–1953), CBS (1953–1970), and NBC (1970–1971). For most of its life, the program was built around a "mega-sketch" that ran for 40 minutes, including commercial breaks, and that featured the characters—The Mean Widdle Kid, Freddie the Freeloader, for example—that Skelton had developed in vaudeville and radio.

Arthur Godfrey went prime-time in December 1948, by permitting the televising of his radio hit *Arthur Godfrey's Talent Scouts*. Up to 1959, there was no bigger star in both radio and TV. Godfrey hosted a daily radio program and appeared in two top-10 prime-time television shows, all for CBS. Arthur Godfrey earned a million dollars a year, making him one of the highest paid people in the United States. Godfrey launched the careers of singers Pat Boone, Tony Bennett, Eddie Fisher, Connie Francis, and Patsy Cline. A month after the debut of *Arthur Godfrey's Talent Scouts* came *Arthur Godfrey and His Friends*, a collection of professional musicians. His shows were cheap to produce but drew high ratings. He seemed to have no talent, but was so effective that through most of the 1950s he was "everywhere" in the mass media until tastes changed. Audiences responded to his personality that seemed casual, warm, and friendly, but he was rumored to be volatile behind the scenes and fired one of "his" singers while on the air.

The *Admiral Broadway Review* 1949 was broadcast on both the NBC and DuMont networks, so it was seen in every city with television facilities (either live or by filmed kinescope). The show dominated Friday night, the way Berle did on Tuesday and Ed Sullivan on Sunday. The format was like a Broadway revue, with guest stars in comedy skits and big production numbers. The show lasted only 17 weeks, from January to June, but its successor, *Your Show of Shows*, was a Saturday night fixture for four years. It had a similar format of monologues, skits, and parodies of movies and plays starring Sid Caesar and Imogene Coca, with a cast of regulars like Carl Reiner and Howard Morris. The writers were Mel Tolkin, Lucille Kallen, Mel Brooks, Larry Gelbart (M*A*S*H TV series), Bill Persky, Sam Denoff (The Dick Van Dyke Show), Neil Simon, and also Joe Stein (Fiddler on the Roof) and Mike Stewart (Hello, Dolly and Bye, Bye Birdie). Caesar and company went on to perform some 160 telecasts—all live, original comedy.

The Colgate Comedy Hour (NBC 1950–1953) was a big-budget musical variety show competing directly with Ed Sullivan's Toast of the Town (CBS). This live Sunday evening series featured vaudeville favorite Eddie Cantor once every four weeks in rotation with the comic team of Dean Martin and Jerry Lewis, and Fred Allen. The fourth show of the month was sponsored originally by Frigidaire with comic Bobby Clark to alternate with Bob Hope. Fred Allen left the series after his fourth disappointing broadcast.

Premiering with Jackie Gleason as a host in its second season, The Colgate Comedy Hour was the highest budgeted, single-sponsor extravaganza on television with a cost of $3 million a year for talent, production, and time. After a few years the cost doubled. Back for their second year were Cantor and Martin and Lewis with Gleason, Abbott and Costello, Spike Jones, Tony Martin and Ezio Pinza. The Colgate Comedy Hour became the first commercial network series to originate on the West Coast when Cantor hosted his program from Hollywood's El Capitan Theatre on September 30, 1951.

NBC's Four Star Revue (1950–1951) starred Danny Thomas with Jimmy Durante, Jack Carson, and Ed Wynn. The format was fast-paced three-minute sketches. For the series' second season, the network ordered a format change, and the four rotating hosts were replaced by a procession of headliners. With all but Ed Wynn's departure, the program became the All Star Revue (1951–1953).

Many of the variety shows borrowed talent from radio. Kate Smith had been an immensely popular singer on radio, but The Kate Smith Evening Hour (NBC, 1951–1952) failed to win a TV audience. In contrast, Herb Shriner, a casual, charming host from the Midwest, made the transition easily with The Herb Shriner Show (CBS, ABC, 1949–1956) in prime-time and went on to entertain audiences in the daytime for many years after that.

Edgar Bergen had done well on radio with his dummy, Charlie McCarthy. It was only natural there would be a TV version of the concept. The Paul Winchell-Jerry Mahoney Show (NBC, 1950–1954) had the comedy of the ventriloquist (Winchell) and his boyish-looking wooden friend along with a variety of guests, but the format and name changed at times. Several of the earliest of the variety shows, such as The Swift Show and The Gulf Road Show Starring Bob Smith (he of Howdy Doody fame; both NBC (1948–1949), changed formats repeatedly: On some weeks they were musical programs, other weeks talent or quiz shows. This indicates that something as taken for granted today as the format of a program was not yet set in concrete, so to speak, during the earliest years of prime-time television.

The most innovative of the comedy-variety genre was *The Ernie Kovacs Show* (CBS, NBC, 1952–1956). The humor was frequently visual, sometimes silly, sometimes sophisticated. Even today, it seems modern.

Country Music Variety Shows

A fair number of variety programs on the related themes of country music and rural humor have appeared on television over the years, mostly concentrated into the earliest days of TV and again during a country music revival that took place in the early 1970s.

"Hillbilly," as country music was more commonly known, gained its initial exposure on shows hosted by regional performers in the Midwest, including Earnie Lee at WLW in Cincinnati (1947), Pee Wee King at WAVE in Louisville (1948), and Lulu Belle at Chicago's WNBQ (1949).

The early network programs came largely from New York City, the headquarters of the television networks. Conditioned as we are by movies, it's easy to form mental images of New York City after dark during the 1940s, peopled with men in tuxedos and women in evening gowns in swanky Manhattan nighteries or hot Harlem jazz clubs. But, though it seems somewhat incongruous, country-and-western music not only existed in 1940s New York, but was popular enough to have clubs devoted to it. One of the programs, *Village Barn* (NBC, 1948–1950), originated live from a nightclub of the same name at 52 West Eighth Street in Manhattan.

Besides New York, country music programs were broadcast from Philadelphia (*Hayloft Hoedown*, ABC, summer 1948); Chicago (*ABC Barn Dance*, ABC, 1949, based on a radio show of the same title that began on the air in 1924); Nashville, of course (*Grand Ole Opry*, ABC, 1955–1956); and Springfield, Missouri (the highly successful *Ozark Jubilee* 1955–1960). Ohio was a significant source of country music programs, with shows originating from Cleveland (*The Pee Wee King Show*, ABC, summer 1955) and from Dayton and Cincinnati (*Midwestern Hayride*, summers on NBC, 1951–1956, and ABC, 1957–1959).

Talent Shows

Talent shows are closely related to variety programs in that both featured numerous performers in short routines of one sort or another. The main difference, of course, is that talent shows presented relatively unknown performers, whereas variety programs showcased those well on the road to success and those who had already arrived.

Talent shows ranged from the obscure, such as *Places Please* (CBS, 1948–1949), one of many musical talent programs that aired three times per week in a 15-minute format, right before the network evening news, to the famous, such as *The Original Amateur Hour,* which had started on radio in the 1930s, ran on all four networks, although not always continuously, in prime-time (1948–1960), and continued on daytime TV until 1970. *The Original Amateur Hour* was significantly different from all the other talent programs in prime-time as it was the only one to feature truly amateur performers. All of the others were showcases for experienced performers who were looking for their big breaks before a national television audience.

The appeal of talent programs to audiences of the time should not be underestimated, something that is perhaps easy to do in the modern television environment—or at least was, until the advent of *American Idol* and similar shows.

DRAMA

Anthology Dramas

Anthologies had different stories, settings, and characters each week, like *Twilight Zone.* The first significant legal drama was titled *Cross Question* during its brief run on CBS in 1949. But when the program moved to DuMont, it was soon retitled *They Stand Accused,* and under that name it caught on and stayed on the DuMont schedule until December 1954, making it one of the longest-lived programs on the fourth network. *They Stand Accused* was a departure from other legal dramas in that it was something of what today would be called a reality program. The cases in the program were fictional, but the lawyers and judges who appeared were lawyers and judges, not actors, and the program itself was unscripted. The case was argued through ad-libbed dialogue, guided by the Assistant Attorney General for Illinois, who had a hand in the program's production, and its outcome was decided by the Chicago studio audience who served as a jury during the live performance. Cases ranged from murder to child custody disputes, and it's said that the program's verisimilitude caused some viewers to believe they were watching a real trial.[5]

The Fireside Theatre was one of the longest-lived anthologies, and it was unusual because it was filmed. The show was on NBC and later ABC from 1949 to 1963. The actress Jane Wyman became the hostess of the program, and it was renamed *The Jane Wyman Show* in 1955.

Prestige dramas, although well-known and fondly remembered by television historians, were relatively rare during this time period, with only about a dozen or so airing on CBS and NBC, fewer on the relatively poorer ABC and none on the poverty-stricken DuMont network, which was saddled with low-budget, low-grade programs.

The live television schedule was a programming vortex with an inexhaustible demand for new shows, 90 percent of which were broadcast live. The remaining dramas were transmitted (usually from the East Coast to the West) via kinescopes. Perhaps the most important reason leading to the success of this new television art form was the high caliber of talent on both sides of the camera. Although many well-known actors from the stage and screen participated in live television dramas as the 1950s progressed, it was the obscure but professionally trained theater personnel from off-Broadway, summer stock, and university theater programs who launched the innovative broadcasts that came to be called television's "Golden Age."

Each week a different play with different characters and different settings was performed. The sponsors owned and controlled the programs, so the shows were not restricted to a particular network or time schedule. As a result of this flexibility, some rotated around the dial whereas others remained firmly entrenched, all in search of the best possible ratings. Anywhere from 30 to 90 minutes, live dramas borrowed specific elements from the legitimate stage, network radio, and the Hollywood film, as most of the producers had backgrounds in those arenas.

From radio came the network distribution system, sound effects, music, theme music, and exposition by a narrator when action had to take place off stage or after commercial breaks. From film came out-of-work former stars and influences on camera techniques. From Broadway there was a large pool of energetic young talent looking for a break—Paul Newman, Joanne Woodward, Robert Redford, James Dean, and so on. Broadway also inspired set designs and acting techniques that gave a sense of immediacy and reality to small-screen performances. But it was live drama in the home that helped to displace radio, the stage, and the movie as the favorite leisure-time activities for more and more families.

These dramas were forced to deal with ordinary people and their problems. Since everything was done live on a stage, it was difficult to have chase scenes, fights, and gun battles. The action had to be small, the pace slow, and the setting commonplace. Fancy costumes and elaborate sets were hard to manage. The focus had to be on the human character in contemporary times and familiar places.

The Philco/Goodyear Television Playhouse (NBC, 1948–1955), produced by Fred Coe, was one of the most distinguished. Toward the end of its first season it became the first anthology program to produce original plays written exclusively for television. Hollywood's film studios bought the rights to popular works and then refused to grant their rival television from doing them; therefore, dramatic programs had to encourage original scripts from young writers. Writers who began in TV and developed critically acclaimed reputations included Paddy Chayefsky, Horton Foote, Tad Mosel, and Gore Vidal. The growing prestige of live dramas attracted established and fading stars from the Broadway stage and Hollywood. Some lent their famous names to an anthology drama program, such as *Robert Montgomery Presents* (ABC, 1950–1957).

Kraft Television Theatre ran on two networks: NBC (1947–1958) and simultaneously ABC (October–January 1955) with 650 live one-hour comedic and dramatic plays. Its scheduling on different nights on different networks—Wednesday on NBC, Thursday on ABC—made it necessary for the cast to perform each play twice, as few episodes were filmed or kinescoped. *Kraft Television Theatre* was also notable for being one of the earlier prime-time programs to be broadcast in color, beginning on an occasional basis in 1954 and going to all-color production two years later at a time when most people had still not seen a color TV set, let alone a color program.

Equally well known was *Studio One*, the dramatic anthology on CBS, which aired from 1948 until 1958, during which time 500 live one-hour plays were telecast. The program was known for its emphasis on visuals, at a time when the low production values that were the norm pushed the emphasis to dialogue, and it featured original scripts and adaptations of other works.

The longest-lived was *Lux Video Theatre*, which had begun as *Lux Radio Theatre* in 1934 before moving to television in 1950. It aired on CBS from 1950 to 1954 and NBC from 1954 to 1957. In its NBC incarnation, it offered one-hour adaptations of such Hollywood films as *Casablanca* and *Double Indemnity*, but not with the original casts. One wonders what the appeal of *Casablanca* with Paul Douglas and Arlene Dahl in the roles played by Humphrey Bogart and Ingrid Bergman would have been, although it should be noted that films such as *Casablanca* were not available on TV until after 1957 when the film studios and television networks came to an agreement about the showing of them, and so audiences had no way of seeing them outside of motion picture theatres.

Serial Dramas

Serials had continuing characters and settings week after week. Of course the most obvious example is the soap opera. One of the first network prime-time programs was *Faraway Hill*, a soap on DuMont (1946). It was followed in prime-time by *One Man's Family* (NBC, 1949–1952), which centered on the activities of a prosperous family San Francisco. The program was simultaneously a radio soap opera heard from 1932 to 1959. The TV version moved to daytime in 1954.

Although most family-oriented dramas centered on intact nuclear families, a single-parent variation existed, beginning with *The O'Neills* (DuMont, 1949–1950). Its focus was on a single mother, a situation somewhat rare in early television but easily explained by making the character a widow—and there were many in the years right after World War II, of course—as widowhood was more socially acceptable than was the shame brought about by divorce or, far worse, by having a child outside of wedlock.

WESTERNS

The first westerns appearing on television were Hollywood films that had played on double-bills in movie houses in the early 1940s. These syndicated films were popular among children and rural audiences. The innovative William Boyd, who completed 66 western features as *Hopalong Cassidy*, secured the TV rights to his Hoppy films and syndicated them. In 1949, his weekly series on NBC, *Hopalong Cassidy*, ranked number seven in the Nielsen ratings. The next wave of made-for-TV westerns was targeted at the juvenile market. Children were a growing demographic segment because of the postwar baby boom. *The Gene Autry Show* (CBS, 1950–1956) and *The Roy Rogers Show* (NBC, 1951–1957) also recycled prominent stars of those "B" westerns.

The Lone Ranger moved to ABC (1949–1957), after beginning on radio in 1933, but westerns were otherwise slow to pick up. It wasn't until the mid-1950s and the advent of the so-called adult westerns that the genre took off. By the 1957–1958 and 1958–1959 television seasons, which form the peak of western popularity, nearly a dozen new series were premiering each year.

Typical of the children's western was *Cactus Jim*, which was stripped on NBC Monday through Friday from 6 to 6:30 P.M. during 1949–1951, just before prime-time but in a time slot, today called early access, often reserved for children's programming. *Cactus Jim* had an eponymous host—on-camera hosts were de rigueur in programming aimed at children—who introduced aging western films that were shown in short segments over several days to fit the running time of the program.

CHILDREN'S TV

The initial appearance of science fiction on television came in deliberate juvenile form as three of the first four prime-time sci-fi programs were produced with children firmly in mind. *Captain Video and his Video Rangers,* a half-hour DuMont network show, was the first science fiction, space adventure program on television. Set in 2254, the show was a live, technically demanding, continuing serial appearing five nights a week with a minute budget. The show took advantage of switching between cameras to

Captain Video and His Video Rangers starred Al Hodge as the captain and Don Hastings as his faithful assistant. The cheaply budgeted show survived six years on the DuMont network. Courtesy of Photofest.

get dissolves, superimpositions, and crude key effects. By 1951, the show was carried by 24 stations and seen by 3.5 million viewers. When Miles Laboratories, Inc., canceled its sponsorship of the Morgan Beatty news program, *Captain Video* was DuMont's only sponsored program in the prime-time hours from 7:00 to 9:00 P.M. *Captain Video* left the air April 1955, and DuMont folded that same year.

Its success sparked the much less successful *Tom Corbett, Space Cadet*, which orbited CBS, NBC, and ABC (1950–1952); it too ran in 15- and 30-minute episodes either once or three times per week. *Space Patrol*, the last of the three children's sci-fi programs, aired on ABC during prime-time during summer 1951 and again December 1951–June 1952, and continued as a daytime program until 1955.

Kukla, Fran, and Ollie (NBC, ABC, 1948–1957) originated in Chicago. This gentle puppet show was a favorite with kids and their parents. The creator was Burr Tillstrom, and his wife, Fran Allison, played the only real-life character. The characters spent their time chatting among themselves and with guests like Beulah the witch.

SITUATION COMEDIES

Radio series became TV successes in 1949: for example, *The Aldrich Family* (NBC, 1949–1953) and *The Goldbergs* (CBS, NBC, DuMont, 1949–1954). The homespun drama *Mama* (CBS, 1949–1956), the story of a Norwegian-American family living in San Francisco in 1910, was told through the eyes of the daughter Katrin. Mama was played by veteran stage actress Peggy Wood, who created one of the warmest characters on television. In 1956, the show was canceled but popular support from the public brought it back for a 13-week run on Sunday afternoons until March 1957.

The Life of Riley was another blue-collar, ethnic sitcom, but Irish. Unlike most series of the time it was filmed in Hollywood. The show was broadcast on NBC from 1949 to 1950 and from 1953 to 1958. In its first TV season, Jackie Gleason played Riley, unsuccessfully. Then William Bendix was cast in the second version, and the series became one of the top 25 most watched programs from 1953 to 1955. (The catch phrase from the show was heard each time Riley finally realized how much trouble he was in and would say in horror: "What a revolting development this is.")

Ethel and Albert (NBC, CBS, ABC, 1953–1956) was another inheritance from radio. Peg Lynch, also the writer, and Alan Bunce starred as a middle-aged couple who lived a normal life with a quiet sense of humor. *My Friend Irma* (CBS, 1952–1954), with Marie Wilson as the ditzy blonde secretary, also made the transition smoothly to television. Not as scatterbrained, but equally as warm hearted, was Ann Southern in *Private Secretary* (CBS, NBC, 1953-1957). Popular culture has always loved the blonde secretary.

The Adventures of Ozzie and Harriet was one of the most enduring family-based situation comedies. Ozzie and Harriet Nelson and their sons portrayed fictional versions of themselves on the program. Nelson and his wife, Harriet, started out on radio as a bandleader and singer, and in 1941 were providing music for Red Skelton's program. In 1944 their proposed show was put on CBS radio by their long-time sponsor, International Silver. Ozzie Nelson himself directed and cowrote all the episodes, as he would most of the television shows. The television program premiered on ABC in 1952 when David and Ricky Nelson were 16 and 13. The program focused on the Nelson family at home and the growing pains of the boys. Domestic comedies were literally house-bound. A family member experienced some sort of lightly depicted minor dilemma, which Ozzie or Harriet then neatly dispatched with some well-pointed words of advice. Eventually the on-screen David and Ricky, unlike their real lives, graduated from college and became lawyers. When the real David and Rick got married, to June Blair and Kristin Harmon respectively, their wives joined the cast of Ozzie and Harriet on television as well as in real life. Rick Nelson, while on the show, became a real-life rock star and teen heartthrob. *Ozzie and Harriet* lasted 14 years on American television, remaining on the air until 1966.

Desi Arnaz and Lucille Ball, in 1950, formed Desilu Productions, expressly to produce *I Love Lucy* on their own terms. The first routinely filmed network television show, *I Love Lucy*, began in 1951. Their crucial innovation of shooting shows on multiple film cameras in front of a studio audience combined the excitement of live performance with the quality control of film. They, not the sponsor or the network, owned their show, which enabled them to control future reruns and syndication. They transformed television economics. But it still took time for the studios to see the advantages and produce their own filmed programs.

Of course, the success of the program led to imitators. *I Married Joan* (NBC, 1952–1955) was about a judge (Jim Backus) and his wife (Joan Davis) with a knack for getting into trouble. A minor variation was *My Little Margie* (CBS, NBC, 1952–1955) about a widower (Charles Farrell) and his daughter (Gale Storm) with a knack for getting into trouble.

Domestic comedies about married couples without kids also existed, beginning with *Mary Kay and Johnny*, a dimly remembered show that ran on three networks (in order, DuMont, NBC, CBS and NBC a second time)

Ozzie Nelson wrote, directed, and acted in *The Adventures of Ozzie and Harriet*. His real-life wife, Harriet, and their two sons, Ricky and David, costarred with him in this gentle sitcom. Courtesy of Photofest.

between 1947 and 1950. *Mary Kay and Johnny* is interesting in that it had significant verisimilitude in that its stars, Mary Kay and Johnny Stearns, were married in real life. Their son, Christopher, became a part of the program when he was born in 1949, and *Mary Kay and Johnny* naturally evolved into a family-oriented sitcom.

Another relatively early childless example is *Heaven for Betsy* (CBS, 1952) about newlyweds in New York City. The program is also a good example of the odd scheduling (to contemporary eyes) of the period. It ran twice a week in a 15-minute format, live at 7:45 P.M. ET Tuesdays and Thursdays, and starred the newlywed-in-real-life Jack Lemmon and Cynthia Stone. It lasted for three months on the schedule.

Young Mr. Bobbin (NBC, 1951–1952) was yet another variation, this time a surrogate family sitcom—of which there were and still are many—in which the title character (Jackie Kelk), an 18-year-old making the transition into adulthood, lived with the two aunts who had raised him. While they functioned as a family, they were not the same sort who populated the traditional nuclear family programs associated with 1950s television.

Another variation on the theme of family deals with the roles of domestic servants, and there is little doubt that television, even today, has many more domestic servants than are found in the real world, perhaps because in the affluent world of the mass media housekeepers are common. The first was *Beulah* (ABC, 1950–1953), which had as its main character the sassy African-American maid of a household of bumbling, incompetent upper-class white folks. The cast featured prominent African-American performers, including Ethel Waters, Hattie McDaniel from *Gone with the Wind*, and Louise Beavers, all of whom played Beulah; Butterfly McQueen, also of *Gone with the Wind* fame; and Dooley Wilson from *Casablanca*. It was among the first network programs to have a largely minority cast.

Comedies set in the workplace also were popular, and one of the most common settings was the school. *Mr. Peepers* (NBC, 1952–1955) was a well-loved sitcom about a slight, balding teacher who wore glasses, a very gentle man played by Wally Cox, but he was respected and liked by his colleagues and even his students.

Amos 'n' Andy

The justly famous, or perhaps infamous, *Amos 'n' Andy* had a brief life on television, airing on CBS from 1951 to 1953. Although it had been a hit on radio, where its stars had been white, the program fared less well on television with its all-black cast and soon became controversial because of its portrayal of African-Americans.

The problem with the program was that the civil rights organizations of the time, including the NAACP, objected to the stereotypical behaviors exhibited by the characters. Kingfish, for example, tried continually to swindle Andy as part of his get-rich-quick schemes. In one episode, Kingfish

African-Americans were rarely seen on television in the
1950s. One exception was the show *Beulah*, in which
Hattie McDaniel and others played the role of a maid who
served the Henderson family and shared her wisdom with
their son Donnie, played by Clifford Sales. Courtesy of
Photofest.

sold Andy a large house that was no more than a false front on a plot of
land on which Kingfish had rigged a fake oil well from a can of motor oil
and a bicycle pump. In another, he sold Andy sheets of the "invisible glass"
that he'd invented; the glass, of course, was nothing but air.

The reaction of the black community was divided. In the program,
released on video recently, there was a clearly deliberate contrast of the

leads with the ancillary characters (e.g., police officer, shop owners, store managers and clerks, pastors) who were shown as competent, intelligent, educated, middle-class black professionals.

But the objection was more complex than a simple complaint over yet another mass media stereotype of African-Americans as lazy and gullible, for the actors on *Amos 'n' Andy* were virtually the only African-Americans to be found on prime-time television. A comparison of the prime-time schedules during the 1951–1953 seasons showed that only *Beulah* (ABC, 1950–1953), another sitcom, had a cast with a significant number of African-Americans and that the rest of the TV schedule was lily white, a situation that wouldn't be rectified until sitcoms starring black actors came along in the 1970s. There was nothing on the air to balance the one-sided portrayal of the characters of *Amos 'n' Andy*.

In 1953, CBS reluctantly removed the program from the air, mainly because of stations in the South. Advertisers and, therefore, television executives wished to avoid appearing to support civil rights. There were instances of stations cutting off network programs that featured black performers on the same program with white performers. Even with so much conflict looming, the *Amos 'n' Andy* show remained in syndication well into the 1960s. The irony was that this was the first and only television series with an all-black cast to appear on prime-time, network television for nearly another 20 years.

DETECTIVE DRAMAS

Detective programs began as live programs, recycling prose fiction, movies, and radio shows. The earliest featured simple versions of the hard-boiled private eye such as *Man against Crime* (CBS, NBC, DuMont, 1949–1956) and *Martin Kane, Private Eye* (NBC, 1949–1954) conceived and produced in New York City by advertising agencies.

Martin Kane, Private Eye (NBC, 1949–1954) was popular both on radio and television. Sponsored on both media by U.S. Tobacco, Kane hung out in Happy McMann's Tobacco Shop. It became a standard practice to get the sponsor's name into its programs by having a poster prominently displayed in a store set, or having a character use the sponsor's clearly identifiable product. By 1950, it had reached 12th spot in the ratings, and later in two seasons was in the top ten. *Kane* became the first TV/comic book tie-in.

Ellery Queen, an American Sherlock Holmes, first appeared in popular novels beginning in 1929, appeared on radio a decade later in a long-running weekly program, and on television in 1950 in a live series, *The Adventures of Ellery Queen* (DuMont, 1950–1951; ABC, 1951–1952). This is the first of four series devoted to Ellery Queen, a mystery writer and amateur detective. *Stand by for Crime* (1949) and *Chicagoland Mystery Players* (WGN 1947, Dumont 1949–1959) provided television's first police dramas, although neither was as influential as their long-running successor, *Dragnet*, which had two network runs.

DRAGNET

"Big Break" opens with the now-iconic close-up of Los Angeles Police Department badge no. 714, Detective Sergeant Joe Friday's, the four-note theme music and a voice-over that says, "The story you are about to see is true—the names have been changed to protect the innocent." This cuts to documentary-style scenic shots of mundane, not-terribly-scenic 1953 Los Angeles and Friday's off-camera line, "This is the city...."

What follows is a mix of visual images that clearly mark the characters as detectives—overcoats, hats, neckties, cigarettes—and staccato dialogue of remarkably precise detail, interspersed with prosaic discussions of the officers' everyday lives. "It was Wednesday, March 18th. We were working the daywatch out of robbery division." Friday and partner Frank Smith are dispatched with two other officers to confront "Hoffman, George R.", an armed criminal wanted for a string of 18 robberies during the past three months. Waiting for the elevator, the four officers look nervous, in contrast to the usual cool, calm, and collected demeanor of TV lawmen. They nervously finger their guns, eyes darting, sweating, and take long drags on their cigarettes. Smith gulps a mouthful of the coffee that Friday's brought him, and then pours the rest into an ashtray as the elevator arrives.

Hoffman is captured after a brief shootout and a tear-gassing that forces him into the handcuffs of Friday. His trial is set for May 14th, but a week before his court date Hoffman escapes by climbing down seven stories inside a ventilator, clinging to its flanges with his exceptionally strong fingers and hands, which he strengthened through vigorous exercise while in custody.

His pursuit takes up the next month. Friday and Smith follow leads until they come across an odd man who seems unnaturally interested in his model trains but who knows where Hoffman is hiding. Friday and Smith go to Hoffman's room at a motor court and occupy it for several tedious hours before learning that he's been arrested elsewhere. On August 16th Hoffman is sentenced to the state pen.

A montage of time passing is presented to viewers. As Friday says that "time went fast," his hand checks off the dates on typed police reports. We learn that in June Hoffman was paroled to the Army with the provision that he be sent overseas (presumably to Korea) and that Smith had the flu in January. Then, the day before he's due to ship out, Hoffman appears in uniform at the police station to tell Friday and Smith that he has no hard feelings over his arrest. He also borrows a few bucks. They've just returned from lunch, and Smith was complaining that he eats too much—three pastrami sandwiches and two plates of fried beans—when Hoffman popped in. Later they learn that he'd escaped military detention just that morning. The chase resumes.

The following Saturday an acquaintance of Hoffman phones to say that Hoffman wants to meet him at the acquaintance's office at the LCD Tool & Die Works. Friday and Smith arrange to be there, along with backup. After a chase through the building and some gunfire, Hoffman is again captured. He boasts that he'll just break out of prison again, but Friday asks him what the point is of doing that. The episode ends with the results of the trial, and as we get one last look at Hoffman, we're told that he's serving life at the California State Penitentiary at Folsom. Dum-da-dum-dum.

Whereas other police dramas emphasized the glamour of the profession, Dragnet focused on the routine with ordinary-looking detectives and stoic dialogue. There was a certain appeal for many in a program that seemed to be more reflective of real life.

Other very early detective programs employed gimmicks to attract viewers. *The Plainclothesman* was shot entirely from the point of view of the protagonist, in the style of the hard-boiled detective film *The Lady in the Lake* (1946) and was one of DuMont's greater successes, airing for almost the entire history of the network from 1949 until 1954. But ABC's *Stand by for Crime* was much less successful. Its gimmick was that viewers could phone in to guess whodunit. And while it lasted for eight months in 1949, it is worth mentioning as it was the first national network program to originate from Chicago and starred a young Mike Wallace, long before he would go on to lasting fame on *60 Minutes*.

REALITY

Ralph Edwards began a new TV program on NBC TV called *This Is Your Life* (1952–1961). Each show began with Edwards surprising some unsuspecting soul. The victim would then be presented on the set with the story of his or her life, complete with friends and relatives who had been brought in for the big occasion.

Arthur Murray can probably be credited with the first infomercial. He developed mail-order dance lessons and the franchise dance business with the Arthur Murray Dance Studios. In July 1950, the balding, silent Arthur Murray bought five 15-minute time periods on DuMont, with his wife, the lively Kathryn Murray hosting and teaching dancing. Before the third show he bought a half-hour summer series on CBS called *The Arthur Murray Party*. By May 1952, the Murrays had televised almost 100 programs and CBS got its first sponsor other than themselves, General Foods. The program continued on NBC from 1953 through 1962.

Candid Camera was the first and longest running reality-based comedy program. On ABC in 1948, under its original radio title *Candid Microphone*, hidden film cameras caught people in embarrassing situations or hoaxes thought up by the show's host Allen Funt. The name changed to *Candid Camera* when it moved to NBC in 1949 and finally got a set time slot when it was moved to CBS in 1960. For the next seven years it was consistently rated as one of television's top 10 shows before it was abruptly canceled.

Reenactment programs, based on real-life crime and still easily found at this writing, came early to television, in part because of the relative ease of developing a script based on real events but also because greater verisimilitude is possible through a recounting of real events; if nothing else, the seeming "reality" of the programs was enough to attract viewers. Two reenactment programs found considerable success during the period, drawing large audiences and staying on the prime-time schedule for years. *Treasury Men in Action* – which also illustrates the "on again, off again" scheduling of the period, as it aired on ABC in 1950, on NBC from 1951 to 1954, and again on ABC from 1954 to 1955—was based on cases that had been investigated by the U.S. Treasury Department. A similar idea was developed in *The Lineup* (CBS, 1954–1960), which recreated cases of the San Francisco Police Department in both half-hour and one-hour lengths. As was typical for the time, the former program used a large number of guest stars in various roles whereas the latter had a relatively stable cast during its run. Each program made it into the top 20 programs during at least one season.

GAME SHOWS

Most quiz show sets were simple in design and structure. A number of early quiz shows were based on stumping experts. The games themselves usually involved a simple question-and-answer format that showed off the panel. Although this authority-centered format dominated the 1940s, it was slowly replaced by audience-centered quizzes in the early 1950s. People from the studio audience became the subjects of the show. The host was the center of attention and main attraction. For example, the quips of Groucho

Marx, the comic quizmaster on the long-running *You Bet Your Life*, kept the show in the top 10 for most of a decade.

Goodson-Todman then produced two different types of quiz shows: celebrity panel shows and celebrations of ordinary people. The Mark Goodson-Bill Todman production *Winner Take All* (CBS, 1948–1950), introduced the concept of a returning contestant who faced a new challenger every round. Thus, attention was directed away from panels and hosts and toward the contestants.

Their first panel show proposal, called "Occupation Unknown," was to see if someone could deduce the occupations of total strangers. CBS bought the idea in 1950 and renamed it as *What's My Line*. The panel was composed of smart, articulate, personable, well-dressed personalities. In its second season, *What's My Line's* format and panelists jelled, and CBS had a hit that would last for 18 seasons, the longest-running game show in primetime. Another of their shows, *Beat the Clock* (1950–1958), let ordinary folk attempt difficult, weird stunts. The prize for completing the stunts started at $100 and finally got to $5,000 by 1958. Goodson-Todman continued to prepare more panel shows such as *The Name's the Same* (ABC, 1951–1955), in which celebrity panelists met ordinary people with famous or unusual names (e.g., George Washington, Mona Lisa, A. Garter).

Two unemployed comedy writers, Allan Sherman and Howard Merrill, created *I've Got a Secret* (CBS, 1952–1976) for Goodson-Todman, and when it debuted in 1952, Sherman became its producer. He managed to be the first to interview Edmund Hillary by phone following his historic ascent of Mt. Everest. He got the Air Force to attempt to break the jet flight speed record from Los Angeles to New York on a Wednesday. The pilot, John Glenn, was then a guest that evening. The show was an example of panel shows that had regular celebrity panelists who appeared in conjunction with noncelebrity contestants. In programs like this, the appeal was in the witty interaction between panelists; prizes, when compared to those of the big-money game shows, were small and of less overall importance to the fun of watching repartee.

Many quiz/game shows had their roots in radio, where the form had originated, and they made the transition to television early in TV history, enjoying considerable popularity. One of the most popular game shows that appeared, *Stop the Music* (ABC, 1949–1956) was an hour prime-time show, in which contestants had to guess the titles of songs after hearing only a few notes. It retained the same radio orchestra, Harry Salter, and emcee Bert Parks. Louis G. Cowan, later to create the *$64,000 Question*, employed Mark Goodson as producer. Goodson would go on to produce more game and quiz shows on TV than any other person.

Although other game shows originated on television and survived through the 1950s, many came and went relatively quickly. The history of the genre is littered with long-forgotten minor shows like *Take a Chance* on NBC for just two months in 1950, with its quaint $5 prizes and jackpots of $1,000 plus a thousand bars of Sweetheart, the sponsor's soap.

NEWS AND DOCUMENTARIES

Most local television stations began creating their own newscasts the day they went on the air to provide instant local community involvement and identity. Early newscasts were brief and nonvisual, for tube cameras were too cumbersome to leave the studio, and live news remotes were all but impossible because of their cost and complexity. Costly 16-millimeter film that required at least three and a half hours to be processed, edited, and set up to play back on a live newscast eventually became the standard. As a result of this new mobility, news visuals became more interesting, and both networks and their affiliates installed their own film developing equipment for speed.

Two roadblocks to making network TV news current were the lack of fast transportation and the networks' inability to do live coast-to-coast broadcasts at first. Developing film and transporting it to New York usually meant that the film available for newscasts was outdated by the time of broadcast. These delays were remedied in 1951, when the coaxial cable link connecting the coasts was completed. The cable enabled the electronic, rather than physical, transportation of television news.

On August 15, 1948, the first network nightly 15-minute newscast, *Douglas Edwards with the News*, debuted on CBS. Still pictures were mounted on easels so that studio cameras could photograph them. When Don Hewitt, who later developed *60 Minutes*, became the regular director of *Douglas Edwards with the News*, he developed techniques to project slides on a screen behind the news anchor. Soon afterward, the R. J. Reynolds Company announced that Camel cigarettes would sponsor a daily television network newsreel on NBC, *Camel News Caravan*, with John Cameron Swayze. He was seldom seen on camera, reading news copy while filmed images filled the screen. The networks had to rely on the movie newsreel companies. Edwards's audience ratings lagged behind the *Camel News Caravan* until the early 1950s. ABC Television, which traced its heritage to the 1943 forced sale of one of NBC's two radio networks, began regular news broadcasts in 1948. The struggling fourth network, DuMont, broadcast news from 1947 to 1949, halted news programming until 1953, then went out of business in 1955.

VICTORY AT SEA

One of the most ambitious documentary undertakings of early network television was *Victory at Sea* (1952–1953), a 26-episode series, shown consecutive Sundays, about the naval battles of World War II. Each episode was composed of archival footage originally accumulated by the U.S., British, Japanese, and German navies. The dramatically edited footage was enhanced by voice-over narration and by Broadway composer Richard Rogers's stirring musical score. *Victory at Sea* received 13 awards, including a Peabody and a special Emmy. The producer was Henry Salomon, who, while serving in the U.S. Navy, had helped historian Samuel Eliot Morison write the Navy's official combat history and learned of the film footage. He came away in 1948 with the idea for a comprehensive historical account of the conflict. He presented the idea to a Harvard classmate, Robert Sarnoff, the son of RCA Chairman David Sarnoff.

The younger Sarnoff was about to take over the network's new Film Division as NBC, which anticipated shifting more of its schedule from live to filmed programming. Production began in 1951, with the substantial budget of $500,000. Veteran film newsreel editors assembled 60 million feet of footage, edited down to 61,000 feet. It was first broadcast without sponsorship; so NBC placed it in the lineup of cultural programs on Sunday afternoon. The company promoted it as a high-prestige program, an example of history brought to life in the living room through the new medium of television. As a film (rather than live), it could be rebroadcast indefinitely, and NBC was able to exploit the program in lucrative residual markets. Since *Victory at Sea* dealt with a historical subject, its information value would not depreciate as would a current-affairs documentary. When *Victory at Sea* went into syndication in May 1953 it played on 206 local stations over the course of 10 years with as many as 20 reruns in some markets. In the mid-1960s one year's syndication income equaled the entire production cost. By 1964, *Victory at Sea* had played in 40 foreign markets. NBC recut the material into a 90-minute feature distributed theatrically in 1954, and that version was broadcast in NBC's prime-time schedule in 1960 and 1963. The Richard Rogers score was sold in several record versions through RCA-Victor and by 1963, the album version had grossed $4 million. One tune from the score, "No Other Love," earned $500,000 just as a single. The combination of prestige and residual income helped establish as a program form, compilation documentaries, programs composed of existing archival footage. (It is now being offered on the History Channel on videocassette to viewers.)

Nonfiction programs of the documentary and public affairs sort, featuring both hard and soft news as well as segments on topics of general interest, have a long history in prime-time television. Public affairs programming was encouraged by the FCC. A 1946 document, "Public Service Responsibility of Broadcast Licensees," (more commonly known as the "Blue Book" because of the color of its cover) made a case for providing viewers with what they needed—as opposed to the "mere" entertainment they presumably wanted— and implied that a certain, though unspecified, amount of public affairs programming would be looked upon favorably at station license renewal time. Due to protests from broadcasters, the document never became official policy, but it did have some influence. It was only natural that the networks, with their greater financial and human resources, would take the lead in providing public affairs programming to their affiliated stations. Moreover, public affairs programming was cheaper for the networks to produce than were the fictional programs that required high-priced actors, costly sets, and expensive props.

The Blue Book also suggested that networks and their affiliates do more sustaining programming. These unsponsored shows became an important part of the industry's push to sell television receivers. Since many advertisers were reluctant to make the commitment to pay all of the costs of producing a program, the networks had to do more of their own productions. And since the financial strategy of many veteran broadcasters was to use radio profits to provide funds for the fledgling television medium, a side effect of increased sustaining programming on television was the decrease in sustaining programming on radio as programs were dropped in favor of sponsored programming. Sustaining programming on television was varied, including dramatic series, educational programs, political events, and public affairs programs. However, many programs that began as sustaining (such as *Howdy Doody*) quickly found sponsors after they became popular. As a result, the amount of sustaining programming on commercial television quickly diminished, notwithstanding the FCC's admonitions.

President Truman was inaugurated in January 1949 with TV cameras covering the ceremonies. Thirty-four stations located in 16 cities composed that first inaugural network.

That year the FCC established a policy that came to be known as the "Fairness Doctrine." It guaranteed (among other things) the presentation of both sides of a controversial issue. Stations became very cautious about the content of programs to avoid controversial subjects. They did not want to have to give free time to balance content by seeking out and encouraging opposing viewpoints, then giving them free time on the air. The doctrine was repealed by the FCC in 1985. Attempts by Congress to reinstate it were vetoed by President Reagan in 1987, but it had a real effect on programming decisions during the period it existed.

The final construction of the first transcontinental relay system between New York and Chicago, and finally extended to San Francisco, was launched from the West Coast on September 4, 1951. The first program carried was a telecast of the Japanese peace treaty conference. The impact of nationwide networking was quickly seen. Edward R. Murrow and Fred Friendly launched one of the most highly praised TV documentary programs in broadcasting, *See It Now* (CBS) in 1951. On the first program, Murrow showed a live camera shot of the Atlantic Ocean, followed by a live shot of the Pacific, and said, "We are impressed by a medium through which a man sitting in his living room has been able to look at two oceans at once."

See It Now (1952–1955) was a television version of the radio program *Hear It Now* created by journalist Edward R. Murrow and producer Fred Friendly. Murrow had made a name for himself as the CBS radio London correspondent during World War II and was perhaps the first TV network superstar news personality.

In a famous broadcast on March 9, 1954, Murrow and Friendly aired an exposé on the notorious Red-baiting tactics of the powerful Sen. Joseph McCarthy. The program spelled the beginning of the end for the senator from Wisconsin. The Army–McCarthy hearings that followed the broadcast, in which McCarthy sought to root out the communists that he believed had infiltrated the U.S. military, and which were broadcast on live daytime TV to high ratings, backfired and in fairly short order McCarthy was censured by Congress. He died shortly after in 1957. But McCarthy had a long-lasting influence on television as the desire to stamp out communistic influences, real and imagined, in all walks of American life led to the blacklisting that continued into the 1960s, and CBS management, nervous in the wake of the McCarthy program, moved *See It Now* back to a Sunday afternoon timeslot that guaranteed it fewer viewers and less influence.

The networks were conscious of their duty to provide public affairs programming but were equally aware of its potential to stir up controversy and displease advertisers. After the death of *See It Now*, CBS created *CBS Reports* (1961–1971), which presented documentaries on a fairly regular basis. One of the most respected was "Harvest of Shame" about the plight of migrant workers. The most debated was "The Selling of the Pentagon," dealing with the military's use of tax dollars for public relations. Throughout the 1960s and into the 1970s, NBC, CBS, and to a lesser extent, ABC presented hour-long documentaries in prime-time about pressing issues on a national and international level, but the programs lost ratings and created contention. They have been replaced by the news magazines that assume an attention span of 15 minutes for any topic except crime and celebrity.

On June 21, 1948, came the first network telecasts of political conventions. Both parties met in Philadelphia that year. Connecting network lines with Philadelphia the coaxial cable ran only from Boston to Washington with a spur to Chicago. The only recording system in use for networks was a film camera pointed at a picture on a TV screen. The film then had to be developed. The resulting "kinescope" had a grainy, jerky, washed-out picture, but for stations not yet connected to the networks, it had to do. NBC sent edited kinescope recordings for next-day telecasts to those stations not yet connected.

By 1952, the networks and affiliates were connected, and the presidential election was given heavy live coverage, with the nominating conventions taking up most of prime-time. In the future, networks would provide less coverage during prime-time, in part because popular programs were pre-empted, riling both viewers and advertisers.

Westinghouse was the convention's sole sponsor. Their on-air spokesperson was Betty Furness. She was in every ad, live. By the convention's end she had logged more air time than any speaker of either party and made her tag line "You can be *sure* if it's Westinghouse" into a national catchphrase. Betty Furness began her television career in 1945, as the host of DuMont's *Fashions Coming and Becoming*. By 1948, she was in front of the television cameras as an actress for an episode of *Studio One*, sponsored by Westinghouse appliances. Like the programs, the commercials were done live, frequently performed on the side of the main set. Furness thought she could do better than the actor hired to do the commercials and offered to take a stab at it. Company executives were impressed and offered her the $150 a week job as spokesperson. Furness's delivery was always smooth and memorized (in the days before the TelePrompTer), and she was given great credit for high sales volumes. She received, on average, 1,000 pieces of fan mail a week. From January to July 1953, Furness hosted *Meet Betty Furness*, a lively, informative daily talk show—sponsored by Westinghouse—on NBC.

The Vice Presidential nominee for the Republicans, Richard Nixon, went on the air September 23, 1952, to deny allegations that he misused political contributions from wealthy California executives. Although it appeared he was delivering the speech to the American public, he was trying to convince Presidential candidate Dwight Eisenhower not to dump him as his vice-president. After an exhaustive defense of his financial dealings, Nixon did admit to accepting one personal donation, for his children, a cocker spaniel named Checkers—a gift he insisted he had no intention of returning. With its mixture of defiance and humility, the broadcast salvaged Nixon's political career.

One significant person in news was Martha Rountree, perhaps the most visible woman in news and public affairs programming during the early period of network television history, in both a genre and time dominated by men. Along with Lawrence Spivak, she was the creator of the long-running public affairs program *Meet the Press*, which aired in prime-time on NBC (1947–1965) and on Sunday mornings for several more decades, often with Spivak serving as a panelist. *Meet the Press* had begun on radio in 1945 as a program to promote "The American Mercury Magazine," which Spivak edited. Rountree was moderator of *Meet the Press* during its earliest years (1947–1953). She and Spivak were also moderator and panelist, respectively, on DuMont programs similar in theme and content: *Keep Posted* (1951–1953) and its successor *The Big Issue* (1953–1954); the pair produced the simultaneous *Washington Exclusive* in 1953.

Rountree was also the creator and producer of the more light-hearted *Leave It to the Girls*, complete with the to-today's-eyes sexist title, which has been described as a once-serious program that "soon degenerated into a one-sided battle of the sexes," that aired on NBC (1949–1951) and ABC (1953–1954). Although the program's panelists are largely unknown today, it's worth noting that the panelist with the longest tenure is listed as Eloise "The Mouth" McElhone,[6] a nickname that implies a stylistic connection between *Leave It to the Girls* and contemporary reality/talk shows. The program had begun on radio in 1945, moved to local New York City television in 1947 and on to the network in 1949. After the collapse of DuMont, Rountree was moderator of *Press Conference* (NBC, summer 1956 and ABC, 1956–1957), before otherwise disappearing from TV screens.

Perhaps the only other personality in the genre to stand out was Walter Winchell, whose eponymously titled, tabloid-like television program provided the same mix of right-wing commentary and celebrity gossip that he had been providing in his syndicated newspaper column and on radio since the 1930s. *The Walter Winchell Show* (ABC, 1952–1955) was heavy on Winchell's pro-McCarthy, anticommunist philosophy and his showmanship as a former vaudevillian.

MOVIES ON TELEVISION

Hollywood theatrical films were shown in often-unrecognizable (to modern eyes) forms on network television from its earliest days. One of the earliest series, if not the first, was the all-but-forgotten *Western Movie* on DuMont, which began toward the end of 1946. Some of the films aired on *Western Movie* were so old as to be silent. The networks that would later become the "big three" all began showing films or film shorts in some form with the half-hour *NBC Presents* in 1948; *Film Theatre of the Air* on CBS in 1949 as a half-hour program; and *The ABC Feature Film* as a one-hour show in 1949. The showing of full-length films, those of roughly 75 minutes or more, apparently didn't begin until CBS brought out its *Summer Cinema* program in 1952.

In 1948 the major movie studios had been forced by the Justice Department to divest themselves of either their theaters or their production facilities. They sold off their movie houses—which greatly weakened their ability to control the distribution of their product. At the same time, they found themselves competing with television. By 1950, television was severely curtailing movie attendance. The movie industry responded by going color and working on large-screen systems.

There was one way to compete with television, and that was to own it. ABC was nearly bankrupt. Leonard Goldenson, manager of United Paramount's' theater division, brokered a merger with ABC TV for $25 million in 1951. He was able to persuade Hollywood film leaders Jack Warner and Walt Disney to provide filmed programs to ABC. The result from Warner Bros. was action shows like *Cheyenne* and *77 Sunset Strip*. Disney brought a variety of programs under the umbrella of *The Wonderful World of Disney*. Variations of this show have appeared at various times on ABC, CBS, and NBC ever since then. The program introduced Davy Crockett, Zorro, and the new Disneyland to the public. Though very concerned about competition from television at the beginning, the big studios were finally convinced to sell or rent production capability in order to reduce overhead.

For the most part the films shown on TV were either short subjects, of less than 30 minutes in length, or features edited into one-hour, half-hour or even shorter time slots. The films were minor efforts by the studios, most if not all made by the smaller independent producers such as RKO, Republic and Monogram during the 1930s, and usually B features—the second film of a double feature—at that.

The major sort of Hollywood film, something with big stars, was a long time in coming to network television. One set of problems that kept them out of the prime-time lineup centered on industrial relations, as agreements over compensation between members of the Screen Actors Guild and other employment guilds and the studios took years to resolve[7] and limited the release of films to those made before 1948.

Other problems were based in the uneasy relationship between the movie studios and the networks. An apocryphal story has it that one Hollywood studio not only banned TV sets as props in its films but forbade its employees from talking about what they'd watched on TV the night before. This poor relationship was based on competition between the movie and TV industries for viewers, an emphasis on live programming in television, and, simply, because the networks either wouldn't or couldn't pay the price for the broadcast rights to Hollywood films. It's not that the films weren't available. The trade publication *Variety* in 1951 estimated that Hollywood held in its vaults more than 4,000 full-length feature films and more than 6,000 short subjects made between 1935 and 1946, and estimated their value to television at a then-astronomical $250 million—although, without being shown on TV, they were worthless studio inventory, too far out of date to be rereleased to theaters[8] and as such unable to generate revenue.

As a result, full-length Hollywood feature films trickled onto television over a number of years. Independent TV stations—those without network affiliations—bought the rights to older films such as *The Hunchback of Notre Dame* (1939) and *Citizen Kane* (1941), and used them to counterprogram the networks, sometimes to great result. Independent WATU in New York City, for example, took 90 percent of all TV viewers in the nation's largest television market one night in December 1956 with a showing of the 1948 Clark Gable World War II film *Command Decision.*

The networks, in turn, counter-counterprogrammed the independent stations and their old black-and-white movies with big budget, all-new specials and spectaculars that they produced themselves. Sylvester "Pat" Weaver of NBC saw these specials as a way of taking away control from the advertisers, who could only buy time within the show and who couldn't control its production or scheduling. The famous Mary Martin version of *Peter Pan* drew an estimated 70 million viewers to NBC in March 1955.[9] The early days of television consisted of many one-time-only programs such as the *Miss Television USA Contest* (1950) and *Amahl and the Night Visitors* (1951), an opera commissioned for television. It was the first *The Hallmark Hall of Fame* and was repeated around Christmas for some years.

But movies weren't major parts of the prime-time network schedule. During the 1953–1954 season, a number of movies made before 1948 began to appear, but it wasn't until ABC in summer 1957 began its *Hollywood Film Theatre* that "A" films with well-known stars began to be seen. Among the offerings that summer were *King Kong, Top Hat,* and the Cary Grant trilogy *Gunga Din, Mr. Blandings Builds His Dream House,* and *Bringing Up Baby;*[10] still, all had been made during the 1930s, except for *Blandings,* the newest of the films and dating from 1948.

LEADERS

There is one person who affected the future of TV programming but did it behind the scenes. At a time when many in the movie business saw TV as the enemy, MCA's Lew Wasserman saw it as an opportunity. He got his first TV set in 1939, deciding even then that TV could be a market for Hollywood products. Eventually he would buy film libraries and license them to TV, making MCA a premier program supplier as well as the largest talent agency.

But in 1948, radio still was the mass medium. Lew Wasserman proposed a deal to CBS's William Paley. By utilizing a loophole in the tax code, Wasserman told Paley, CBS could likely obtain the services of most of NBC's top radio stars (his clients). NBC had been the frontrunner in radio ratings with CBS coming up just behind. Wasserman explained that under the newly revised tax code, performers were assessed 77 percent of all personal earnings over $70,000. But by incorporating themselves as businesses and selling their companies to the network, the tax bite would only be a 25 percent corporate capital gain.

Paley jumped at the chance to beat his rival at NBC, David Sarnoff. After Charles Correll and Freeman Gosden (*The Amos and Andy Show*) were signed, Paley offered the deal to Jack Benny. Wasserman then told Sarnoff about the CBS offer to drive up the price. Paley prevailed but had to get Benny's sponsor to permit the move as they had a contract with Benny that they controlled which network he would appear on. Paley promised the sponsor, American Tobacco Company, that he would compensate them for every rating point that was lost. Paley was not in favor of sponsors having control over programming but at that time he could not see how to prevent it.

The Internal Revenue Service challenged the arrangement, but the Supreme Court declared the contracts legal. Jack Benny, Red Skelton, Bing Crosby, George Burns and Gracie Allen, Edgar Bergen (with Charlie McCarthy), and a number of other MCA clients jumped to CBS radio.

The importance of just this one event, known as "The Talent Raid," is that CBS experienced a tremendous profit increase. This made it possible for Paley to launch CBS into TV with 12 of the top 15 radio stars to appear exclusively on his TV network. The impact was that CBS held a lead over all the other networks for the next 25 years.

There were other key people who had a great influence on the development of television programming. Edward Petry founded the first station sales representation company in 1931 for independent radio stations to gain access to national sponsors. Petry was also the first rep firm to open a separate television division in 1948. He developed the commercial spot business, whereby sponsors could just buy 60-second "spots," in shows rather than paying for the complete program.

Bing Crosby helped build radio and TV businesses into the powerhouses they became. As a singer and actor, he was among the first rank of radio stars. He went on to produce television with Bing Crosby Productions and sped the introduction of videotape as an early investor in Ampex.

THE THAW

TV advertising increased throughout this period. But the TV networks and individual stations operated at a heavy loss. By 1952, no more than half of all TV stations were earning a profit. Then came the TV thaw. After almost four years, on April 14, 1952, the FCC issued its *Sixth Report and Order.* The freeze on granting new licenses for TV stations had given the FCC time to deal with the linked technical problems of allocation and signal interference. The questions were straightforward: Where should TV stations be located, both on the broadcasting spectrum and physically? And how can one station be kept from interfering with another? But the answers were fairly complex.

Exactly where television signals would be placed on the electromagnetic spectrum had been partially solved by the time the freeze began in 1948. The FCC had earlier decided for technical reasons to allocate space for television in a part of the spectrum deemed Very High Frequency, known most often as VHF, originally comprising channels 1–13. In time channel 1 was reallocated for the radios of various public safety agencies, leaving VHF with the familiar range of channels 2–13. The FCC added 220 more VHF stations.

But it was apparent that there was a need for additional spectrum space—that is, more channels in more cities. The FCC expanded to Ultra High Frequency (UHF) on channels 14 to 83, establishing 70 UHF channels providing 1,400 potential stations. The problem was that UHF stations could not be successful unless people had TV sets that could receive UHF. None of the sets already in people's homes had UHF tuners, and set manufacturers did not plan on putting UHF tuners in new sets, citing cost. People would have to purchase an adaptor to receive UHF signals, but why would they spend the extra money when there were so few UHF stations offering so little programming?

Between 1952 and 1959, there were 165 UHF stations that went on the air; however, 55 percent went off the air. Of the UHF stations still on the air, 75 percent were losing money. UHF's problems were (1) technical inequality of UHF stations as compared with VHF stations; (2) VHF and UHF stations had to compete with each other in the same market with the millions of VHF-only receivers; (3) the lack of confidence in the capabilities of and the need for UHF television.

Suggestions were made that each market should have either all VHF or all UHF rather than some of both. This would force people to buy sets or adaptors that would pick up their local TV stations or go without. This idea was not adopted, because the VHF owners fought hard to keep their frequencies. Ultimately all TV sets were required to have UHF tuners under an All Channels Act. However, more than four decades later, UHF is still considered inferior to VHF. Despite cable television, ratings on VHF channels are generally higher than those of UHF channels. The allocation between VHF and UHF in the 1950s, and the lack of UHF tuners is entirely analogous to the dilemma facing digital television more than fifty years later.

Channel interference was solved by implementing strict rules of separation for stations broadcasting on the same channel, which had to be at least 190 miles apart. A few existing stations had to change channels to meet the requirements. Channel allocation took the form of city-by-city assignment of one or more channels based on the general criterion of fair geographic apportionment. The "assignment table" that was produced gave some cities—New York and Los Angeles, for example—many stations. Less populated locales were allocated a smaller numbers of outlets. The average-sized market had three VHF channels allocated, and that decision meant that for many years, only three networks could survive.

The FCC also set aside 242 potential channels throughout the country for education, most of them of in the UHF band. The reservation of channel space for noncommercial, educational television was spearheaded by FCC Commissioner Frieda B. Hennock. When the channel reservation issue was raised for radio during the deliberation leading up to the Communications Act of 1934, the commercial industry view prevailed. Broadcasting was considered too valuable a resource to entrust to educators or others who had no profit motive. Would they be able to spur the development of the medium to reach high technical standards? The FCC acquiesced to Hennock because it reasoned that if the educators succeeded, it would be viewed as prescient; if the educators failed, at least the FCC had given them an opportunity. In addition, Hennock and her forces were seen as a nuisance: The noncommercial channel issue was helping keep the freeze alive, and there were powerful industry and viewer forces waiting for it to end.

This, then, was the climate in which the freeze was rescinded in 1952. The effects of its end were almost immediate. The number of stations on the air jumped from 108 in 1952 to 334 just a year later. Suddenly television, something that up to that date many people had only heard about, was available to 24 million households, the stations situated so that almost everyone in the United States could get at least one. Those 24 million television households represented about 45 percent of the total number of households in the United States at the time, and the percentage of homes with TV increased rapidly, reaching 90 percent by 1962, just a decade after the freeze ended.[11]

CONCLUSION

The age of awkward adolescence for TV programming was 1948–1952. The ties to the parent radio networks were still strong. Stars and genres were inherited from the elder medium. Frequently, TV programming was little more than minimal visualization of the audio. But even more importantly, the structure of the radio industry was passed on. The same companies—ABC, CBS, and NBC—continued to dominate. The advertising agencies were still the main source of programming. Production facilities were headquartered in New York City, allowing Broadway to be more of an influence than Hollywood. Most programming was still done live; film was rarely used and videotape was still being developed. The shows were black and white, and the networks didn't reach from coast to coast until 1951.

Perhaps the biggest change during this period was the growing audience. People quickly switched their loyalty from radio to TV. They bought sets as the prices came down and sat in the living room, their eyes glued to the moving images. But the number of choices in most cities was limited to one or two TV stations. When the FCC lifted the freeze on new applications, more stations went on the air, and the TV industry was poised to become the dominant medium for the audience.

CHAPTER 4

The Rise and Fall of Live Drama and Quiz Shows (1953–1959)

Television was still new in the early 1950s but growing in its importance to everyday life. If contemporary stories are to be believed, a television set was such a status symbol that husbands who couldn't yet afford them bought antennas to attach to their roofs to keep up with the Joneses, and wives followed the lead of women's magazines and redecorated their homes to incorporate television rooms in which TV dinners could be served while the family sat on furniture slip-covered in plastic.

The first generation of television superstars arose during this time period. Lucille Ball, Milton Berle, and the cast of *Amos 'n' Andy* kept millions of Americans glued to their tiny screens watching grainy images that faded in and out as primitive antennas struggled with the vagaries of over-the-air reception.

But by the end of the decade, much of the innocence that TV, and perhaps viewers, had was gone. Increasing amounts of news and public affairs programs brought the problems of the world into living rooms, and the revelation that highly popular quiz shows were in fact rigged brought about a scandal that changed the way programming was produced.

SITCOMS

Comedy is difficult to write about, because the inevitable question—*why is any given program funny?*—is unanswerable. All that can really be said about any successful comedy is that audiences at the time took it to be humorous, and that failed programs simply weren't considered funny. As such, it becomes impossible to look back into television history and divine reasons for the success or failure of any comedy program.

Perhaps the most enduring television genre is the situation comedy, a form born in radio and familiar, because of endless repetition, to all television viewers. All sitcoms share a similar form in that they all revolve around "'timeless' didactic narratives on the foibles and frailties of family life and social relations"[1] and, if not family-centered, then are grounded in the "family" of coworkers in the major sitcom variant, the workplace comedy. There are structural similarities as well—chiefly the half-hour format, divided into two or three acts with commercials between. The conventions of character, setting, and so on that govern sitcoms change over time, of course, but their continued appeal lies in the way that they, like genre films, "repeatedly flesh out and reexamine cultural conflicts"[2] of the sort that most of us deal with on a day-to-day basis, filtered through a gauze of comedy. For example, the entry of large numbers of women into the workforce in the 1970s generated a series of workplace comedies centering on young, independent women who aimed to "make it after all," à la Mary Tyler Moore.

Looking Back: The Older Audience and 1950s Sitcoms

For most of its existence, and unlike today, this television genre was far from trendy, hip and up-to-date. Instead, it looked backwards with programs in the mid-1950s that seem today to be trapped in a time warp, although with presumed appeal for TV-owning older audiences afflicted with nostalgia. For example, the sitcom *It's a Great Life* (NBC, 1954–1957) centered on two World War II veterans looking for jobs in Southern California, as if the war had just concluded instead of having ended in 1945, and would no doubt have been of interest to people who had lived through the war years themselves and who with the passage of time could now laugh about it.

Many of the sitcoms from before the 1960s appear to have older actors and to have been aimed at an older audience; for example, Gale Gordon, who was in his 50s, played a bachelor who owned a San Francisco photo shop with his brother in *The Brothers* (CBS, 1956–1957). It seems fitting, somehow, that fifty-something bachelors would be fodder for humor during the 50s. In another example of actors playing roles too old for them, the then 34-year-old movie star Mickey Rooney was cast as a young NBC page looking for his big break in show business (he'd starred in the *Andy Hardy* series of films during the 1930s and 1940s) in the eponymous *The Mickey*

Rooney Show (NBC, 1954–1955. Hollywood followed a similar tactic at the time, routinely casting people in their late 20s and early 30s to play teenagers in movies, to sometimes unintentionally comic results, as when high school teachers and their students appeared to be the same age.

Happy Family Sitcoms

Happy family sitcoms, which were sometimes as dramatic as they were humorous, are among the television programs lodged in our collective memory as typifying the 1950s, a largely mythical era when dad put on his necktie and went off to the office (he would continue to wear it at home after work) and mom stayed home, cooking and cleaning in pearls and a pleated dress, with every hair perfectly in place, like Donna Reed.

The exception, of course, was *The Honeymooners* (CBS, 1955–1971). The program spent most of its life as a sketch in other shows and survived as a series only a short time, but its reruns remain classics. The characters were Ralph Kramden (Jackie Gleason), his wife (Audrey Meadows), the best friend (Art Carney), and his wife (Joyce Randolph). The setting was a barely furnished apartment in Brooklyn. And the plots were mainly about the efforts of the blue-collar Ralph to raise his status in the world and about his failures. He yelled at the others, and they responded with sarcastic comments, but somehow the overall tone wasn't about his frustration and anger, but about his one success—getting people to see beyond his bluster into his heart of gold.

The Danny Thomas Show (ABC, CBS, 1953–1971; also called *Make Room for Daddy*), told about the life of an entertainer, his wife (lovely, lots of common sense, and a high tolerance for nonsense from a husband), and two children (the usual charming brats). The familiar formula had to change when the original wife (Jean Hagen) left the show. Thomas became a widower who married a woman (Marjorie Lord) very similar in temperament to his first wife.

Father Knows Best did break the mold in one way. Whereas most of the sitcoms of the 1950s were about foolish fathers and wise mothers, this show had an intelligent dad with some insight into his children's problems. He could offer advice without making the audience laugh, and his family respected him. It was even understandable why his wife married him. In *The Donna Reed Show* (ABC, 1958–1966), the mother was clearly the source of wisdom, but the dad was a respected pediatrician and his viewpoint could be considered seriously sometimes. And *Leave It to Beaver* (CBS, ABC, 1957–1963) followed that pattern. Both parents (Hugh Beaumont and Barbara Billingsley) had good judgment. The program added another

LEAVE IT TO BEAVER

Leave It to Beaver is a rare program that can truly be called iconic as it informs our view of what we think American families were like during the 1950s, based on memories of the gentle happy family sitcoms of its era. Located within the comforting world of the suburbs, it opens with typical-for-its-time visual and verbal introductions of the characters, beginning with central character Theodore "Beaver" Cleaver. Of particular interest is June Cleaver, the very picture of 1950s TV motherhood, a housewife in pleated dress and necklace, whose household is so efficiently run that Beaver and older brother Wally clean their already tidy rooms and help with after-dinner dishwashing.

The "Wally's Test" episode focuses on Wally instead of Beaver. Its plot involves an exam on World War I that Wally and his friends Eddie Haskell and Lumpy Rutherford, a dimwitted jock who's been left back, have to take. Whereas Wally does the right thing by studying, Eddie and Lumpy try the easy route and plant exam answers inside a paper towel dispenser in the boy's rest room. Wally goes to the restroom first, though, and discovers a note on a paper towel that reads "To thine own self be true . . . ," signed "Polonius and Mr. Gannon," their teacher. Eddie and Lumpy, of course, fail to find their notes, do poorly on the exam—Lumpy in fact scoring lower than he did on the same exam the year before—and conclude that Wally got to them first.

They confront Wally, who goes home and in expository dialogue tells Beaver about the sudden decline in his friendship with Eddie, although without mentioning cheating. Gannon telephones Wally and orders him to a meeting at which Gannon tells Wally that an anonymous note accusing Wally of cheating has been left on his desk. Wally recognizes the handwriting and calls Eddie a "no-good bum," then immediately apologizes for using such shocking language in front of a teacher. But Gannon is wise to the old notes-on-the-paper-towels trick, and tells Wally that he found the notes and substituted the cryptic message, which he thought was humorous. Wally says he didn't realize it was supposed to be funny.

Wally asks his father, Ward, for advice. Ward—a typical 1950s television dad, in necktie and cardigan, wisdom always on his lips—tells him that people like Eddie sometimes see the error of their ways and that Wally should leave him to it, even if he never does reform. Eddie arrives unexpectedly and, surprisingly, apologizes to Wally for his behavior. Eddie says he's learned the value of studying honestly, which Wally passes on to Beaver in additional expository dialogue that underlines the episode's lesson.

In the dénouement, Gannon advances an argument blatantly in favor of 1950s-era, buttoned-down conformity. He tells the class that cheating is always discovered within what he calls "the system" and advises them that since the real world is much like the system, they must learn to get along in it. The class listens in rapt attention, heads bent over notebooks, taking the advice to heart and looking forward to careers at IBM and as homemakers.

quality that made it in an enduring success: children who almost seemed real, not escapees of a nightclub act. They acted and talked like authentic kids ... at times.

By the end of the 1950s, television programmers were beginning to admit that another culture existed beyond the suburbs: an urban counter-culture where people sat around coffee houses, listened to jazz music and poetry, and snapped their fingers in appreciation. They wore black sweaters, black slacks, and black berets. They weren't really so much opposed to the mainstream society as bored by it. Maynard G. Krebs (Bob Denver) was a more casual version of the beatnik—sweatshirt, jeans, beard, bongo drums, and a strong aversion to work. This character on *The Many Loves of Dobie Gillis* (CBS, 1959–1963) imparted his laid-back insights to the lead, a teenager trying to understand women, parents, school, and the world, while his parents struggled to make him satisfied with ordinary middle-class life.

But while the most popular and longest-lived of the happy family programs—namely, *The Adventures of Ozzie and Harriet* (ABC, 1952–1966), *Father Knows Best* (CBS, NBC, and ABC, 1954–1963), and *Leave It to Beaver* (CBS and ABC, 1957–1963)—focused on the home life of traditional nuclear families who overcame their everyday trials and tribulations in a warm and wholesome manner, a large number of similar programs were built around less traditional families, run by single parents, often widows but more often widowers, or even housekeepers. It should also be noted at the outset that none of the big three aforementioned programs survived the tumultuous 1960s (except on cable) and the social changes that the decade brought to the real world and to television.

In the skewed world of prime-time television, widowers vastly outnumbered widows, the opposite of the case in the real world, where women generally outlive men. Reasons for this are unclear, but it may simply be that at the time, single fatherhood was seen as being riper for comedy than single motherhood: Men, as the stereotype went, tended to be inept outside the workplace, so what had greater potential for humor than a man bumbling his way through raising children? Typical dad-only sitcoms included *Bonino*, on NBC for just three months in 1953, which followed the everyday life of a widower opera singer with eight children, and starred the real-life opera singer Ezio Pinza. *The Dennis O'Keefe Show* (CBS, 1959–1960) was similar in nature, focusing on a syndicated newspaper columnist, a widower with a typical-for-television precocious 10-year-old son.

The most popular program about single fathers who weren't widowers was *Bachelor Father* (CBS, NBC, and ABC, 1957–1962). In it, wealthy Hollywood bachelor attorney Bentley Gregg (John Forsythe) raised his niece Kelly (Noreen Corcoran) after she was orphaned as a teenager. The program lasted long enough that Kelly went through high school and entered college.

The single mother variant was represented by *It's Always Jan* (CBS, 1955–1956), which was also one of a number of show biz family variants of the happy family sitcom, and which centered on war widow/nightclub singer/single mom Janis Stewart (singer Janis Page) and her precocious 10-year-old daughter Josie (Jeri Lou Aimes). The program featured songs by Paige. Another example is *The Betty Hutton Show* (CBS, 1959–1960), which dealt with manicurist Goldie Appleby (Hutton), who inherited both the estate and the teenaged children of a wealthy client.

A similar theme was found in *Jamie* (ABC, 1953–1954), about 11-year-old orphan Jamie McHummer (Brandon DeWilde) who, after being shuffled about, landed in the household of a loving aunt where he bonded with Grandpa (Ernest Truex), a kindred spirit.

In the days before targeting the young audience became the goal of programmers, people over 60 years old were allowed to star in a series. *December Bride* (CBS, 1954–1961) was about a widow (Spring Byington) with grown children who adored her and with a number of suitors. In contrast, *The Real McCoys* (ABC, CBS, 1957–1963) was about a hillbilly family with a crotchety old grandfather (Walter Brennan) who headed up the clan.

Of course, some shows resist categorization. *Topper* (CBS, ABC, NBC, 1953–1956) told the weekly trials and tribulations of a respectable man (Leo G. Carroll) who finds his house haunted by a sophisticated young couple (Robert Sterling and Anne Jeffreys) and their St. Bernard, Neil. All of the ghosts, including the dog, had a taste for martinis and champagne.

The comedy built around the workplace was not quite as popular as the family sitcom. *Our Miss Brooks* (CBS, 1952–1956) starred Eve Arden as a wisecracking high school teacher. Like Mr. Peepers, she was well liked by her students and never had any problems winning their respect. *The Phil Silvers Show* (CBS, 1955–1959) (also known as *You'll Never Get Rich*) was a view of the peacetime army. Sgt. Ernie Bilko spent his time trying to play con games on everyone, sometimes for virtuous reasons, but most often just for the sheer joy of winning. Underneath his bluster was a reluctantly decent human being, which made his antics forgivable.

Another sort of scamp was the lead character in *The Bob Cummings Show* (NBC, CBS, 1955–1959). He played a handsome bachelor with a roving eye for lovely young women. Luckily, for him, he was a photographer and met plenty. (In the 1950s, such a character was considered charming, even admirable, not a male chauvinist pig.) He did live with his sister and her son, but the emphasis was usually on his attempts to win a date for the evening.

Taken together, these programs indicate that television reflected not only the received view of domestic life, that of traditional families composed of father, mother, and the statistically correct 2.2 children, but also some of the other realities of family life in the 1950s as well.

I Love Lucy

Perhaps the most iconic of all sitcoms is a set of programs often thought of collectively as *I Love Lucy*, the title of the first set, but that includes several similar series that aired in prime-time from the 1950s to the 1970s and that continue to attract viewers to the present day.

The content of *I Love Lucy* places it in what has been called the "show-biz family" sitcom, a subgenre that includes *The Danny Thomas Show* and *The Dick Van Dyke Show*. Lucy was forever attempting to break into Ricky's nightclub act, or trying out jobs outside the home, and episodes centered on Ball's revival of comic routines honed in vaudeville and silent movies. The enduring appeal of the programs is such that inexpensive DVDs of episodes of *The Lucy Show* could be found for $5.99 in the merchandise-stuffed foyers of Cracker Barrel restaurants in 2005, where they've become part of the chain's good-old-days-in-a-simpler-time theme. The DVDs are sold next to bright pink T-shirts emblazoned with a scene from an episode, the one where Lucy has to gobble chocolates in order to keep up with the too-fast production line.

I Love Lucy, which ran on CBS from 1951 until 1961 in both new episodes and as several years of prime-time reruns, and its successor program *The Lucy Show*, also on CBS from 1962 to 1974, were among the most highly rated programs of their, or any, time. *I Love Lucy* peaked at an unheard of 67.3 rating during the 1952 season and *The Lucy Show*, while drawing many fewer audience members in a time of much greater programming choice,

In *I Love Lucy*, Lucille Ball created the classic zany lady. In one memorable episode, she and her friend played by Vivian Vance found themselves desperately trying to keep up with a never-ending supply of chocolates on the assembly line. Courtesy of Photofest.

was a top 20 program through most of the 1960s and was still the number-three program of the 1970–1971 season, with a 26.1 rating. Its popularity during the 1950s led to a spin-off film, *The Long, Long Trailer* in 1954, directed by no less a personage than Vincente Minnelli, and the source of the famous publicity photo of Lucy, Desi, Fred, and Ethel singing as they drive along in their convertible.

The Long, Long Trailer was not the first excursion onto the big screen for Ball. She had been cast not only in 1930s Bob Hope comedies, but also as independent, intelligent women in post-World War II films noir, such as *The Dark Corner* (1946), in which she played the brainy, beautiful secretary to a private detective investigating a series of art thefts. The contrast between her character in that film and the Lucy persona is dramatic.

Also prior to television, Ball had starred as Liz Cooper in the 1948–1952 CBS radio sitcom *My Favorite Husband*, in which she first developed her persona as a "frantic, endearingly spacey" housewife[3] who annoyed her long-suffering husband with her antics in much the same way that Lucy would drive Ricky to the brink of exasperation on television.

The pairing of Lucille Ball and Desi Arnaz—who in real life were married, of course, was also groundbreaking in the conservative world of 1950s television. Arnaz was perhaps the most visible Hispanic in television, and the story is told that network programming executives didn't think that Arnaz would be "believable" as Ball's husband—that is to say, they were uncomfortable with the idea that the all-American and very Caucasian Ball would be married to someone from outside her ethnic group, such things simply not being done in the early days of TV. Ball and Arnaz overcame the network's ethnic bias by a tour in which they performed live to the delight of audiences.

Pregnancy was taboo in 1950s television, but the power of Ball and Arnaz was such that her real-life pregnancy became a part of I Love Lucy when Lucy Ricardo gave birth in January 1953 in an episode that aired on the same day as the birth of Ball's real child, Desi Jr. The episode that night is said to have drawn a rating of 70 and a share of 92 percent, perhaps the highest rating and share of any television program ever aired, and such was the public interest in the blessed event that a photo of the newborn babe graced the cover of the following week's TV Guide.

The significance of I Love Lucy in the way television programs are made is not to be understated. The sitcom was among the first to employ production techniques that were later standardized across the industry. It was shot on film instead of being performed live. Its producer, Jess Oppenheimer, adapted the three-camera technique; instead of using one camera, as films had done; the multi-camera technique allowed multiple angles to be shot simultaneously and the best chosen during editing. And the series was filmed in front of a live studio audience. All three of these things changed the way the program looked, compared with other contemporary shows, and allowed it to enter the lucrative world of unending (thus far) international syndication.

The long, long history of the various incarnations of what generically could be called The Lucy Show came to an ignominious end when, after being off the air for years, Ball tried a comeback in the 1980s. Airing for only two months on CBS during fall 1986, Life with Lucy reunited Ball, then age 75, and long-time costar Gale Gordon, age 80, in what has been called an "embarrassing" and "unimaginative rehash" of the earlier wackiness. Sadly, Ball must take the blame for the program's failure, as she had complete creative control over it and, unlike most other network shows of the time, it went on the schedule without the pilot that could have been used to gauge audience interest.[4]

VARIETY SHOWS

Vaudeville in Prime-Time Television

For reasons that are difficult if not impossible to fathom today, programs with a vaudeville theme could be found semiregularly on the prime-time schedule from the late 1940s until, surprisingly, the early 1970s, long past the time period of the 1880s to the 1920s during which vaudeville itself had flourished. Although the form of vaudeville held perhaps some appeal for viewers old enough to remember it firsthand, the television industry was catering to the tastes of younger viewers as the 1950s turned into the 1960s and TV entered its "mature" (i.e., "appealing-to-youth") phase. Attempts to interest the young in an entertainment form, disguised as variety programs or sitcoms, which dated back to the days of their parents, or even their grandparents, were largely unsuccessful.

Early variety programs appropriated the form of vaudeville shows, as the idea of various acts putting on brief performances worked well on television (as it had in radio during the 1920s). It offered viewers a variety of things to look at in rapid succession. After a gap of a few years, ABC tried to emulate Milton Berle's vaudeville-style success with the aptly titled *Vaudeville Show*, which had just four episodes broadcast in December 1953, whereas NBC's similarly themed *NBC Comedy Hour* lasted for the six months between January and June 1956.

Oddly, NBC continued its attempts to breathe new life into vaudeville through the 1960s and into the 1970s. The network ran *Mickie Finn's* in the spring and summer of 1966, a program based on a real life Gay 90s-themed nightclub (run by husband-and-wife vaudevillians Fred E. and Mickie Finn), which, remarkably, coexisted with the burgeoning counterculture of San Francisco, shortly before 1967's "summer of love." The network's final attempt at resuscitating vaudeville came in the form of *NBC Follies* in 1973, which was also a late entry into the ranks of variety programs, a genre that in general was moribund at the time.

The Pinky Lee Show (NBC, 1950) starred, obviously, Pinky Lee, who played a bumbling stagehand in a vaudeville theater. *It's a Business?* (the question mark is correct in the title) aired on DuMont in 1952; it was set at turn of the twentieth century and followed the comic activities of two song publishers on Broadway. Later in the 1950s CBS tried *Willy* (1954–1955), about a young New Hampshire woman who split her time between a small-town legal practice and a position as legal counsel to a vaudeville company in New York City. Despite this relative lack of success, the theme of vaudeville would continue in sitcoms for years; for example, Fred and Ethel Mertz, the neighbors of Lucy and Ricky Ricardo in *I Love Lucy,* were retired vaudeville performers.

Vaudeville-as-sitcom was last seen on the little screen in *Harry's Girls* (NBC, 1963–1964), which was improbably based on the notion that vaudeville was more popular in contemporary Europe than it was in the United States. In reality it was, of course, dead everywhere by the mid-1960s.

COMEDY AND MUSIC VARIETY

Some comedy variety shows earned an audience. *The George Gobel Show* (NBC, CBS, 1954–1960) followed the usual successful formula: Find a host with some talent, a little charm, and a soft-sell style; then add whatever acts you can find. If the audience likes the host enough, they'll sit through the less interesting performers. *The Garry Moore Show* (CBS, 1958–1967) was another example of how well the format could work. The most successful member of his TV family was Carol Burnett, who went on to host her own show. In both programs, the emphasis was on humor and the skits could sound like mini sitcoms at times.

On the musical side, one of the most popular stars was singer Dinah Shore. She hosted several different programs, but her most successful was *The Dinah Shore Show* (NBC, 1951–1957). Audiences liked her sunny personality. At the end of each show, she'd throw them a big kiss. One of the longest-lived successes was *The Lawrence Welk Show* (ABC, 1955–1971). The host's band played standard tunes of the day, plus polkas while bubbles arose behind them. Instead of a variety of performers, there was a group of regulars, who danced, sang, and played musical instruments.

One interesting failure was *The Nat "King" Cole Show* (NBC, 1956–1957). He was a popular singer who was African-American. His show was filled with stars from the music world but was quickly canceled. The rumor was that southern affiliates of the network didn't think their audiences and advertisers would approve of a show starring a black man, especially one who could be seen singing with white women.

DRAMA

Family Dramas and General Dramas

Two major categories of dramas that defy attempts to pin down their generic conventions are family dramas, in which problems and resolutions take place within a family, and general dramas, a category so broad that the programs in it seem unrelated to one another other than by dint of being somehow dramatic in nature. What makes the first category somewhat vague is that, television being television, the focus on the family is found across all genres of programming, and the boundary lines, if such things exist, between family dramas, family dramedies (which blend elements of comedy and drama) and family-based sitcoms are difficult to detect. The problem with the second category is that it appears composed of a mishmash of programs

The Adventures of Robin Hood, starring Richard Green, was unusual for television in the 1950s because it was made in Great Britain and was filmed. Most of the network series then were produced live in New York City. Courtesy of Photofest.

without a coherent theme to connect them other than that all are, like the family dramas, dramatic in some respect, and some blend of humor and seriousness can be found in all of them.

Adventure Dramas

Programs in which characters have various sorts of adventures have been popular throughout the history of television, although the number of adventure programs increased as time passed, as ever more portable equipment allowed location shooting and as production budgets grew. As with the general dramas described previously, the adventure programs are a mixture of themes with great breadth but little in common with one another.

Early adventure dramas were often historical in nature and, unusually for American TV, were filmed in the United Kingdom. CBS had two British-originated and largely self-explanatory series, *The Adventures of Robin Hood* (1955–1958) and *The Buccaneers* (1956–1957). Meanwhile, NBC ran the equally self-evident and equally British *The Adventures of Sir Lancelot* (1956–1957), but branched into American history with the French and Indian War–themed *Northwest Passage* (1958–1959), the sole domestic entry in the lot.

SCIENCE FICTION DRAMAS

Science fiction (sci-fi)—a part of American pop culture since the earliest days of the silent cinema and, perhaps more notably, the sci-fi short story magazines of the 1940s with their famously lurid covers—was reflected in prime-time television in forms designed to appeal to children and to adults, although the boundary between what exactly constitutes a children's program and its counterpart for adults is at best hazy. Nevertheless, sci-fi programs aimed deliberately at children lasted only a relatively short time before being phased out in favor of programs that either directly appealed to adults or could be watched by a mixed audience of children and adults.

ANIMALS

Animals of various types—horses, bears, elephants, dolphins, lions—have been the focus of several dramas over the years, not to mention being found, like *Mr. Ed*, in the occasional sitcom. But it's dogs, of course, which have found the greatest success on television in two programs, *The Adventures of Rin Tin Tin* and *Lassie*.

Both programs premiered in 1954, and *Lassie* went on to be a Sunday night institution for CBS until 1971, an astounding 17 years, making it not only the longest-running animal drama but one of the longest running programs of any type in network television history. This was more than time enough for it to enter Baby Boomer pop culture, and familiarity with the program, even to those who haven't actually seen it, is reflected, for example, in episodes of *The Simpsons* in which Homer compares the Simpson's dog, Santa's Little Helper, unfavorably to Lassie.

Rin Tin Tin itself lasted a significant five years, leaving the CBS lineup in 1959. Both programs had their roots in earlier forms of mass media, with the Rin Tin Tin stories beginning as Hollywood films in 1922 and Lassie starting off as a novel in 1940 before moving into films and radio.

PRIME-TIME SOAP OPERAS

Some have claimed that soap operas were the only original programming created by radio, and they made an easy transition to television's daytime schedule. Their target audience was women who stayed at home. The stories were serial, with plotlines that could continue for decades. The subject matter was the family and the neighbors, and the atmosphere was frequently filled with overwrought emotion. Nighttime dramas, at that time, wrapped up their stories at the end of each episode; frequently, characters even seemed to be unaffected by the past week's events. The subject matter and the setting were broader in scope than the soap opera. And the tone of the drama was more restrained.

Soaps had trouble making the transition to prime-time, possibly because of the serial nature of their stories, which require viewers to watch the episodes in order, unlike the more self-contained narrative of series programs. Despite earlier experiments with the form, it wasn't until the 1970s that soap operas became truly popular during prime-time, when four major soaps—*Dallas, Dynasty, Knots Landing,* and *Falcon Crest*—would begin runs of between 9 and 14 years.

MEDICAL DRAMAS

Although many medical dramas have aired over the years, only a relative handful have lasted for longer than a season or two. Just two prime-time medical series aired during the 1952–1959 period. The earlier and rather more interesting *Medic* was on NBC (1954–1956). *Medic* was what today would be termed a reenactment program that dramatized real cases from

Los Angeles. It was filmed on location in hospitals and sometimes had actual doctors and nurses in its cast. The later *Man and the Challenge* (NBC, 1959–1960) was a rather far-fetched medical/adventure program (note how easily television genres blend, and how early in TV history such genre-blending took place) about Glenn Barton (George Nader) who, in the best multi-tasking tradition of fictional TV heroes, was a government medical doctor, a research scientist, and an athlete to boot.

DRAMA AND RELIGION

A side road, so to speak, that didn't go anywhere in prime-time was *This Is the Life*, a religious family drama that illustrated "the Christian solution to the problems of life" and centered on the Fisher family, who lived somewhere in the heartland of America. The show, a rare example of a prime-time program with an overtly religious theme, jumped back and forth between DuMont and ABC during 1952 and 1953 before becoming a dramatic anthology program and going into first-run syndication, where it remained for 30 years, finally ceasing production in the 1980s. Religion tended to be kept submerged in most prime-time programs, and still is today, although it was allowed to surface at Christmas (when it was a "safe" topic), and in moralistic homilies on programs such as *The Loretta Young Show*.

QUIZ AND GAME SHOWS

The quick birth and near-death of prime-time quiz and game shows mostly took place during the 1952–1959 time period, although the ramifications of their demise would affect all of television for decades.

Genre boundaries for quiz and game shows, like all other forms of programming, are somewhat blurry. They came in a bewildering variety of types. In some of them, such as the paired *The $64,000 Question* and *The $64,000 Challenge*, contestants—often the ordinary sort of person but with unusually detailed knowledge of particular subjects—vied for large prizes and the accompanying celebrity that came with success. Others, such as the notorious *Twenty-One*, asked contestants a range of questions on many subjects and required more broad knowledge.

The immensely popular *The $64,000 Question* (1955–1958) was the number-one program during its first season. Despite its title, it was possible, although no one quite managed it, to win up to $256,000 on *The $64,000 Question* by competing in increasingly difficult "plateaus" of questions. The two biggest winners of the era of big-money game shows were Teddy

Nadler, whose winnings of $252,000 on the spin-off quiz show *The $64,000 Challenge* (CBS, 1956–1958) and humble background as a $70-per-week civil servant epitomized the American dream, and Robert Strom, an 11-year-old who won $192,000 from *The $64,000 Question*.[5]

The Quiz Show Scandals

Given the amount of money involved and the networks' battle for the all-important ratings, it's not surprising that scandal would attach itself to the quiz shows, which had begun to offer massive prizes by the mid-1950s. Programs before then tended to have small—sometimes embarrassingly small—prizes for contestants. *Sit or Miss* (ABC, 1950), for example, was a televised version of musical chairs that paid winning contestants a jackpot of $75. Although there should be little reason for contestants to cheat or for producers to rig a show with a $75 prize, there would also be little viewer incentive to watch, and musical chairs seems to have been rather unappealing, even in the unsophisticated early days of TV when viewers would, according to legend, watch nearly anything, including test patterns.

The quiz show scandal erupted in 1958 when it was revealed that two of the most popular and exciting big-money games were rigged; that is, certain contestants were coached on the correct answers while others were either instructed to lose or simply not coached. Viewers, of course, were not told about this and watched the programs in the innocent belief that what they were seeing was a contest of intellectual equals.

The scandal had started with *Dotto* (NBC, summer 1958), a program in which players' correct answers were used to connect a series of dots that would eventually reveal a portrait of a notable person. A would-be contestant named Edward Hilgemeier, Jr., had found, while waiting for a chance to appear on the daytime version of the program, a notebook that contained a set of correct answers for another player. He complained to the show's producers and accepted a payoff of $1,500. But Hilgemeier, who never actually appeared on *Dotto*, later discovered that another contestant had gotten $4,000 to remain silent and, apparently miffed at being shortchanged, went to the attorney general of the State of New York with an official complaint.[6]

A somewhat similar set of circumstances brought *Twenty-One* (NBC, 1956–1958) to its sudden, and infamous, end, as well. Herbert Stempel was in the midst of an unfairly earned winning streak on the program when he was told to give an incorrect answer that would throw victory to Charles Van Doren, who went on to win $129,000 and a lucrative five-year, $250,000 contract with NBC as a "programming consultant" with no specified duties.[7]

Like Hilgemeier, Stempel was angered at not getting what he considered his just desserts and blew the whistle on how the game was rigged.

The motives of Hilgemeier and Stempel appear to be that both felt they were not sharing in the riches and fame that were going to others, something rather different from taking umbrage at the morality of rigging the programs. But it's understandable. Stempel, for one, had been coerced into signing an agreement with the producers of *Twenty-One* that he would actually be given less than the $50,000 he had won.[8]

The rivalry between Stempel and Van Doren on *Twenty-One* was not merely intellectual in nature. It reflected assumptions and prejudices in 1950s American society, touching on personal appearance and social class, issues deeply meaningful in American life but seldom discussed in what used to be called polite company. Simply put, Stempel was less handsome than Van Doren. Stempel sweated profusely in the isolation booth—a

Before the quiz show scandals of the 1950s, *Twenty-One* was highly popular. In one of the most interesting matches, host Jack Barry asked the tough questions to Charles Van Doren and Herb Stempel while they were in isolation booths. Later, Stempel blew the whistle on the game show. Courtesy of Photofest.

soundproof, stuffy box allegedly designed to keep contestants from hearing anything should the audience shout out an answer, but really a prop to bump up the level of excitement—while Van Doren perspired in a more gentlemanly fashion, dabbing genteelly at his face with a handkerchief as instructed. Stempel was swarthy and ethnic, and Jewish; Van Doren the northern European-American ideal, fair-haired and Christian.

In social terms, Stempel was a commoner, an adult college student on the GI Bill; Van Doren was an instructor at Columbia University, a doctoral student in English and scion of a family of intellectuals. Stempel was apparently rather unlikable, according to comments attributed to the producers of *Twenty-One*;[9] Van Doren was just the opposite, friendly and outgoing. In short, Van Doren had the quintessential sort of 1950s "class"; Stempel didn't.

The question of why quiz shows appealed to so many television viewers during the late 1950s is of interest, especially given that *Twenty-One* probably drew more viewers than did the iconic *I Love Lucy* and that at the beginning of the 1956–1957 television season the top five programs were *The $64,000 Question, The $64,000 Challenge, Do You Trust Your Wife? What's My Line?* and *I've Got a Secret*—all game or quiz shows.

The programs didn't really celebrate intellectualism, a subject that critics debated with some enthusiasm at the time. Instead the shows rewarded people who had vast stores of information, whether that information was in narrow or broad categories. And the reward, of course, was money, something much a part of American values at the time, which tended to assign practical value—if not a dollar value—to intangible things like knowledge. In this way, the programs didn't celebrate the intellectual goal of knowledge for its own sake; instead, they celebrated the financial success that came with knowledge. If knowledge is power, as the cliché says, then in the 1950s knowledge was money, and even Van Doren was quoted in *Life* magazine as having said there was a lot of money "lying around" during the Eisenhower years.[10]

The questions quiz show contestants answered were factual in nature; for example, the so-called intellectual battle between Stempel and Van Doren on *Twenty-One* included the names and fates of the wives of Henry VIII. Analysis was not involved. No one asked them why Henry VIII married eight times, nor were they asked to explain how the marriages related to the Reformation or the history of England. Instead, the questions called for straightforward recitation of the names, dates, and fates of the eight wives, factual knowledge taken at the time as a mark of intelligence.

The notion continues in the present day in the long-running syndicated game show *Jeopardy*, which during 2004 gained huge publicity when it changed its rules and allowed contestant Ken Jennings to win $2.5 million in a string of appearances (previously limited to one week, but now with no such limit) by answering questions that deal with largely unconnected bits of information.

Investigations into what would soon come to be called the quiz show scandals began shortly after Hilgemeier, the angry contestant from *Dotto*, went to the attorney general of the state of New York with his complaint. A grand jury was seated and during the course of its inquiry the first crimes were committed as producers and contestants perjured themselves. Van Doren got additional publicity when he temporarily fled into rural New England to avoid a subpoena to testify. When he surfaced he recanted his earlier public statements that he had never in any way been coached. His grand jury testimony to the same effect opened the floodgates and the truth about rigging soon spilled out. Even Edward R. Murrow's interview program, *Person to Person*, was criticized as being dishonest because some elements were rehearsed.

PERSON TO PERSON

Person to Person (CBS, 1953–1956) was independently owned and produced by John Aaron, Jesse Zousmer, and Edward R. Murrow. This successful program made Murrow rich. This forerunner of the celebrity interview supposedly showed the private lives of public people in their homes. Guests included Fidel Castro, Marilyn Monroe, and Senator John Kennedy and his wife, Jackie. Murrow stated goal was "to "revive the art of conversation." Murrow, in the studio, informally greeted two guests a week in 15-minute interviews in their homes. In 1956 CBS Television bought the series from Murrow, at that time sole owner. *Person to Person*, more than *See It Now*, elevated its host to celebrity status. But Murrow was criticized. Some felt that he had sold out by doing an entertainment program.

The show was a technically complex and advanced use of the medium. Employing two to six large, cumbersome cameras, a program showed different parts of an individual's home. It took time and effort to get to different locations in a time of presatellite technology and set up a signal from the guest home to a microwave transmission tower. The production staff went so far as to build tall relay towers for one-time remotes broadcasts and had to obtain FCC approval each program for a special high frequency wireless microphone. A split screen was used on each show to let the audience see Murrow and the guest.

It was common knowledge that guests were "talked through" the movements to be made from room to room. Answers to the questions were supposed to be spontaneous. But Murrow's journalistic integrity was questioned. Frank Stanton, then president at CBS, accused *Person to Person*'s production practices of deceit and dishonesty as the guests were coached on the questions. This charge came just after the quiz scandals and showed the personality conflicts that estranged Murrow from the executive branch at CBS.

In the fall of 1959, Charles Collingwood became the host. For some nine years the show was in the top 10. It was the first to focus on the cult of the personality in news programs.

The grand jury was followed by Congressional and FCC hearings. The Communications Act, the guiding document under which broadcasting is regulated, was amended to make "rigged or otherwise deceptive programming" illegal. In the meantime, the networks performed penance for their sins by agreeing to an FCC proposal to increase the amount of public service programming during prime-time.

But the real and longest-lasting effect of the quiz show scandals came in changes in the way network TV programs were produced, sponsored, and put on the air. The networks had, since their radio days, done little more than simply rent airtime to advertising agencies and sponsors, who filled it with programs they had developed and produced. This was at the heart of the quiz show scandals, as it became readily apparent that the networks had taken a laissez-faire attitude about the manner in which the programs they aired were produced and were content to simply sit back and collect the money as it rolled in. The scandals, with other factors, would bring this to an end. To prevent further embarrassment, and further regulation, the networks adopted "magazine" format advertising, in which they sold commercial time to numerous advertisers in programs that the networks either developed themselves or bought from independent program producers—the system that exists today.

There appear to have been several reasons behind the quiz show scandals. For one, the producers no doubt had a desire, natural to anyone in the entertainment industry, to, for want of a better word, entertain their viewers by making the shows as exciting as possible. The coaching of contestants, which had apparently begun on *Tic Tac Dough*, evolved from this need as it avoided the problem of a boring program in which the players consistently gave the wrong answers and no one won anything, which had actually occurred on early episodes of *Twenty-One*.

This desire ties directly into the commercial aspects of the quiz shows. Producers had a vested interest in pulling a big audience, and sponsors and networks shared in it, for the simple reason that the larger the audience, the more money there is to be made by all and sundry. By making the quizzes exciting, producers would draw the large audience needed for their financial success and their continued place on the prime-time schedule.

But audiences played a role in the collusion, as well. Viewers in the 1950s retained a certain amount of naïveté. Television was still relatively new—regularly scheduled prime-time programs had been a part of American life for little more than a decade when the scandal broke—and before the scandal the boundaries between fictional and nonfictional programming had been relatively well defined. Then the rigged quiz shows came along, blurring the line between what seemed to be real and what was staged: What appeared to be an honest competition that pitted one person against another was in fact managed to make it better than reality.

Although the scandals certainly highlighted the unfairness of games that appeared to be honest, criminal actions didn't take place until legal investigations into the games began: Rigging a game show may have been dishonest and unethical, but it was not illegal at the time or a violation of FCC rules. Criminal activity came about when producers and contestants committed perjury by lying about their roles in the scandal. At that point, the whole system began to unravel.

The bottom line for quiz shows is that they were all but banished from the networks' prime-time schedules until *Who Wants to Be a Millionaire?* came along in 1999. Game shows of various types continued to be mainstays of daytime programming, but the era of the prime-time quiz show was over by the start of the 1959 television season.

WESTERNS

It should come as no great surprise that westerns, a staple of the movies since *The Great Train Robbery* (1903), came along early in the history of prime-time television. The appeal of the television western was no doubt the same as the continuing appeal of the western film. Americans—not to mention many people around the world, including in communist East Germany (and in united Germany today)—have long been fascinated with the 1860–1890 time period in American history, the period during which westerns are most usually set. Wright attributes this great interest to the fact that many adventurous ways of life were possible then and there, and that this forms the basis for stories in which people of different viewpoints and personality types can act out "fundamental conflicts."[11] Beyond this, the conflicts (sheepherders vs. cattlemen, the law vs. outlaws, East vs. West, etc.) take place during a historical time period that is uniquely American and that still has its influences today; for example, the cowboy imagery used in the advertising of many products both nationally and internationally, and the continuing popularity of cowboy boots and denim jackets.

The height of the popularity of Hollywood westerns stretched from the 1930s through the 1950s, and overlapped with the prominence of the television western during the late 1950s. Television picked up much of the western formula from the movies, just as the movies had earlier appropriated much from the music, folk tales and novels that related to the frontier and that could, in turn, be dated to as early as the Colonial era of the eighteenth century.

One of the aspects of the western that was appealing was the presence of a clear-cut enemy—the Indians. As time went on and our view of history changed, the Indian became more victim than villain. In *Broken Arrow* (ABC, 1956–1960), a government official (John Lupton) worked with the Indians (headed up by Michael Ansara) to improve their lives. But this program was clearly an exception to the usual portrait of Native Americans.

In the earlier westerns, the hero was frequently a wanderer with no home and no family. Whereas the situation comedies of the era emphasized the importance of family, these westerns seemed to celebrate the lone man who remained always a stranger, but despite (or because of?) his status as an outsider, he was the one who made sure right was done. Examples include *Sugarfoot* (ABC, 1957–1961) about a young cowboy (Will Hutchins) fresh from the East, and *Bronco* (ABC, 1958–1962) about a Civil War veteran (Ty Hardin). *Cheyenne* (ABC, 1955–1963) added the element of male cheesecake to the formula; in almost every episode, the well-built star, Clint Walker, had to take off his shirt for some reason not always justified by the plot.

Perhaps the quintessential wanderer was Josh Randall, bounty hunter, played by Steve McQueen on *Wanted: Dead or Alive* (CBS, 1958–1961). No one could play the outsider with as much edgy charm as Steve McQueen. A smoother version of the same type of hero was seen in *Have Gun, Will Travel* (CBS, 1957–1963). The hero, known only as Paladin (Richard Boone), lived in luxury in San Francisco but would make periodic forays into the wild part of the west to bring justice and satisfy his clients.

The wanderer concept was also occasionally expanded to include a core group. Together these groups faced new locations each week, but their values remained constant. Each season, the *Wagon Train* (NBC, ABC, 1957–1965) would leave the East and traverse the West. Although the settlers varied, the wagon master (Ward Bond), his scouts, and his cook were there week after week. *Rawhide* (CBS, 1959–1966) was another example. Each season the cowboys (including Eric Fleming and Clint Eastwood) would take the herd to the market and then head home to begin the journey again.

The Lawman (ABC, 1958–1962) had the marshal (stern-faced John Russell) and his young deputy living in a town, where the evil had to come to them on a weekly basis. *Bat Masterson* (NBC, 1958–1961) (Gene Barry) had the same concept, but its hero was more of a fop. He carried a fancy cane, which could be used, if necessary, to fight crime, but he tried hard not to mess up his clothes too badly.

But as the 1950s advanced, the cowboy with a home and a family became more popular, as though the zeitgeist of the situation comedy had settled out west. Chuck Conners played *The Rifleman* (ABC, 1958–1963), a homesteader who could shoot down the bad guys on the main street of town with his special rifle, but who could also give his son (Johnny Crawford) wise advice on growing up to be a good man. In *Laramie* (NBC, 1959–1963), the rancher had a brother and later a ward to take care of, a hired hand, and a grandmother figure, all of whom form a family of sorts.

The phrase "adult western" (which has a vaguely pornographic connotation today as the word *adult* has been co-opted to refer to sexual content) serves to distinguish programs in the genre from earlier, more child-oriented and often non-prime-time. The western genre holds some of the longest-lived programs in television history. *Gunsmoke* spanned three decades, airing on CBS from 1955 to 1975. It was the top-rated program each year from 1957 to 1961, and during the 1957–1958 season, its peak in terms of viewership, it had an average rating of 43.1. And although its ratings declined during the 1960s and 1970s, as viewers' interests shifted to other genres, it remained on the CBS schedule because, legend has it, it was the favorite program of the wife of William Paley, the long-time and immensely powerful chairman of the board of the network. It was also among the first of the long line of adult-oriented westerns that would dominate prime-time television during the late 1950s and early 1960s.

These adult westerns, naturally, differed in structure, plot, and theme from those aimed at younger viewers through an emphasis on "character and incident rather than on the old action-adventure, good versus bad, of children's programs."[12] One need only think here of the substantial differences between, say, *The Lone Ranger* and *Gunsmoke* and to mentally compare and contrast the former's masked hero (Clayton Moore), Indian companion Tonto (Jay Silverheels), and faithful horse (Trigger) with the latter's more complicated relationship between noble sheriff Matt Dillon (James

The western moved away from the lone hero to the
family man. In *The Rifleman*, Chuck Connors played a
rancher who was willing and able to use his weapon,
but only in a good cause, and Johnny Crawford played
his son. Courtesy of Photofest.

Arness) and saloon-keeper—or was it actually brothel-keeper?—Miss Kitty
(Amanda Blake), and its darker, more ambiguous worldview in which right
and wrong weren't always clearly distinguished. As well, a comparison of
the two programs that takes into account the years in which they aired
points to Leo Braudy's notion that the "evolution" of a genre is characterized
by increasing complexity over time[13]; in this case it should be noted that
The Lone Ranger was coming to the end of its trail as *Gunsmoke* was getting
underway.

GUNSMOKE

Critics have suggested that some TV shows become popular by allowing the audience to project their concerns safely on to fictional characters (i.e., the programs are relevant). And the wise producer will create a series that allows liberal and conservative interpretations of the same material. For example, the "Murdoch" episode of the long-running western *Gunsmoke* illustrates how contemporary social concerns manifest themselves in fictional programming set in the past, in this case the twin 1970s themes of law-and-order and the generation gap transplanted back 100 years.

The arrival in Dodge City of famous U.S. Marshal Lucas Murdoch (Jack Elam) and his deputies sets the stage to compare and contrast the shoot-'em-all-and-let-God-sort-'em-out philosophy of Murdoch and the rule-of-law orientation of Matt Dillon (James Arness). Murdoch—left eye cocked at a 45° angle because of a gunshot wound to the head, greasy and untrimmed hair, drooping moustache—is set to entrap the notorious Carver gang with a bogus shipment of $42,000 in gold that he's planted in Dodge City. He's armed with a two-year-old John Doe warrant for the gang that allows him to fill in the names *after* the arrests have been made. *If* any arrests are made, that is, for Murdoch has already explained to Dillon that his standard procedure is to hang criminals without trial, something that shocks the noble Dillon.

The situation becomes further complicated when we learn that the youngest member of the gang, Scott (Bob Random), is actually Murdoch's son gone wrong. Scott is an obnoxious, long-haired little snot, an 1870s hippie, who traces his life of crime to the 13th birthday party that Murdoch missed because of work. When Pa failed to show up for cake and presents, Scott stole a watermelon and Murdoch had him thrown in jail for three days. To add insult to injury, Scott tells Murdoch to his face that gang leader Amos Carter (Jim Davis, who later played Jock Ewing in *Dallas*), is the closest thing to a father he's ever had. Murdoch now faces the dilemma of either hanging Scott or bending the rules because the apprehended criminal is his son.

It's soon time for the situations to be resolved through gunfire. Scott agrees to guide Murdoch to Carver's hideout, but on the condition that they go alone. They arrive to find a red-haired woman in an off-the-shoulder peasant blouse asking Carver for $3.50 for ironing, wine, and food, but he pays her $10 "just in case you forgot something," an unambiguous reference to prostitution. Their happy scene is interrupted, though, when Murdoch calls Carver out for their showdown.

At this point, Murdoch's cocked eye becomes a factor when in a point-of-view shot we learn that Murdoch's vision is badly blurred. As Carver says, Murdoch couldn't possibly get off a shot without hitting the woman. But she flees and gunfire erupts. Murdoch misses, Carver shoots him, and Murdoch falls to the street, Scott rushes out of hiding to pick up his gun, Scott also misses, Carver shoots him too, Dillon arrives just after the nick of time, gets off two rounds at an impossible distance and Carver falls dead into the dust. Murdoch and Scott reconcile—nothing like gunfire to make you realize you have something in common after all—and the episode ends in the visual style of a Sergio Leone spaghetti western, with an extreme close up of the redhead, who cries quietly as tumbleweeds roll by.

The audience can sympathize with Marshall Murdoch, the man who is tough on lawbreakers, but who finds doing his duty estranges him from his son. Or they can sympathize with the young man, who is willing to commit crimes to get back at his father. It was a story from the Old West that resonated with the audience of the Vietnam era. And the moral seemed to be: the generations should work together against true evil. Of course, the comforting thought was that traditional moral forces, like Dillon, would save both generations from their mistakes.

Gunsmoke was a mixture of action and melodrama that kept the audience's attention for two decades. Dennis Weaver played the deputy, Chester; Amanda Blake, the saloon keeper, Miss Kitty; James Arness, the marshal; and Milburn Stone, Doc. Courtesy of Photofest.

Contemporary westerns, that is to say westerns set during the twentieth century, form another distinct subgenre. The contemporary western began with *The Roy Rogers Show* (NBC, 1951–1957), which was set on Roy and Dale's ranch in the 1950s, far in time from the Old West of the late nineteenth century but not far in spirit, as Roy was cast as a noble sort of sheriff.

In contrast, *Maverick* (ABC, 1957–1962) ran episodes in which other television programs, both westerns and detective dramas, were parodied, and it was one of the more popular programs of its time, which indicates that audiences were not entirely opposed to variations on the western theme and had become sophisticated enough by the late 1950s to accept references about television in TV programs.

DETECTIVES

Detective dramas existed from the earliest days of television. They offered on their surface mystery and suspense, the eternal struggle between good and evil, exciting chases, fistfights and shootouts, and on a deeper level an examination of the "countercurrent of anxiety and alienation" that was part of urban life in the 1950s. Their iconography was easily recognizable, as characters looked and acted much like the detectives and criminals who had peopled Hollywood films for years, especially since the rise of the "gangster and urban crime films" that had become popular during the Depression era.[14] And they grew in number of programs and size of audience as westerns went into a rapid decline early in the 1960s.

There was no "typical" detective program during the time period at hand. The most popular programs of the 1952–1959 era embodied a combination of forms carried over from Hollywood movies, such as the Bogart-like hard-boiled private detective—although the television detectives were usually more handsome, less disheveled, and younger than their film counterparts—and reenactment dramas that, for want of a better word, dramatized the cases of real-life law enforcement agencies.

The first incarnation of *Dragnet* appeared during this time period, airing 1952–1959 on NBC, following a life on NBC radio that had begun in 1949. Jack Webb, who created the program and was its executive producer, starred as reticent Detective Sergeant Joe Friday of the Los Angeles Police Department, and the program itself was visually quite radio-like, with actors speaking large amounts of dialogue while standing about. There was minimal physical action. Although to contemporary eyes its static nature would be a handicap, the program's popularity was immense. It was a top 10 program through the end of the 1955–1956 season, and had peaked in

In the 1950s, *Dragnet* was one of the first filmed crime shows on the networks. The show used dramatic lighting, unusual camera angles, voice-over narration, and music to take advantage of being filmed. The stars were Ben Alexander and Jack Webb, who created the concept on radio. Courtesy of Photofest.

the 1952–1953 season in the number two position with a spectacular 53.2 rating, second only to *I Love Lucy*'s rating of 58.8 that season.

It was also during this period that the Federal Bureau of Investigation (FBI) became something of a force in television. *Wanted*, a program not only based on open cases the FBI was investigating, but which used actual FBI agents in its some of its episodes, aired on CBS (1955–1956). It set the stage for later Bureau-sanctioned programs, including *The F.B.I.* (ABC, 1965–1974) and the Discovery Network's *The FBI Files*, which remained in production through in 2004, some 50 years after *Wanted*.

Typical also of early television were attempts that turned out to be failed subgenres. CBS had tried a private investigator sitcom titled *Detective's Wife* during the summer of 1950, but it failed to catch on, perhaps because audiences at the time were somewhat confused by the clash of police work and humor, perhaps because the program simply wasn't very good. NBC would be somewhat more successful at fusing comedy and the grim work of criminal investigation in its version of *The Thin Man* (1957–1959), although audiences were already familiar with the Nick and Nora characters from the Dashiell Hammett novel and the six film adaptations made between 1934 and 1947. The police-themed sitcom was tried repeatedly, but it wasn't until *Barney Miller* came along in the mid-1970s that a program of this type would be truly popular.

The smooth, debonair detective was seen on *Richard Diamond, Private Detective* (CBS, NBC, 1957–1960). David Janssen played the man tough enough to catch the bad guys and smooth enough to win the women. He was the opposite of the Sam Spade school of detectives—not the hard-boiled, hard-living type of man. But perhaps the "coolest" of all of the 1950s detectives was *Peter Gunn* (NBC, ABC, 1958–1961) (Craig Stevens). He hung out in a nightclub and remained nonchalant in every situation. He could shoot a gun and use his fists, but he preferred to enjoy the company of the women who flocked around him. The jazzy theme music by Henry Mancini became a hit record.

ANTHOLOGIES

The time period before the late 1950s is frequently referred to as The Golden Age of Television, a title that reflects a rather elitist view of programming. There were more quality dramas on the air then than at any later time—"quality," that is, if one defines the word as referring to dramas written and performed by people with Broadway theatrical connections—but this was due in part to the existence of an educated and affluent highbrow (to use 1950s cultural terminology) urban class that was able to afford the then-expensive television receivers. The networks, logically, scheduled programs that appealed to them or, more precisely, to the advertisers who wished to reach them. Alongside the quality dramas there existed wrestling and roller derby, unsophisticated comedies and banal variety shows—the sort of lowbrow entertainments that the working classes, the people who couldn't yet afford their own TVs, viewed in neighborhood taverns over glasses of cheap beer.

Anthologies are programs in which different actors appeared from week to week in episodes that were unconnected to previous or future episodes. Anthologies existed in both half-hour and one-hour formats, with the rare program opting for the 15-minute format that was common in the early days of television. The aptly named *Short Short Dramas* (NBC, 1952–1953) used the 15-minute format, but 15 minutes was apparently not suitable for even a one-act play, as the program aired for less than a year.

As was the case with most programming in the early days of TV, anthologies were usually live, but many went to film and videotape when the technology became available, in order to take advantage of the obvious benefits of producing a recorded program; for example, errors could be edited out, camera angles could be selected during editing for maximum emotional impact, and kinescoped, videotaped, or filmed shows could be rerun at little additional cost. The long-lived *Fireside Theatre* (NBC, 1949–1958) was perhaps the first anthology to go to film, during fall 1949, making it one of TV's earliest filmed programs, and *Playhouse 90* (CBS, 1956–1961) was among the earliest television programs to utilize the newer and easier-to-work-with videotape in 1959.[15]

But most anthologies, like other forms of programming, were short-lived. For every *Kraft Television Theatre*, which lasted for 11 years on NBC and ABC (1947–1958), there were a number that barely made it through a full year. Anthology history is composed of such failed programs as the obscure

Playhouse 90 offered live drama each week in prime-time. For example, *The Miracle Worker*, starring Theresa Wright and Patty McCormick, told the story of a blind, deaf girl, Helen Keller, and her teacher. Courtesy of Photofest.

Showcase Theatre (ABC, 1953) and the undistinguished *Damon Runyon Theatre* (CBS, 1955–1956).

Although live dramas are nowadays thought of as being "quality" productions in some way, the truth is that most were mundane general anthologies that presented a mix of everything from comedies to melodramas and which existed by the dozen. These were not in the least highbrow. For example, *General Electric Theatre*, which aired for a credible nine years on CBS (1953–1962), was known for "simple dramas and diversionary entertainment."[16] The most dramatic opening for an anthology belonged to *The Loretta Young Show* (NBC, 1953–1961), in which the host of the show would fling open French doors and enter with a swirl of her skirts in a fashionable outfit. Her anthology centered on morally uplifting stories, and she frequently starred in them.

To stand out from the crowd, some of the general anthologies resorted to gimmickry. For example, *Dark of Night* (DuMont 1952–1953) was broadcast live at 8:30 P.M. from various locations in New York City. This reportedly consumed most of its budget and necessitated the use of little known, and hence low-paid, writers and actors. Likewise, *Gulf Playhouse 1st Person* (NBC summer 1953) employed a subjective camera to represent one of the characters; viewers saw whatever the character saw, a technique also used in the detective drama *The Plainclothesman* at the same time.

An interesting frame was provided by *The Millionaire* (CBS, 1955–1960). Each week a millionaire (seen only from the back) would give his faithful employee a million-dollar check to hand out to a person who was seemingly chosen on a random basis. The plot then would describe the recipient's reaction to the unexplained windfall, whether good or bad.

Other, more minor subgenres existed alongside the general and prestigious dramatic anthologies. Some were general sorts of mysteries, such as *The Web*, a rather long-lived and well-regarded half-hour anthology, seen live on CBS (1950–1954) and as a filmed series on NBC in 1957. Episodes of the program were written by members of the Mystery Writers of America, and it won the Edgar Allen Poe Award for excellence in the presentation of suspense stories on television during the 1951–1952 season.[17]

Suspense anthologies existed in relatively small number, as well. Perhaps the best known of the programs in this subgenre was the macabre *Alfred Hitchcock Presents*, which ran on CBS and NBC (1955–1965) in both half- and one-hour forms, and which had the added appeal of droll on-camera introductions and conclusions featuring Hitchcock himself.

Other anthologies specialized in magazine and film adaptations. Magazines adaptations were found in *My True Story* (ABC, 1950), with its first-person tales from the magazine of the same title; *Cosmopolitan Theatre* (DuMont, 1951), which dramatized stories from *Cosmopolitan* magazine; and *Newsstand Theatre* (ABC, 1952), a half-hour anthology focusing on short stories from various magazines. None of the programs aired for more than three months. A bit later in the time period *The 20th Century Fox Hour* (CBS, 1955–1957) offered one-hour adaptations of its movies, such as *The Ox-Bow Incident* and *Miracle on 34th Street* at a time when, again, the original films were unavailable to television.

Anthologies on a theme of patriotic Americanism also existed. *Cavalcade of America* started on radio in 1935 under DuPont sponsorship before moving to television in 1952; for a year it ran on both radio and TV. *Cavalcade* was on NBC (1952–1953) before moving to ABC, where it stayed through 1957. Throughout its life, it specialized in dramatizing major American historical events. *TV Reader's Digest* (ABC, 1955–1956) was a similar entry on the theme of American history. It is significant that both programs aired during the era of McCarthyism, television and movie blacklists, and a pervasive fear of Communist subversion in American society.

Others anthologies ran stories of a particular type that frequently existed in series of their own; for example, the western anthology *Frontier* (NBC, 1955–1956); the children's anthology *Shirley Temple's Storybook* (ABC, 1959 and NBC, 1960–1961), hosted by Shirley Temple herself; and romance anthologies such as the aptly, if not creatively, titled *Romance* of November and December 1949 on CBS. There were two police anthologies: the rather short-lived *The Men behind the Badge,* which dramatized the cases of a number of police agencies on CBS (1953–1954), and the even more short-lived *The Mail Story* on ABC for two months in 1954, based on United States Postal Service investigations; these inevitably become confused with the various police reenactment dramas that may or may not have had the same cast week after week.

The era of live dramas came to a fairly rapid end. By the time videotape was introduced in 1957, the dramatic anthology format was already fading, as if the fact that the programs were live was part of their appeal. There is, after all, something more magical about a live performance than a recorded one, perhaps because of a perception that it takes more skill for actors to act in a live setting than if they had the safety net of film or videotape. If nothing else, the chances of amusing on-camera errors are greater, and anecdotes abound about mistakes that went out over the air.

Another factor in their decline is that the new night-at-the-movie prime-time programs, showing Hollywood movies old and recent, and which began in 1961, displaced many of the dramatic anthologies. A third factor is that by the late 1950s, as prices fell, television ownership had spread to classes of people with less interest in quality or prestigious Broadway-type dramas, and the networks began to cater to their tastes. After all, the predictability of a serial format was easier to sell to the audience and the advertisers.

VARIETY PROGRAMS

The variety show—with its combination of comedy, music, dance, mimes, jugglers, and plate-spinners—was a staple of American prime-time television programming through the 1970s. The programs today seem largely interchangeable, and little of note jumps out from among the number of variety programs that aired over the years as topicality, in the form of audience familiarity with performers popular at the time, was their chief attraction. This now out-of-date atmosphere makes finding the programs today nearly impossible, as they are of little interest to cable networks that otherwise rerun vast amounts of old network programming.

Talent shows are nonetheless largely an artifact of the 1950s. Only two of them, *Talent Scouts* (CBS, summers 1962 and 1963) and *Hollywood Talent Scouts* (CBS, 1965–1966) continued into the 1960s; *Dick Clark's World of Talent* nearly made it into the new decade, but ended its one-season run in December 1959. Those programs that did survive did so only with the addition of recognizable celebrities who had "discovered" the underpublicized talent and who "presented" them to the audience. But by the mid-1960s there was little interest in the genre, and talent shows as part of prime-time entertainment came to an end, not to be revived until the syndicated *Star Search* began its 12 years of production in 1983.

MUSIC PROGRAMS

Music programs built around a specific singer and musical "interludes" of between 5 and 15 minutes were common during the early years of television, but largely disappeared by 1960. The appeal to viewers of music programs was no doubt much the same as it is today with music videos; that is, actually seeing the performer is (usually) more interesting than just listening. The appeal to the networks was that the programs were inexpensive to produce and air, as they required only minimal sets and scripts, hence the large number of them on ABC and DuMont, the poorest networks, although they were also seen on CBS and NBC. To modern eyes, though, most of the shows have long since passed into obscurity, along with their now forgotten stars, people like Jane Pickens, who starred in a short-lived eponymous program on ABC (1954) and Stan Kenton, who with his band headlined *Music 55* on CBS during summer 1955.

Women figured prominently in music programming, of course, with performers who still have name recognition today, like Dinah Shore, whose TV career covered five decades, as well as those now more obscure, like Ina Ray Hutton and Her All-Girl Band, of the all-woman *The Ina Ray Hutton Show* (NBC, summer 1956). Even African-American performers had a place, though only for a brief time, with *Georgia Gibbs and Her Million Record Show* (NBC summer 1957); the program was 15 minutes in length, aired at 7:30–7:45 P.M. But for the most part music leaned toward safety in the form of "standards" and show tunes, at the white end of the spectrum, with programs typically starring such middle-of-the-road singers as Vaughan Monroe, Jo Stafford, and Pat Boone.

Besides standards, other, less popular forms of music were sometimes to be found. ABC programmed the self-explanatory *Polka Time* (1956–1957) and *Polka-Go-Round* (1958–1959), both of which originated in Chicago. Limited amounts of jazz and blues programming also existed. *Opera vs. Jazz* (ABC, summer 1953) was one example, although the program featured popular music and opera, but no jazz; *Stars of Jazz*, hosted by jazz musician Bobby Troup on ABC in 1958, made up for the omission.

Your Hit Parade didn't survive the transition to rock music that came in the wake of Elvis's appearance on the NBC musical variety program *Stage Show* on 28 January 1956, his first network TV appearance and one that was followed by the more famous above-the-waist performances seen on *The Ed Sullivan Show*. The transition from standards to rock and roll is evident in the fact that the hosts of *Stage Show* were Tommy and Jimmy Dorsey, the brothers who were emblematic of the Big Band era of the 1930s and 40s and as such representatives of a generation that was losing its appeal to the advertisers who supported prime-time television.

By the late 1950s, with rock firmly established on radio and in the popular culture, rock musicians finally began appearing on network programs. Alan Freed, perhaps the best-known disk jockey of the 1950s and the man who claimed to have invented the phrase "rock and roll," packaged four rock-oriented half-hour spectaculars under the title *The Big Beat* on ABC during summer 1957. The programs featured rock performers like Chuck Berry and Jerry Lee Lewis, but also more middle-of-the-road musicians like Connie Francis and Andy Williams.[18] Richie Valens, shortly to become one of the victims of the airplane crash that also killed Buddy Holly and the Big Bopper, appeared on *The Music Shop* (NBC, January–March 1959), another of the rare and brief forays of 1950s network prime-time television into the world of rock and roll.

Music programs eventually blended with musical variety shows that offered more than one performer per episode and included comedy and guest stars to broaden their appeal; for example, *The Patti Page Show* (NBC, summer 1956) and *The Patti Page Olds Show* (ABC, 1958–1959) were compilations of song and dance, centering on one of America's most popular vocalists and someone who had appeared on dozens of other variety programs. Programs like these would in turn blend with straight variety programs that incorporated music amongst the jugglers, comedians, and circus acts.

Lip-Sync Programs

A dead end, but a nonetheless interesting one, is the lip-sync program genre that enjoyed a surprising amount of popularity during the 1950s, long before Milli Vanilli horrified the music industry and was forced to return a Grammy award for Best New Artist in 1990. Paul Dixon's specialty was making funny faces while pantomiming the top hits of the day, and after doing so on local television in Cincinnati for a couple of years, he moved to ABC and *The Paul Dixon Show* (1951–1952). The shtick was popular enough that he continued on daytime TV on DuMont through April 1955 and the collapse of the network, and later turned up as a regular during 1957–1958 on the successful country music variety program *Midwestern Hayride* (NBC and ABC, 1951–1959).

Dotty Mack had a similar act, and had begun as a regular on *The Paul Dixon Show* before moving on to her own program, *The Dotty Mack Show* (DuMont and ABC, 1953–1956). *This Is Music* (ABC, 1958–1959) continued the network's tendency to air lip-sync programs. *This Is Music* distinguished itself by airing live from Cincinnati and having a group of lip-syncers instead of a single performer. But the program proved quite unpopular, and ABC affiliates in larger markets simply refused to air it.[19]

None of the lip-sync programs really made the transition to rock and roll, however, and they faded from prime-time TV as rock music grew in popularity. Although a great many performers would themselves lip-sync during television performances—or on stage during supposedly live performances—an argument could be made that *The Paul Dixon Show, The Dotty Mack Show*, and *This Is Music* were honest in that the programs were upfront about it and that audiences were fully aware. The same can't be said about variety programs in which audiences weren't told that they weren't hearing a live rendition of a popular song or in live concerts in which "backing tracks" are employed to help vocally challenged performers sound better than they really are.

DOCUMENTARIES AND PUBLIC AFFAIRS

A vast number of interchangeably dreary discussion/interview public affairs programs, most of which logically originated from Washington, D.C., aired on ABC and DuMont, the poorest of the big four networks, no doubt due to their low production costs. Little serves to distinguish one from another, although sincere attempts to include the interests and views of teenagers formed a brief offshoot of the genre. ABC, CBS, and NBC simultaneously aired the youth-oriented discussion programs *Junior Press Conference* (aka *College Press Conference*), *Youth Takes a Stand,* and *Youth Wants to Know,* respectively, in prime-time between 1951 and 1954; the latter two programs survived for several more years when they moved to the Sunday afternoon "ghetto" time slots reserved for public affairs shows.

THE BLACKLIST

The great ideological struggle between the communism of the USSR and the entrepreneurial capitalism of the United States affected television during the 1950s, just as it had affected all aspects of the popular culture. How serious the communist threat actually was to the American way of life is difficult to assess some 50 years after the fact. Suffice it to say that those on the right reviewed the evidence and saw a credible threat, while those on the left didn't.

The situation that faced television was similar to that facing the film industry. There was at the time considerable fear that left-leaning actors, writers and producers, of which there were many in show business, would somehow slip pro-communist messages into the movies and TV programs that unsuspecting Americans would watch and be subliminally influenced by. As a result, the political beliefs of people in Hollywood were scrutinized, and when suspicions were raised, the parties who failed to adequately toe the capitalist line were blacklisted—that is, prevented from working in the entertainment industry. The blacklist in the television industry continued into the 1960s, and in film it hung on into the 1970s.

The blacklisting process was inherently unfair. Actors, writers, and producers were the subject of anonymous letters, and apparently one anonymous letter was enough to provoke an investigation and end a career. The sponsors of television programs at the time controlled the content of the programs, and it was their call as to who worked and who didn't. Although many Hollywood workers had in fact flirted with communism during the depression of the 1930s—Lucille Ball among them—most, if not all, had long since put the association behind them. Or so they thought.

The stage was set for the blacklist when the U.S. House Committee on Un-American Activities opened a series of hearings on "subversive" activities surrounding the Hollywood film studios in 1947, just two years after the end of World War II, and a time of record film attendance and the birth of network television. Shortly after this the FBI reported to the Federal Communications Commission that it was investigating what it termed a growing communist influence in the broadcasting industry.

Blacklisting began soon after three former FBI agents working under the benign-sounding name American Business Consultants published "Red Channels: The Report of Communist Influence in Radio and Television," a 200-page book that named some 151 "questionable" people then working in broadcasting. By a stroke of remarkable luck, the credibility of "Red Channels" was immensely boosted when North Korea invaded South Korea on 25 June 1950, just three days after publication,[20] making the communist threat seem suddenly very much alive and sparking American and NATO military involvement on the Korean peninsula.

To modern eyes, it's difficult to believe that the television workers who were blacklisted had ever had the opportunity to spread communist propaganda, even if they'd wanted to. For example, Ireene Wicker, the first television performer to be blacklisted, was the hostess of a gentle children's program called *The Singing Lady*, which had begun on radio around 1930 and moved first to local television in New York before going on the fledgling ABC network in 1948. The program would have been long forgotten had it not been for its association with the "witch hunt" for communists. Wicker's "crime," such as it was, was an allegation that she had signed a petition in support of a communist candidate for local office in New York City. That fact that she hadn't signed failed to clear her of the charge, and the question of how, even if she had, it would have influenced the content of *The Singing Lady* apparently was never raised.

It was the same with the other on-screen talent who were blacklisted. Jean Muir, whose career in radio and movies stretched back to the 1930s, had been hired to play Mrs. Aldrich in the CBS sitcom *The Aldrich Family* before being removed from the program after the first episode of the 1950 season. She never returned to television. John Henry Faulk, who later won a lawsuit over the blacklist and was awarded $3.5 million that he never collected, was a panelist on two discussion programs, *It's News to Me* on CBS and for a few months in 1954 on *Leave It to the Girls* on NBC. The blacklist ended his television career until 1975, when he began appearing on the syndicated comedy-variety program *Hee Haw*. Louis Untermeyer, a literary critic and poet, was forced from his role as a panelist on the long-running quiz program *What's My Line* in 1951 in another case in which it's difficult to imagine how he could have inserted pro-communist messages into the program, whose point was to guess the occupation of a contestant by asking him or her questions that could be answered with yes or no.

But the most tragic blacklisting case was that of Philip Loeb. Dropped from the cast of the sitcom *The Goldbergs*—which had begun on radio in the late 1920s and was seen on three of the four television networks (CBS, NBC, and DuMont)—at the start of the 1952 season, he committed suicide after being without work for three years. Like the others, Loeb appears to have never been in a position to make an ideological statement of any sort, let alone a pro-communist one.

The search for communist-influenced subversion continued in many areas of American life, of course, through the 1950s and into the 1960s, although it lost steam with the 1954 censure of Sen. Joseph McCarthy of Wisconsin, whose communist-hunting career had been fueled—and ended—by televised hearings.

But the blacklist nonetheless had lasting effects on the prime-time television programming. The battle for hearts and minds was directly reflected in at least three largely forgotten, topical dramas that for short periods of time dealt overtly with the task of rooting out the red menace: *The Hunter* (CBS, 1952 and NBC, 1954); *The Crusader* (CBS, 1955–1956); and a rather late entry in the genre, *Five Fingers* (NBC, 1959–1960). None of the programs lasted more than a few months. Another effect was that the networks again questioned the wisdom of having programs controlled by advertisers and their agencies. The networks had failed to show much courage, but some of the advertisers had been downright cowardly. They had insisted on firing people with little evidence of wrongdoing.

The other effects were more subtle, but the desire of producers and networks to avoid controversial programming during the years of the blacklist led to large numbers of the rather bland, "safe" programs that seem today to characterize the 1950s, programs such as *The Honeymooners* that contained no overt ideological commentary and instead concentrated on the domestic sphere of home and family. Bus driver Ralph Kramden and sewer worker Ed Norton, after all, never discussed casting off the chains of their oppression.

LAW AND REGULATION: COLOR

Color television was an ideal, perhaps from the beginning of monochromatic (i.e., black-and-white) TV experimentation in the 1920s. Big-budget blockbuster Hollywood movies had been routinely filmed in color since *The Adventures of Robin Hood* was released in 1938—although the studios continued to produce significant numbers of black-and-white films well into the 1960s—and color television seems a natural parallel to color film for its ability to better represent the real world of experience.

But the problem with color in television was compatibility. Because the television system already in place in the United States in the 1940s was monochromatic, it was considered necessary that color broadcasting be done in such a way that people who already owned monochromatic TV sets would be able to receive black-and-white reception of broadcasts originating in color. If this was not possible, then millions of viewers would be forced to purchase at considerable expense color-compatible TV sets in order to watch color shows, and networks would be forced to choose between monochromatic or color broadcasting. The economics of the networks at the time virtually guaranteed that CBS and NBC could afford color, whereas ABC and DuMont would remain mired in black-and-white broadcasting.

CBS and RCA had independently developed color TV systems, and the FCC had surprisingly accepted the noncompatible CBS system as the national color standard in 1950. This would have forced viewers to buy CBS-manufactured or-licensed television sets in order to see color shows and also forced the other networks to either adopt the CBS system themselves, at presumably great expense, or convince viewers to buy two television sets, one for color programs and one for everything else. Fortunately for consumers, war intervened, and in 1951 the production of color TVs was deemed nonessential for the conduct of the Korean War and was halted. By the time the war was halted by a cease-fire in 1953, the FCC had changed its mind, and rescinded the adoption of the noncompatible CBS color system in favor of the compatible system developed by RCA. Equally fortunately, CBS had seen the error of its ways and had begun cooperating with RCA, so that Admiral was able to put on the market TV sets that could receive both monochrome and color signals shortly after the end of hostilities. Unfortunately, at a retail price of over $1,100 there were few takers; by comparison, a new Ford two-door sedan sold for a little more than $1,700 the same year. At the same time, few programs were being broadcast in color as the networks dealt with the chicken-or-egg question of whether color broadcasting would drive the sale of color televisions or the ownership of color sets would create a demand for color programs. Whatever the answer, color broadcasting and viewing were possible, and prices of sets began to fall in short order as demand for them increased.

Full conversion to color would take some time, though, and even more time would pass before the networks became color-equal. By the start of the fall 1965 TV season, NBC had 95 percent of its prime-time programs in color, whereas CBS and ABC lagged behind at 50 percent and 40 percent, respectively. (DuMont was long gone by this time.) And while the number of color sets being sold outstripped the sales of monochrome sets for the first time in 1966, only one-sixth of households had color TVs in 1967.

CONCLUSION

This early period of prime-time history saw the advent of programs that are still part of our collective cultural memory. Indeed, when politicians talk about how family life used to be, they're referring to the sitcom fantasies of the 1950s usually, not the realities of the decade. We tend to forget that the violent genres of the western and the detective show were equal in popularity to the wholesome sitcoms.

By the end of the decade, the industry's pattern was set for the next few decades:

1. Live programming was replaced by shows presented on film or video-tape, which could be syndicated and endlessly repeated.
2. Production facilities moved from New York City to Hollywood to be near the expertise and experience of the film industry.
3. Anthologies went out of style and were replaced by serial programs.
4. The advertisers and their agencies went out of the production business. They merely bought seconds within the programs. The quiz show scandals and the increased cost of producing filmed programs were two of the reasons. The networks finally controlled their own schedules.
5. Instead of producing their own prime-time series, the networks usually relied on the major film studios, independent producers, and talent agents who acted as packagers, with the networks sometimes getting part ownership. The packagers would put together a deal with a star or a writer and sell the concept to the networks.
6. Ratings became more important as the mass audience became available to advertisers.

CHAPTER 5

Detectives, Cowboys, and Happy Families (1960–1969)

Social changes that affected many aspects of American life during the 1960s were reflected in television as the medium entered what could be called its mature phase. Programming coalesced around the Big Three networks—ABC, CBS and NBC—as they were not only the dominant but the only players in prime-time television.

A significant change that came about was a shift in the audience in which advertisers were interested. The prime-time audience, which had been thought of as a truly mass audience that included everyone everywhere, was reconfigured through programs that appealed to the urban, affluent, and above all young audience that advertisers lusted after. The westerns that were numerous during the 1950s died out, replaced by programs that centered on the adventures of urban detectives, and usually young urban detectives at that. ABC, the youngest-skewing of the Big Three networks, went to an almost entirely sitcom prime-time schedule in an effort to attract youthful viewers. Meanwhile, bracketing the sitcoms were news programs offering a continual flow of images of Vietnam, domestic rioting and assassinations.

Discussions about the influences, good and bad, but mostly bad, that TV had on its viewers came to be part of public discourse. Congress held hearings into televised violence, scholars studied its effects, parents banned their children from watching the worst of the violent programs (which made them only more appealing), and FCC Chairman Newton Minow made a speech that still resonates today in which he called television a "vast wasteland."

SITCOMS

ABC went to virtually all sitcoms in 1964, and the other networks soon followed, so that soon the entire prime-time television schedule was laden with sitcoms, most of which proved to be unpopular and were rapidly canceled. Although most sitcoms had a life of something between a handful of episodes and a season or two, a few lasted for five to six years. Others live on in the twenty-first century as part of the popular culture and can be found in endless rotation on cable.

One exception to the usual sitcom was *That Girl* (ABC, 1966–1971). Marlo Thomas played an attractive, young woman who was not married. She had a boyfriend but was more interested in pursuing a career than in getting him to the altar. Before *The Mary Tyler Moore Show*, the program was one of the few to treat being single as though it were not a disease needing desperate efforts for a cure and to view the single woman as being admirable, not the butt of all of the jokes. Another exception was *My World and Welcome to It* (NBC, 1969–1972), based on James Thurber's stories. William Windom played a cartoonist with an active imagination, who viewed his marriage from a whimsical viewpoint.

Happy Family Sitcoms

The locus of the happy family sitcom was ABC. Its Thursday night prime-time lineup in 1962, the high point of the happy family genre, was a solid block from 7:30 to 9:30 P.M. of programs that today typify what we think of as wholesome entertainment from a time long past: the distinctly unadventurous *The Adventures of Ozzie and Harriet, The Donna Reed Show, Leave It to Beaver* and *My Three Sons*, the lattermost being an all-male, single-father variant, whereas the other three were firmly rooted in the traditional, somewhat mythical, intact family unit. In *My Three Sons* (ABC, CBS, 1960–1972), Fred MacMurray played the gentle father who seemed temporarily bewildered occasionally but always came up with wise advice by the end of the show. The series lasted long enough that some of the sons married, an orphan was added, the housekeeper changed, and Dad remarried. But despite the evolution of the family, it was typical in that every boy wanted to join it and every girl wanted to marry into it.

But CBS was home to two of the most loved sitcoms—*The Dick Van Dyke Show* (1961–1966) and *The Andy Griffith Show* (1960–1968). The shows were different in some obvious ways. The former was clearly a show about suburban New York. The father had a glamorous job and an attractive wife, and usually he was the one who was the source of the humor. The latter was equally clearly about small-town North Carolina. Andy was a sheriff, a widower, and the source of wisdom. But both combined characters in the workplace and the home to make us laugh; both were anchored by the father figures; and both avoided controversial topics and radiated with a humanity that made viewers feel good about the world. In both shows, the supporting characters—like Mary Tyler Moore, Morey Amsterdam, and Rose Marie in *Dick Van Dyke* and Don Knotts, Ronnie Howard, and Frances Bavier in *Andy Griffith*—were important in creating laughter and warmth.

The single-parent variation continued, as it had in the previous time period, to focus on single fathers. *Accidental Family* (NBC, 1967–1968) was not about a failure of birth control but rather combined generic program elements so that a motherless show biz family moved to the country in search of a better life. It followed nightclub comedian/widower Jerry Webster (Jerry Van Dyke) as he raised his son (Teddy Quinn) on a farm in the San Fernando Valley. Similar as well were *The Governor and J.J.* (CBS, 1969–1972) and *The Courtship of Eddie's Father* (ABC, 1969–1972); in both, single fathers—the governor of an unnamed state and a magazine writer—interacted with, respectively, an early-20s daughter and a 7-year-old son. *Family Affair* (CBS, 1966–1971), added the themes of death and substitute parents into the mix as three siblings—15-year-old Cissy and the 6-year-old twins Buffy and Jodie—were shipped off to live with their uncle (Brian Keith), a rich bachelor complete with English manservant (Sebastian Cabot), after their parents had died. *Family Affair* is today firmly ensconced in the morbid pop culture due to the sad end of child star Anissa Jones, who had played Buffy: She died from a drug overdose after the program went off the air but when she was still a teenager.

The domestic servant variant, of which *Family Affair* was one because of the presence of butler Mr. French, was also seen in *Hazel* (NBC, 1961–1965 and CBS, 1965–1966), in which the competent housekeeper (Shirley Booth) ran the incompetent family. *Hazel* was based on single-panel cartoons published in *The Saturday Evening Post* when it was one of the most popular of the mass circulation magazines in the United States.

Rural Comedies

The 1960s saw CBS schedule a number of rural comedies during prime-time, and the form would come to be associated with the network and not occur elsewhere. The trend began on ABC by way of *The Real McCoys* (1957–1962), a program in which a West Virginia mountain family moved to California, with the expected clash-of-culture results. CBS had begun its own rural sitcom programming at about the same time, with the gentle *The Andy Griffith Show*, but when *The Real McCoys* moved to CBS for the 1962–1963 season, it touched off a succession of other programs on the same theme.

The guiding force behind rural sitcoms was producer Paul Henning, who masterminded what could be called "the big three" rural comedies: *The Beverly Hillbillies, Petticoat Junction*, and *Green Acres*. It was Henning's signature, so to speak, to be able to tap into a distinctly non-urban point of the view that has always been somewhat unusual in prime-time television.

GREEN ACRES

It is sometimes difficult to understand the appeal of comedies, especially those being viewed several decades after they first aired. Such is the case with *Green Acres* (CBS, 1965–1971), a program popular enough to reach the number-six position in the ratings during the 1966–1967 television season and no. 19 in 1968–1969. It was one of CBS's "rural sitcoms" during the time.

The title sequence introduces the main characters and sets up the conflict at the heart of the program. Oliver Wendell Douglas (Eddie Albert) is a Manhattan attorney who forsakes urban life for a ramshackle farm in Hooterville (also the location of *Petticoat Junction*), located somewhere in the television version of rural America, a place simultaneously Southern and Midwestern, but in a vague sort of way. His wife, Lisa (Eva Gabor), is a Hungarian immigrant, thoroughly urbanized and completely horrified, in a comedic way, by their new life in the country. The song they perform during the opening sequence—yet another example of memorable television theme music—spells out their views on the situation and establishes them both as fishes out of water, something illustrated as well by their clothing. Oliver usually wears a three-piece suit and Lisa a glamorous gown, in contrast to the bib overalls and plaid shirts of the country folk.

The episode "The Great Mayorality Campaign" is about local politics. Sam Drucker (Frank Cady), who runs the general store and has been mayor of Hooterville for 37 years, has decided against running for reelection. For no particular reason, the men in town decide to back Oliver for mayor, while the women support Lisa, so they end up running against each other for a job that neither particularly wants. The plot, then, revolves around real-world contemporary gender conflicts, albeit on a simplistic level.

Dirty campaign tricks soon arise, this being the mid-60s and the beginning of the age of heightened political cynicism. Mr. Haney (Pat Buttram) flattens the front tire on Lisa's campaign car—a postwar wood-bodied station wagon that represents the sort of ancient car that rural types on TV drive—and in retaliation Ralph Monroe (Mary Grace Canfield), a masculine woman in white painter's overalls, squirts Oliver with a garden hose while he makes a tedious speech about the need to drill a municipal well. Annoyed by such shenanigans, Douglas demands that Lisa campaign against him "on an intellectual level"—an absurdity given Lisa's complete lack of intellectual capability—a statement that provokes an argument complete with much comical slamming of doors by both parties (and also by an on-looking mouse in a sight gag repeated twice during the episode).

The women say that because Hooterville has more men than women, they'll lose the election unless some men vote for Lisa, so they contrive for her to ride a white horse through town à la Lady Godiva. Meanwhile, the men scheme to have Hank Kimball (Alvy Moore) marry Ralph so that she'll be out of town on a honeymoon during the election, which will somehow throw the vote their way. Hank, a happy (of course) bachelor, doesn't want to go through with the wedding, but Ralph, an unhappy (of course) spinster, does; after all, everyone knows that what women really want is to get them a man. Oliver and Lisa argue repeatedly over their campaigns, but then both independently announce that they'll drop out of the race to preserve their marital harmony.

In the final scene, Hank has come to the Douglas's house to hide from Ralph, who is in literal pursuit of him even though the election appears to be over. He tries to crawl under the Douglas's low couch in a desperate attempt at escape as the episode ends. The sequence is in fast motion, in the style of silent films, in an apparent attempt to make it look funnier.

Much of the humor in the episode comes at the expense of Lisa, who is incompetent at the things women are supposed to be able to do. She's shown to be a terrible cook—in once scene she's making hot chocolate by melting candy and pouring the resulting sludge into china cups so that it overflows—and her limited command of English leads to malapropisms, such as her misreading of a newspaper headline about the mayoralty race as a "morality race." She wonders aloud what qualifies Oliver to run in a morality race. On the other hand, Oliver comes off little better, as a pompous blowhard who thinks himself much more intelligent and important than in fact he is. Interestingly, the rural natives are neither much smarter nor much stupider than the urban Douglases; everyone seems to be equally unintelligent and silly, regardless of their origins in the city or the country. The world of *Green Acres* looks normal on the surface; only the sense of logic is skewed; therefore, the program is the perhaps the perfect reflection of life in the late 60s.

The Beverly Hillbillies (CBS, 1962–1971) was by far the most popular of the lot, ranking as the most popular program in the country during its first and second seasons, when it was seen by an estimated 60 million people per week. The concept of *The Beverly Hillbillies* was simple and familiar to anyone who has seen the show: Jed Clampett (Buddy Ebsen) had struck oil on his hardscrabble farm in Arkansas and moved to "Californey" with mother-in-law

The Clampett clan drove from the backwoods of the Ozarks to become *The Beverly Hillbillies*, but the change in location didn't mean a change in lifestyle or values for them. The show had Bea Benadaret as a frequent guest star, and Donna Douglas as Elly May, Irene Ryan as Granny, Buddy Ebsen as patriarch Jed Clampett, and Max Baer as Jethro. Courtesy of Photofest.

Granny (Irene Ryan)—in this way he was another in a long line of widower fathers on TV—to seek a better life for the young'uns. Daughter Ellie Mae (Donna Douglas) was the tight-jeaned precursor of tight-shorted Daisy Duke in *The Dukes of Hazzard*, and cousin Jethro (Max Baer Jr.) was muscular, reasonably handsome, but not very bright.

The Beverly Hillbillies would soon be joined by *Petticoat Junction* (CBS, 1963–1970), a rural sitcom with a proto-T and A opening sequence that featured apparently naked young adult triplet sisters bathing in a water tower in a town with the suggestive name of Hooterville. The nudity was implied by bare shoulders, the program airing during an age when such things were left to the imagination of viewers. Two years later, a straight-laced New York City attorney (Eddie Arnold) and his glamorous Hungarian-born wife (Eva Gabor, an instantly recognizable celebrity and one of the Gabor sisters) moved to Hooterville in the spin-off *Green Acres* (CBS, 1965–1971), a program that reversed the rural-to-urban migration of *The Beverly Hillbillies* and which again presented the city folk as the fishes out of water.

At the same time, *Gomer Pyle, U.S.M.C.* (CBS, 1964–1969) was bringing rural humor to the peacetime military in a hybridized prime-time sitcom, and *The Andy Griffith Show* was spinning off its successor, *Mayberry R.F.D.* (CBS, 1968–1971), which continued with some of the cast of the original.

And then it all came crashing down. In the belief that the rural comedies were reaching a rural audience too old and too poor to buy the products advertised during the programs, CBS president Jim Aubrey purged the network's prime-time schedule, canceling *The Beverly Hillbillies*, *Green Acres*, and *Mayberry R.F.D.* so that, when the new season began in September 1971, no rural comedies were to be found. *Petticoat Junction* had ended its run a year before, and *Gomer Pyle* the year before that. The age of the rural sitcoms had come to an end, and changes to the sitcom landscape of the 1970s were soon to get underway as two overlapping categories of sitcoms—the independent young woman comedy and the workplace comedy—came to prominence.

Silly Sitcoms

A certain level of silliness was reached in sitcoms of the mid-1960s, which should not be taken as an implication that earlier sitcoms traded in more intellectual or refined humor; after all, the heyday of slapstick and humor appropriate to the vaudeville stage was still relatively recent, and performers employing those styles—Milton Berle, Red Skelton, and the Three Stooges, among others—were still fixtures in television and film.

There seems to be no coherent theme among the sillier of the 1960s sitcoms, but all offered escapism in one form or another and served, if nothing else, as a means of distraction from the social changes—women's lib, hippies, civil rights, and so on—that characterized American life at the time. Many of the programs remain familiar to viewers as episodes run continuously on cable.

Perhaps the most well known of the silly sitcoms was *Gilligan's Island* (CBS, 1964–1967), a program that formed part of the childhood of Baby Boomers, who can outline the basic plot of the show, and perhaps even act out episodes, even if they haven't seen it since it left the air. As everyone knows, *Gilligan's Island* focused on a three-hour boat tour that inexplicably turned into a three-year stranding on the proverbial desert island. The program featured the antics of Gilligan (Bob Denver), the first mate of the chartered boat Minnow, as he interacted with the skipper (Alan Hale Jr.) and passengers: the fabulously wealthy Thurston Howell III (Jim Backus) and his wife Lovey (Natalie Schafer); a high school science teacher usually referred to as The Professor (Russell Johnson); and two sexy women, movie star Ginger (Tina Louise) and girl-next-door Mary Ann (Dawn Wells). Episodes centered on personality clashes among the disparate castaways and various wacky situations that would routinely befall them as they utterly failed in their every attempt to get back to civilization.

Get Smart (NBC, 1965–1969 and CBS, 1969–1970) was a spoof of the highly popular James Bond movies, and their inevitable clones, such as the four Matt Helm films in which Dean Martin starred,[1] and perhaps even a spoof of the spoof spy series *The Man from U.N.C.L.E.* Its central character, the ironically named Maxwell Smart (Don Adams), was the polar opposite of the suave, international and above all highly competent spies embodied in the characters of Bond and *U.N.C.L.E.*'s Napoleon Solo (Robert Vaughan) and Illya Kuryakin (David McCallum). Whereas the men from U.N.C.L.E. had highly sophisticated technological devices, Smart spoke into his shoe, which "concealed" a telephone, a parody of the miniature devices that were part of the iconography of spy films.

Two sitcoms dealt with the humorous ownership of women, something a bit jarring given that the time period in which they aired included the early stages of what was called at the time the women's liberation movement. Neither woman was actually human and therefore was somewhat more "controllable" by men: *I Dream of Jeannie* (NBC, 1965–1970) was, of course, about a beautiful genie (Barbara Eden) owned by, and later married to, an astronaut, and *My Living Doll* (CBS, 1964–1965) was about a beautiful android (Julie Newmar) "programmed to do anything she was told—absolutely anything"[2] a phrase that needs only a Monty Python "wink wink nudge nudge" to complete its innuendo. It doesn't seem to be much of a stretch of the imagination to see both programs as male reactions against the burgeoning women's movement. Readers interested in repressed sexuality may wish to ponder the ramifications of sex objects who despite their beauty are not actually human.

Other programs, although influenced by the social milieu of the times, are more difficult to probe for deeper layers of meaning. *My Favorite Martian* (CBS, 1963–1966), in which a newspaper reporter (Bill Bixby) had a Martian (Ray Walston) as a houseguest, seemed linked to a contemporary societal

Barbara Eden played the insubordinate genie and Tony Hagman was her "master" in *I Dream of Jeannie*. The question is: What does this series say about the role of women in the 1960s? Courtesy of Photofest.

interest in UFOs and science fiction, but what can be made of *My Mother the Car* (NBC, 1964–1965), a sitcom in which the main character's mother had somehow been reincarnated as a 1926 automobile, a mythical "Porter"? Or *Mr. Ed* (CBS, 1961–1965), the famous program about, of course, of course, a talking horse?

Occult Sitcoms

Even more difficult to plumb than the silly sitcoms are the sitcoms built around what could be termed "occult" themes, which although quite benign, followed witches and families of monsters as they went about their day-to-day activities in parodies of viewers' daily lives and routines. Although the programs seem on their surface to present a world very much different from the world of everyday experience, they were as conservative in their construction of the family unit as any 1950s-era happy family program. *Bewitched, The Addams Family,* and *The Munsters* all reflected the standardized television family, in which dad went off to work while mom stayed home, as had the parents of "the Beav" and many others. The main difference in the occult sitcoms was that mom and dad were decidedly not Donna Reed and Robert Young.

BEWITCHED

A pre-credit introduction of characters opens the first episode, "I, Darrin," and explains how Samantha, a modern day witch, and Darrin Stephens, an advertising executive, met and fell in love. An animated title sequence with the program's memorable theme music follows.

Witchcraft is illustrated through primitive visual effects, the "trick photography" of the time. For example, viewers see Darrin making repeated attempts to walk from the living room of their honeymoon suite to the bedroom, but each time he opens the door he immediately arrives, to his confusion, in the hotel lobby in his pajamas and robe. This is the result of a spell cast by Endora, Samantha's mother, who has appeared in the bedroom to try to dissuade Samantha from going through with (i.e., consummating) her marriage. The sequence begins with Darrin swallowing the last of his drink with a look of sexual anticipation on his face as he heads toward the bedroom; the episode has a surprising amount of sexual innuendo for 1964, although safely within the confines of marriage.

Samantha tries but fails to cast a spell to send Endora away, doing the wiggling-nose gesture that is a signature of the program's visual language.

Endora tells Samantha that "normal" people don't understand witchcraft, and viewers learn that Darrin doesn't know that Samantha's a witch. Samantha cuts off Darrin's sexual advances to tell him. He doesn't believe her, of course, so she does tricks, such as making a drink appear in his hand.

Darrin, naturally, is confused and confides in a bar to bachelor friend Dave, whose advice is useless and generic. He goes home to Samantha, and while it at first appears that he may reject her, he doesn't. Instead, he tells her that she must become "a suburban housewife" who cooks and cleans and goes to his mother's every Friday night for dinner, thus blatantly spelling out the proper role for women in 1964. She readily agrees. The premise for the entire series is set up at this point, as Samantha promises, for the first of many times, to not perform witchcraft.

Meanwhile, the glamorous Sheila arrives at McMann and Tate, Darrin's ad agency, and invites him and Samantha to a dinner party. Sheila makes derogatory comments during dinner about Samantha and insists on referring to her by the demeaning title "Darrin's little bride." Samantha takes revenge via witchcraft—making Sheila's hair fall into her face, moving a plate of soup so she leans her elbow into it, breaking the zipper on her strapless gown so that Sheila has to hold it up, and finally stirring up a wind that blows the front door open and Sheila's wig off in the episode's climax.

In the dénouement, Darrin and Samantha arrive home where he says she broke her promise to him, and she again promises no more witchery. He wants Samantha to ignore the kitchen, which is piled with dirty dishes, and to "come to bed," but she pushes him off, saying "that's what you said last night," thus hinting at nightly newlywed sex. Samantha then uses witchcraft to instantly clean the kitchen and walks through the door, smiling, as the episode ends.

The moral of the story seems to be that a clever woman will pretend to be submissive to her husband and without his permission use her skills (whether magic or not) as she wishes. What he doesn't know . . .

The most popular of the occult sitcoms was *Bewitched* (ABC, 1964–1972), a program that reached the lofty position of being the second-most popular prime-time program during its premier season. *Bewitched* took the familiar form of the married couple sitcom, but its hook was that the wife was literally a witch, Samantha (Elizabeth Montgomery), who used her powers to make life better for hubby Darrin (played first by Dick York and later by Dick Sargent), a rather run-of-the-mill advertising executive. The program eventually added children and morphed into a family-oriented sitcom that continued its theme of nonthreatening witchery in the twentieth century.

The day after *Bewitched* premiered in September 1964, ABC debuted *The Addams Family*, which would stay on the prime-time schedule for two years, much less time than the eight-year run of *Bewitched*. In this case the family was modeled on characters created by Charles Addams in his morbidly humorous cartoons in *The New Yorker* magazine—and as such much, much different than the Stephenses in *Bewitched*. The program centered on Gomez Addams (John Astin), the father of the extended family, who had oddly bulging eyes, wore pinstriped suits and staged model train crashes as a hobby, and Morticia Addams (Carolyn Jones), the mother, who bore a striking resemblance to the actress Maila Nurmi, who as Vampira had appeared in campy 1950s films like the dreadful *Plan 9 from Outer Space*, with long black hair, dead white makeup and a form-fitting gown with plunging neckline. The family unit was filled out with two odd children, son Pugsley (Ken Weatherwax) and daughter Wednesday (Lisa Loring); Uncle Fester (1920s child actor Jackie Coogan); Cousin Itt (Felix Silla), an ambulatory pile of hair; the butler Lurch (Ted Cassidy); and a disembodied hand (also Ted Cassidy) that lived in a box and was called, appropriately, Thing.

The Munsters premiered on CBS during the same week as ABC's *The Addams Family* and *Bewitched*, and like the former it would be part of prime-time through 1966. Thematically, *The Munsters* and *The Addams Family* were quite similar. Both programs took the happy-family-with-children model and inverted it so that family members were not the sort of people, if that's the word, who lived next door to viewers. In the case of *The Munsters*, the father (Fred Gwynne) was a Frankenstein monster; the mother (Yvonne DeCarlo) a corpse in a shroud (or perhaps a female vampire—it was hard to tell); the son (Butch Patrick) a werewolf; the grandfather (Al Lewis) a vampire in the Bela Lugosi mould; and the niece (played by Beverley Owen and Pat Priest) the most unfortunate of all as she was entirely, completely normal. All of the character types in both programs were familiar to viewers from decades of horror films, and both utilized the iconography of such films with, for example, *The Munsters'* house being a ramshackle mansion draped in spider webs and bearing the doubly ominous house number of 1313 Mockingbird Lane.

One should probably not try to read too much into the occult sitcoms. The programs were comedies, after all, not serious investigations into the role of the occult in American life during the 60s, and as such don't appear to reflect societal fears or concerns. Instead, they seem to be part of the desire of the television networks to offer viewers something novel to watch, if only to make the commercials more palatable.

Military-Themed Sitcoms

Growing anxiety about American involvement in Vietnam in the early 1960s was reflected, although in disguise, in a number of military-themed sitcoms, some successful, but most not. Many of them were set during World War II, a much more "popular" war than the conflict then escalating in Vietnam, a setting in which good and evil were more ambiguous and which was in the process of polarizing American political and social life. By the 1960s World War II had receded far enough in history to be a safe topic, and perhaps for the first time American television viewers, many of whom had lived through it, were ready to laugh about their wartime experiences while simultaneously dealing, at an unconscious level, with their Vietnam–related fears and concerns.

The most popular World War II–themed sitcom of the period was *Hogan's Heroes* (CBS, 1965–1971), a comedy improbably set amidst a group of Allied prisoners of war in a Nazi prison camp. Modeled on the 1952 film *Stalag 17*, but played more for laughs than the film had been, the prisoners of war in *Hogan's Heroes*, led by Col. Robert Hogan (Bob Crane), continually outsmarted their slow-witted Nazi captors under the command of Col. Wilhelm Klink (Werner Klemperer). The Nazis, one and all, were figures of ridicule and comedy, hardly representative of a feared and cruel master race that had conquered much of Europe after 1939. Although many sitcoms fail in part because of their setting—for example, viewers found nothing funny about unemployment offices in the single-season *Calucci's Department* (CBS, 1973)—*Hogan's Heroes* was a hit despite, or perhaps because of, its bleak physical setting.

The other highly successful military-themed sitcom of the era was *Gomer Pyle, U.S.M.C.* (CBS, 1964–1969), which centered on the cultural clash between the hillbilly Gomer Pyle (Jim Nabors), who, of course, had been a character in *The Andy Griffith Show*, and his hard-ass career drill instructor, Sgt. Vince Carter (Frank Sutton), in the contemporary peacetime Marine Corps. The casting of *Gomer Pyle* is worthy of note. Nabors was himself a study in contrasts, his hick-accented comedy persona contrasting with the booming, highly trained singing voice viewers heard on variety shows and records. And in an example of the Mobius strip-like way that television bends back in on itself, the actor William Christopher, who played Pvt. Lester Hummel in *Gomer Pyle*, would later be seen as the gentle Fr. Francis Mulcahy in the long-running anti-war military sitcom *M*A*S*H* (CBS, 1972–1983).

Other military sitcoms came and went, all or most of them originating around the mid-1960s as US military involvement in Vietnam was growing.

Several were safely located during World War II, as *Hogan's Heroes* had been, and in the Navy, which seemed somehow funnier than did the land-based forces. *McHale's Navy* (ABC, 1962–1966), starred Ernest Borgnine as the humorous Lt. Cmdr. Quinton McHale, thus inverting viewers' associations with Borgnine's sadistic character Sgt. Fatso Judson in the 1953 film *From Here to Eternity*. At about the same time, *Broadside* (ABC, 1964–1965), with its to-cringe-at sexist title (although considered acceptable at the time), dealt with the Women Accepted for Volunteer Emergency Service or WAVES; both *McHale's Navy* and *Broadside* had been created by Edward J. Montagne.

Other military sitcoms were set in contemporary times, but none dealt with the too-scary-for-comedy subject of troops training for combat in Southeast Asia. The curiously titled *Don't Call Me Charlie* (NBC, 1962–1963) (the title referred to the unusual name of the character Col. U. Charles Barker) was a short-lived sitcom in which a veterinarian (Josh Peine) was for some reason drafted and stationed in Paris. *No Time for Sergeants* (ABC, 1964–1965) followed the lead of the film of the same title, its hillbilly main character (played by Sammy Jackson) safely in the Air Force of the day and safely in the United States. *Mona McCluskey* (NBC, 1965–1966) was another short-lived sitcom with something of a military theme, this one about a beautiful actress (Juliet Prowse) who married a United States Air Force sergeant (Scott Miller) and pretended to let him support them on his measly $500-a-month salary. Its central conceit was, of course, that no real man would allow his wife to support him.

Most of the military sitcoms came and went by the mid-1960s, with the exceptions noted above. As the situation in Vietnam worsened after 1968, and as the continued involvement of the United States in that conflict further polarized American society, sitcoms centering on the military no longer seemed all that funny and they faded from the prime-time schedule.

DRAMA

General Dramas

General dramas dealt with an enormously wide range of subjects and most, but not all, were firmly centered on the nuclear family. But everything else under the sun could be found in the general drama, as well. State and municipal government were featured in *Slattery's People* (CBS, 1964–1965) and in the pretentiously titled *Man and the City* (ABC, 1971–1972), in which film actor Anthony Quinn was cast as the mayor of a small city. George C. Scott was a social worker on the mean streets of New York City in *East Side/*

West Side (CBS, 1963–1964). But the relatively short runs of the programs indicate that government employees, mayors, and social workers were of little interest to audience members.

Just as the networks had experimented with sitcoms set in World War II, ABC also tried dramas from the same era. *Combat* (1962–1967), *Rat Patrol* (1966–1968), and *Twelve O'Clock High* (1964–1967) were three of the efforts, but it was expensive to shoot on location, find the right period equipment, and recreate battle scenes. And the audience response didn't justify the outlay.

Single-parent dramas were mixed amongst the family-oriented dramas, just as single parent sitcoms coexisted with family sitcoms. Perhaps typical was *The New Loretta Young Show* (CBS, 1962–1963), a half-hour drama in which the glamorous Ms. Young played the widowed mother of seven who supported her family by writing for magazines. She remarried in the final episode of the series, at which point, had it continued, it would have become something closer to a happy family drama. *The New Loretta Young Show* was much less of a success than *The Loretta Young Show* (NBC, 1953–1961) had been; the earlier program was a dramatic anthology that for years offered stories that ended with a moral, a reflection of Ms. Young's Catholicism and her belief that TV should be uplifting. Oddly, though, for a conventional widow in suburban Connecticut in the early 1960s, the children in *The New Loretta Young Show* had the unusual names Maria, Judy, Marnie, Vickie, Binkie, Dirk, and Dack, the latter two names also being the names of the actors who played them, the brothers Dirk and Dack Rambo.

Espionage Dramas

Espionage dramas, with their cloak-and-dagger political intrigue, peaked during the 1960s, in some ways the high point (or perhaps the low point) of the Cold War. The genre is of interest because of the number of programs that originated in the United Kingdom and the spoofs that grew from audience familiarity with the genre's conventions.

CBS ran three series, all British and all starring Patrick McGoohan as probably the same character, John Drake, during the 1960s. Drake was the central character in *Danger Man* (1961), in *Secret Agent* (1965–1956) and most likely was the unnamed title character in *The Prisoner* (summer 1968), a man identified only as "No. 6" and being held against his will in a mysterious village somewhere in the United Kingdom. *The Prisoner* was highly stylized and difficult to understand, nearly to the point of incomprehensibility. Although viewers never learned who the characters were, why they were imprisoned, or what exactly was going on, the program is seen today to epitomize 1960s cool and was actively promoted by BBC America as being retro in summer 2004, when the program made a rare reappearance. ABC's contribution from Great Britain was the stylish *The Avengers* (ABC, 1966–1969) with Patrick Macnee and Diana Rigg as two suave British agents who were chic, cool, and self-mocking.

The espionage genre had become so familiar to viewers from television programs and James Bond movies, and from the inevitable clones that follow

In the era of the Cold War, spy dramas with action and a twist of comedy were a relief from the tension. In *I Spy*, Bill Cosby and Robert Culp were in the business of saving the free world, playing tennis, and trading wisecracks. Courtesy of Photofest.

any success, that espionage spoofs inevitably developed during the 1960s. These played with the generic conventions of secrets and technological gadgetry and veered close to comedy, something that occurred simultaneously in espionage films. NBC's successful *The Man from U.N.C.L.E* of 1964–1968 spun off the unsuccessful *The Girl from U.N.C.L.E.*, which lasted for less than a year from September 1966 until August 1967, indicating that while viewers might enjoy one spy spoof, two is apparently too many.

Several espionage-themed programs of the time period had long runs. Besides the four years of *The Man from U.N.C.L.E.*, *Mission: Impossible* followed the adventures of the Impossible Missions Force under the able command of white-haired James Phelps (Peter Graves) on CBS for seven years (1966–1973), while *I Spy*—famous for its then unusual pairing of a Caucasian and an African-American actor in the lead roles and for bringing Bill Cosby to national attention—ran for three years, 1965–1968, on NBC.

Adventure and Historical Dramas

Historical adventures largely passed by the wayside during the period 1960–1969, with the notable exception of *Daniel Boone* (NBC, 1964–1970), a program that could well be classified as a western if it weren't for its being set along the Tennessee–Kentucky–North Carolina border area at around the time of the Revolutionary War. Fess Parker—who had played Davy Crockett in the Walt Disney films that started the coon-skin cap fad of the mid-1950s—starred as Boone, with singer Ed Ames as Mingo, his Native American companion.

Historical dramas were replaced by programs with contemporary settings that, if nothing else, required fewer historical props and were, therefore, more economical and easier to produce. As with the other genres, most adventure series died early deaths; for example, *Mr. Garlund* (aka *The Garlund Touch*, just one of many programs that had more than one title during their run) followed the adventures of a mysterious, rich do-gooder (Charles Quinlivan) and his foster brother (Kam Tong, in a rare major role for an Asian at the time) from October 1960 until January 1961 on CBS. Other contemporary dramas were much more successful and ran for years. *Route 66*, about two young men (Martin Milner and George Maharis), their stylish Corvette, and the famous two-lane highway that runs from the American Midwest down to the Southwest, aired on CBS (1960–1964); toward the end of its run the program incorporated a character who was a Vietnam war veteran, an early reference to that conflict in prime-time television. Attorney Paul Bryan (Ben Gazzara), a man afflicted with an incurable disease and two years to live, ran for his life for three years in *Run for Your Life* (NBC, 1965–1968). But nobody did a better job of being on the run than Dr. Richard Kimble (David Janssen) in *The Fugitive* (ABC, 1963–1967). He was convicted of his wife's murder and escaped. As he traveled across America, he did good deeds and dodged the detective on his trail.

An American veterinarian and his daughter (Marshall Thompson and Cheryl Miller) lived and worked someplace in Africa—the continent represented by a theme park in California—in the exotic *Daktari* (CBS, 1966–1969), a program associated both thematically and linguistically with the 1962 John Wayne adventure-comedy *Hatari!* as the film title is said to mean "danger" and the program title "doctor" in Swahili.

Science Fiction Dramas

By the period 1960–1969 it had become difficult to tell if science fiction (sci-fi) programs were aimed at children or adults, as programs had elements that would appeal to both in terms of plots, the casting of handsome men and beautiful women, and the presence of the ubiquitous rubber monsters. The most successful sci-fi programs of the era lasted for years—*Voyage to the Bottom of the Sea* (spun off from the film of the same title) (ABC, 1964–1968), the juvenile *Lost in Space* (CBS, 1965–1968), and *Star Trek* (NBC, 1966–1969)—even though none of them approached the ratings of the most popular programs of the era. *Star Trek*, by far the most well remembered of the period's sci-fi programs and the source of the franchise that includes theatrical films and numerous spin-off television series that continue through the present day, was never ranked higher than as the number 52 program of the television season. It was, of course, still popular in syndication years later; for example, episodes of *Star Trek* shown at 6 P.M. on an independent station in Jackson, Mississippi regularly had a larger audience than did the ABC affiliate's local newscast during the mid-1980s.

Despite these examples, there were relatively few science fiction programs on the prime-time schedule, despite large numbers of sci-fi films, the hugely expensive space race between the United States and the USSR, and the massive news coverage of NASA's manned space flight program that culminated in the real-life, yet eerily science fiction-like, lunar landing of 20 July 1969.

Legal Dramas

The legal drama that stands out from all others was, of course, the iconic *Perry Mason*, the CBS program whose nine-year, 245-episode run from 1957 to 1966 continues to be the longest for any legal drama in prime-time.

The usual formula for a *Perry Mason* episode was that in the first half of the program the crime in question and Mason's client would be introduced, and the client would be wrongly charged with the crime. During the second half, a detailed investigation, preliminary hearing or a trial would be held and Mason would, inevitably, clear his client and expose the guilt of the real criminal, who would promptly break down and confess on the spot. Along the way would come much didactic legal dialogue; for example, in "The Case of the Illicit Illusion" careful explanation of the role of fingerprints and gunpowder residue tests was necessary as the case hinged on the questions of whether what appeared to be a suicide was actually a murder, and, if it was, who had fired the murder weapon.

PERRY MASON

"The Case of the Pint-Sized Client" follows the *Perry Mason* formula in that Mason's client is wrongly accused of a crime but cleared at the last moment when the guilty party breaks down and tearfully admits all. As usual, handsome Perry Mason, aided by ever-faithful secretary Della Street and virile private investigator Paul Drake, defends, in this case, an old immigrant man wrongly accused of robbery and murder. Appearing for the prosecution are the decidedly less handsome district attorney, Hamilton Burger, and elderly homicide detective Lt. Arthur Tragg. All of the main characters are introduced in a standard courtroom opening sequence, during which the striking theme music is played.

Three men in stocking masks (one of them film noir baddie Elisha Cook Jr.) rob an insurance office in which the significance of an exceptionally loud air conditioner is foreshadowed through close-ups and audio. While one of the robbers expertly cracks the safe, another covers the employees and the third pistol-whips the office manager. The scene then jumps to an abandoned building into which a man in a dark suit enters, secretly observed by teenager Nicky. The next scene jumps again, to a sequence in which Nicky shows his grandfather, the immigrant, the suitcase full of money he's found. Nicky's already bought Grandpa a new warm coat for winter (a bit incongruous in Los Angeles), but just as Grandpa says they should "take-a da money to da police," Tragg arrives and arrests Grandpa for the murder of the man in the dark suit—he was one of the robbers—and the robbery. The evidence is a tool engraved with Grandpa's initials that has been found at the crime scene and his identification by one of the office workers, a flighty woman, as the safecracker.

At Nicky's request, and after a discussion of the legal precedent of finders-keepers, Mason agrees to defend Grandpa. He soon learns that the case against him is built on three things: Grandpa's prowess as an inventor of what seems to be a perpetual motion device, which gives him the technical skills needed to crack a safe; the testimony of a friend who says Grandpa told him that he'd be coming into a good deal of money in a few days; and the earwitness testimony of the woman from the office, who swears under oath that she heard Grandpa's voice during the robbery. After a lengthy courtroom sequence that includes the usual expository dialogue about the functioning of the legal system, Mason manipulates Burger into allowing an expert witness to attempt to crack the safe under real-world conditions—that is, in the office with the exceptionally loud air conditioner on full blast.

The trial moves to the office. When the expert is unable to accomplish the task because of the noise, it proves that the flighty woman could not possibly have heard the safecracker's voice, but also that the safecracker in fact had the combination. As this points directly to the complicity of the office manager, Mason accuses him. The manager immediately confesses while Berger registers the usual astonishment. Grandpa is freed, and Mason tells him in the dénouement that he's waiving his usual high attorney fees, thus underscoring the unspoken, comforting notion that America is the land of equal justice for all and of attorneys who work pro bono for poor immigrants.

Mason was aided by his ever-faithful legal secretary, Della Street, and his private investigator, Paul Drake, each of whom had important roles to play in the resolution of the case. The enjoyment for viewers came from trying to guess exactly how Mason would prove the innocence of his client, who always appeared to be guilty, and just how and when he'd name the real criminal from among the suspects.

Much of the appeal of the program grew from its cast, of course. Raymond Burr, whose persona as Perry Mason was so strong that he reprised the role in a series of made-for-television movies during the 1980s and 1990s, long after the series had ended, had a commanding stage presence—it was difficult to not look at him when he was on camera. The characters played by Barbara Hale (as Della Street) and William Hopper (as Paul Drake) were clearly subordinate to Mason, but served as surrogates for the audience. Episodes usually ended with a dénouement in which Mason explained clearly to them (and us) how he'd cleverly discovered the evidence that lead to the identity of the real criminal.

Over the nine years that *Perry Mason* aired, the actors visibly aged and their relationships changed to some degree. In early episodes Street was a combination of legal secretary and general caretaker, clearly in love with the bachelor Mason; by the end of the series their relationship was affectionate, but more on the lines of old friends than potential romantic partners.

While no other legal dramas lasted as long on the prime-time schedule as did *Perry Mason*, the CBS series *The Defenders* came close, but even then managed only the four years from 1961 to 1965, perhaps because it was scheduled simultaneously with and on the same network as *Perry Mason*. The program focused on Lawrence and Kenneth Preston, father and son attorneys, played by television mainstay E. G. Marshall and Robert Reed, who would later gain lasting fame as the father on the blended happy family sitcom *The Brady Bunch*. They worked together in their small law firm, where they handled topical subjects, including an episode in 1964 that dealt with the blacklist, which despite plaguing television and the movies since the 1950s was a subject generally avoided by TV. As an example of the way television series are developed, *The Defenders* had originated a few years earlier as an episode of the dramatic anthology *Studio One*, and had starred two relatively unknown actors at the start of their careers, William Shatner, later of *Star Trek*, and film actor Steve McQueen.[3]

Medical Dramas

The highpoint of the medical drama came during the 1960s, when the competing programs *Ben Casey* and *Dr. Kildare* were at their zenith. The parallels between the programs are remarkable. Both premiered at the start of the 1961 television season, on NBC and ABC respectively, and both survived until 1966. Both programs had handsome male leads, Richard Chamberlain as Dr. James Kildare and Vince Edwards as Dr. Ben Casey, whose TV careers would be largely defined, and therefore limited, by their roles. Neither's television success continued after their respective series left the air. Both dramas ranked in the top 20 most-popular programs during their first two seasons, with *Ben Casey* being ranked seventh in popularity and *Dr. Kildare* 11th for the 1962–1953 season. And both had links to the past. *Dr. Kildare* had begun as a series of movie dramas during the 1940s, while *Ben Casey* was produced by James Moser, who had produced *Medic*, one of the earliest medical dramas, during the 1950s.

Psychiatry, a part of the culture of affluent, suburban Americans during the 50s and 60s, played only a small role in medical dramas. As a dramatic subject, it seems never to have resonated with run-of-the-mill television viewers whose social backgrounds, perhaps, did not include psychiatry. During the 1960–1969 period, two programs about psychiatrists overlapped in time,

Eleventh Hour (NBC, 1962–1964) and *Breaking Point* (ABC, 1963–1964). But viewers clearly preferred their TV doctors to deal with physical problems.

Soap Operas

During the period 1960–1969 only three attempts were made at bringing soap operas back to prime-time—and of the three, one went on to great success while the other two failed so miserably that it would be more than a decade before the networks would attempt another prime-time soap.

The success, of course, was the famous *Peyton Place*, based on the two Hollywood movies *Peyton Place* (1957) and its sequel *Return to Peyton Place* (1961). The series ran on ABC from 1964 to 1969, airing three times per week at the height of its popularity in 1965–1966 and lasting five seasons. Among the hundred or so cast members is a laundry list of names old and new—Mia Farrow, Ryan O'Neal, Dorothy Malone, Mariette Hartley, Gena Rowlands, Dan Duryea, Leslie Nielsen—names associated with television programs and movies before, during and after the production of *Peyton Place*. Its plot, as is the case with all soap opera plots, was convoluted, but it centered on relationships between the characters and problems caused by those relationships, beginning with that of Constance MacKenzie (Dorothy Malone) and her illegitimate daughter Allison (Mia Farrow). At that time, illegitimacy was not the subject of polite middle-class conversation, let alone of a prime-time television program. It generated a certain amount of controversy in its day, and the author of this chapter was expressly forbidden by his mother from watching *Peyton Place* as a child, despite the fact that no ABC television affiliate could be picked up in the small town in which he lived.

The two duds were also based on earlier works. *Our Private World*, a failed attempt by CBS to compete with *Peyton Place* during summer 1965, was a spin-off from the daytime soap *As the World Turns* and starred Eileen Fulton in the role of young divorcée Lisa Hughes from the daytime version. *The Survivors*, a big-name—Lana Turner and Kevin McCarthy were the two leads—big-budget ABC soap opera, based on a Harold Robbins novel, followed *Peyton Place* in September 1969 but ended its short run the following January.

QUIZ AND GAME SHOWS

The quiz show scandals of the late 1950s had spelled the end of quiz and competitive game shows in prime-time for all intents and purposes, with the sole exception of ABC's premature attempt to breathe new life into the quiz show. *100 Grand* lasted just three episodes in September 1963, and its top prize of $100,000 went unawarded.

In contrast, several prime-time versions of daytime game shows were successful, although they were much different in nature from the troublesome quiz shows of the previous decade. CBS, which had premiered *Password* in daytime in 1961, moved it to prime-time from 1962 to 1967; the program would rotate through non-prime-time syndication, NBC and ABC, until 1989. *Let's Make a Deal*—which required bizarrely costumed contestants to choose between whatever was lurking behind doors numbers one, two, or three—aired throughout the 1960s, 70s and 80s in network daytime slots and in syndication, was a prime-time program during summer 1967 on NBC and a regularly scheduled series on ABC (1969–1971), thus ensuring host Monte Hall a lasting spot in pop culture.

ABC was the network that had the greatest success with new variations on the game show theme. It aired in prime-time *The Dating Game* (1966–1970) and *The Newlywed Game* (1967–1971), with the programs forming a block between 7:30 and 8:30 P.M. on Saturdays during 1967, 68 and 69. Both programs also ran for years in daytime time slots, as well. But they were a new form of game show, based on contestants answering questions about their personal relationships, and as such much different than the more specialized, more knowledge-based quiz shows of the 1950s.

THE POSTMODERNS

By the 1960s, television was evolving into its postmodern period, as several programs came along that emphasized in viewers' minds the notion that they were not watching "real life" play out before their eyes but were instead actually watching a television program. Although elements of this had been tried earlier—both Jack Benny and George Burns existed simultaneously as themselves and as characters named Jack Benny and George Burns in their programs in the 1950s[4]—it didn't really catch on until three popular postmodernist programs, *The Monkees*, *Batman* and *Rowan & Martin's Laugh-In*, shared among themselves this new style of prime-time TV.

While the word *postmodernism* is notoriously difficult to define, in television it is perhaps represented by a "pretense of reality" that goes beyond the realism that movies and television have long traded in. A TV program such as *Bonanza* is realist in nature in that the events on the screen seem part of a plausible world that is something like the world in which viewers live (even if outdoor locations are clearly sets with Styrofoam boulders). While audiences are watching it on television, they're playing a game, so to speak, in which they pretend they're watching real events happen to real people instead of actors acting out a script—what Coleridge in the nineteenth century had called "the willing suspension of disbelief."

Postmodernism breaks down this game, and postmodernist TV programs encourage viewers to acknowledge that they are in fact watching a television program that is not a literal representation of the real world of sensate experience. This is similar to what had happened with Hollywood genre films, which, according to scholars, were reworked through several stages of development before arriving at a "baroque" stage in which their stylistic embellishments themselves came to be the substance of the films; for example, *Singin' in the Rain* is a musical that is more about the conventions of musicals[5] than about its erstwhile plot, which deals with Hollywood as it made the transition from silent to talking motion pictures.

The Monkees (NBC, 1966–1968) bears only a passing resemblance to other sitcoms and is therefore difficult to place within the conventions of the sitcom genre. Stylistically related to The Beatles' 1964 film *A Hard Day's Night*, the program centers on a pop band called The Monkees. But reality begins to get a bit wobbly as the members of The Monkees in the TV program are portrayed by the members of The Monkees from the real world. Or is it the real world? The Monkees didn't exist as a band before the program but were assembled for it, culled from the auditions of 500 potential actor-musicians. The boundary between fiction and nonfiction blurred even more when they began recording pop music, with the actors at first supplying only voices, but, as every teen in the 1960s knew, later playing the instruments themselves. They were popular enough to have two top 10 songs, "I'm a Believer" and "Last Train to Clarksville" in 1966, and were only the fifth band to have two top 10 songs in one year. Moreover, the actors—Mickey Dolenz, David Jones, Mike Nesmith and Peter Tork—played characters by the same names, making it difficult to distinguish between them as real world human beings and as TV characters; for example, how does one sort out the relationship between the person Peter Tork and the male equivalent of the dumb blonde that was the character Peter Tork within the narrative of *The Monkees?*

And to further complicate things, the comedy in *The Monkees* was itself unreal as the characters acted out far-fetched plots—and even the word plot is insufficient to describe what happened during an episode of the program—and were seen in normal, fast- and slow motion sequences, which made the program look televisual or cinematic and as such not a part of the real world of everyday experience.

The real world and the TV world gets even more jumbled, if that's possible, with the historical note that Dolenz, drummer of The Monkees, had

The Monkees' authenticity as a band was questioned, but the show succeeded as a hip, fun, happening event. The stars were Davy Jones, Peter Tork, Michael Nesmith, and Micky Dolenz (on the drums). Courtesy of Photofest.

starred in *Circus Boy* (NBC, 1956–1957 and ABC, 1957–1958) as a child under the stage name Mickey Braddock, making him at least potentially recognizable to older viewers of *The Monkees* and further conflicting the differences between Dolenz as person and Dolenz as character(s).

Batman (ABC, 1966–1968) was based, of course, on the eponymous masked hero who had originated in comic books in the 1930s and was heard on radio and seen in movie serials during the 1940s. The television version of Batman was something different from the serials and from other masked-hero programs, such as *The Green Hornet* (ABC, 1966–1967), which were played somewhat straighter. *Batman*'s adult viewers were apparently sophisticated enough to not take it entirely seriously—the producers and actors certainly didn't—although children may have seen it as simply a comic book-based superhero adventure program. Comic book-like in visual style, it came complete with the now famous on-screen words *bam!* and *biff!* during fights, which served to remind viewers that what they were seeing was far from "reality." *Batman* aired on Wednesdays and Thursdays in its first season with two-part stories, then reverted to a single night in the second season before burning out rather quickly and being canceled, its oddness not attracting viewers for long periods of time.

Both *The Monkees* and *Batman* spun off into the world of movies with films that followed the pattern of the television shows. *Head* (1968) starred The Monkees, again as "themselves" in a non-linear assemblage of sight gags and music, while *Batman* (1966) united all the TV show's villains in an evil plot to eliminate Batman and Robin once and for all.

Rowan & Martin's Laugh-In (NBC, 1968–1973) is also difficult to describe. It was a sort of comedy variety program, but one unlike any other that had aired before it or, for that matter, unlike any others on the air at the time. *Laugh-In* was a loud, colorful, freeform program that battered viewers with a rapid-fire barrage of verbal and visual humor with no time to process incoming information. It was simply gag after gag after gag after gag, with no rest, no let up, until a commercial broke the flow. The program managed to encapsulate the 1960s with a whirlwind of topical humor, performances by ukulele player Tiny Tim, go-go dancers in bikinis, anti-Vietnam war statements (on the episode of Thanksgiving week 1968, cohost Dick Martin said he wouldn't celebrate until "the boys come home") and sets dressed in psychedelic oranges and purples. It even got the dour President Nixon to appear in a fleeting shot in which he spoke the catchphrase "sock it to me" as a question.

WESTERNS

The adult western was the site of a number of contractual disputes between Warner Bros., which produced several highly rated series during the late 1950s and early 1960s, and the stars of the programs. Clint Walker, star of *Cheyenne*, quit the series in 1958, but after being prevented from working elsewhere returned in 1959. The star of *Colt .45*, Wayde Preston, did the same, also in 1958, and also returned to the series but with his character demoted to second-banana status. And, more famously, James Garner, star of *Maverick*, also entered into a contract dispute with Warner Bros. But unlike the others, however, Garner successfully broke his contract in 1960 and went on to star in other series, notably *The Rockford Files* (NBC, 1974–1980) and to a lengthy career in movies. His *Maverick* character was replaced by one played by Roger Moore, the only British subject to ever star in an American TV western, something Moore had managed to do twice as his role in *Maverick* was preceded by a less-successful starring role in *The Alaskans* ABC, 1959–1960. All three of the programs with contract problems suffered declining ratings during the disputes and were soon canceled, while Warner Bros. itself continued to have contract problems with one of the stars of the youthful detective series *77 Sunset Strip*.

The popularity of westerns was such that they were often among the top 10 programs during the late 1950s, peaking with seven of the top 10 in 1958–1959, the season during which the four most-popular programs were the westerns *Gunsmoke, Wagon Train, Have Gun, Will Travel*, and *The Rifleman*. Audiences were enormous: *Gunsmoke* averaged a 39.6 rating, *Wagon Train* a 36.1, *Have Gun Will Travel* a 34.3 and *The Rifleman* a 33.1 rating that season.

Bonanza was second to *Gunsmoke* in terms of length of time on the schedule and audience size, airing on NBC for 14 years, 1959–1973. It was the first western to be filmed in color for its entire run and was used by the network and its owner, RCA, for the promotion of color programs and to encourage the purchase of color TV sets. It reached the lofty most-watched position every year during 1964–1967, with a rating of 36.3 during its peak season in 1964–1965 when it was a Sunday night institution, its episodes discussed on Monday mornings in schoolyards around the country, if not elsewhere in the adult world of work. The Cartwrights—patriarch Ben (Lorne Greene) and sons Little Joe (Michael Landon), Hoss (Dan Blocker), and Adam (Pernell Roberts)—were as familiar as real family members to large numbers of Americans of the time, and the memorable theme song formed part of the background to 1960s pop cultural life.

The popularity of westerns, though huge, was somewhat restricted in time. Adult westerns became so popular during the late 1950s that it was common for the networks to block-program them across prime-time. ABC took the lead, for example, in 1958 running *Maverick, The Lawman* and *Colt .45* on Sunday nights from 8 P.M. to 9.30 P.M. *Cheyenne* and *Sugarfoot* ran on alternate weeks in a block with *The Life and Legend of Wyatt Earp* and *The Rifleman* on Tuesdays at the same time. This trend expanded the following year, when ABC's 1959 Sunday night lineup was a solid three-and-a-half hour block of five westerns from 7 P.M. to 10:30 P.M. The programs were *Colt .45, Maverick, The Lawman, The Rebel* and *The Alaskans*, for a full evening of western-themed programming.

But the end, when it came, was fairly rapid. Whereas 12 new westerns had premiered in 1957 and 11 in 1958, the 1962 season saw the cancellation of 10 westerns, and 2 more went in 1963. The bloom was clearly off the rose as the always-fickle viewers moved to other genres for whatever dramatic satisfaction the westerns were no longer delivering. Some of the casualties had been major programs just a few years earlier. *Maverick*, which had premiered on ABC in 1957 and was the number-six program during the 1958–199 season, was canceled in 1962. *The Rifleman*, first seen on ABC in September 1958 and the no. 4 program of 1958–199, was canceled in 1963. And CBS's *Have Gun, Will Travel*, the no. 4 program in 1957–1958 and the no. 3 program each year during the 1958–199, 1959–1960 and 1960–1961 seasons, went off the air in September 1963.

The westerns that replaced the classics followed the *Bonanza* model. They were family dramas that just happened to be set out West. Horses and guns were secondary to the melodrama. *The Big Valley* (ABC, 1965–1969) starred Barbara Stanwyck as the matriarch of the family. *Lancer* (CBS, 1968–1971) had Andrew Duggan as the patriarch of the family. *High Chaparral* (NBC, 1967–1971) and *The Virginian* (NBC, 1962–1971) followed the same pattern.

Subgenres inevitably developed as years of western programming went by. Western dramatic anthologies, similar in format to the dramatic anthologies described elsewhere, had some success during the highpoint of western popularity in the late 1950s, although they were often summer replacement series used to fill the time slot of a regular program that had "gone on vacation," as was standard operating procedure at the time. CBS carried *Frontier*, a half-hour anthology that aired 1955–1956, *Dick Powell's Zane Grey Theatre* (1956–1962) and *Frontier Justice*, composed of reruns of *Zane Grey*, during the summers of 1958, 1959, and 1961. ABC ran western pilots that didn't develop into series under the title *Pall Mall Playhouse* during summer 1955, while NBC continued to recycle ancient Columbia Pictures westerns from the 1930s and 1940s as *Cowboy Theatre* during summer 1957.

Contemporary westerns, with their focus on the twentieth century, could also be found. Modern-day ranching in New Mexico was the subject of *Empire* (NBC, 1962–1963) and its short-lived spin-off *Redigo* (the surname of the main character) (NBC, 1963). In at least two cases, seemingly interchangeable contemporary westerns ran during the same season on different networks. NBC and ABC directly competed with programs about modern-day rodeo riders, with NBC premiering *Wide Country*, with Earl Holliman, in September 1962 and ABC premiering *Stoney Burke*, starring Jack Lord, a month later. Both programs aired until September 1963 and reflected the theme, if not the spirit, of *The Misfits*, the (somewhat) rodeo-related 1961 film that was the final movie of both Marilyn Monroe and Clark Gable.

A few western parodies were seen through the years, but aside from *The Wild, Wild West* (CBS, 1965–1970)—a spoof of the then-popular James Bond films but set during the corrupt presidential administration of Ulysses Grant—they failed to catch on, perhaps because viewers who enjoy programs in "their" genre don't like to see them made the butt of satire, but also because people who aren't fans of the genre would be unlikely to watch a parody of it. *The Hero,* an NBC series that parodied western TV series, failed to catch on, as have most television programs that take television as their subjects. It lasted only from September 1966 until January 1967.

Western comedies have historically been rather unsuccessful as audiences in general didn't appear to enjoy programs that mixed generic elements, so that the inclusion of humor into the usually humorless westerns became somewhat jarring. Nonetheless, several western comedies were attempted during the 1960s at about the same time that large numbers of sitcoms that can only be described as silly were airing. They included *F Troop* (ABC, 1965–1967), which was loosely structured around the U.S. Cavalry in the post-Civil War west; *Pistols 'n' Petticoats* (CBS, 1966–1967), set in the mythical Wretched, Colorado, and having as its central joke the improbable (at the time) notion that the women in the program were better shots than the men; and *The Rounders* (ABC, 1966–1967), a contemporary-era sitcom based on a Max Evans novel and a 1965 comedy-western film of the same title that starred Glenn Ford and Henry Fonda.

Two other western comedies were also produced during the 1960s. The risible Texas Rangers sitcom *Rango* (ABC, 1967), starring Tim Conway, is notable for what today would be characterized as egregious stereotyping in the form of an effeminate Native American character named Pink Cloud (Guy Marks). The rather more successful one-hour comedy *Here Come the Brides,* also on ABC, made it through the two full seasons of 1968–1970. The program is interesting for its typical-for-the-time construction of gender in which women were treated as chattel, as in the contemporaneous *I Dream of Jeannie* and other series. The plot dealt with the introduction of 100 prospective brides from back East to an all-male, all-heterosexual 1870s logging camp. Otherwise, it is only worthy of note that *Here Come the Brides* served to introduce the soon-to-be teen-heartthrob Bobby Sherman to American teenage girls, and was as well the first starring role for David Soul, who went on to lasting pop culture significance as Detective Ken Hutchinson in the hip young detectives series *Starsky and Hutch* during the mid- to late-1970s.

DETECTIVES

Detective programs, like westerns, increased sharply in number during prime-time at the end of the 1950s, but unlike westerns they would retain their popularity through the present day. Thirteen detective dramas premiered during the 1959–1960 television season alone, a clear indication of their popularity, and were coincident with the decline of the western.

The standard detective drama—with its generic conventions of men in shiny suits in the employ of urban police departments—remained at the center of the genre through the 1960s. There were few significant changes in the programs, although there were many variations on the theme. The decade began with the humorless detectives of an unnamed city, in the unequivocally titled *The Detectives, starring Robert Taylor* (ABC, 1959–1961 and NBC, 1961–1962), and ended with the rise of *Hawaii 5–0*, about humorless detectives in Honolulu, which became the longest-running police drama in television history, airing on CBS (1968–1980). Although the crimes investigated in *Hawaii 5–0* were usually quite routine—murder, arson, the stealing of babies for sale on the mainland—their setting in a location that juxtaposed the island paradise of tourist brochures and the grubby streets of Honolulu drew viewers in large numbers.

HAWAII 5–0

The first Earth Day on 20 April 1968 brought environmentalism into the American consciousness, and environmental issues rapidly became part of prime-time TV programs, cropping up even in the unlikely ground of detective shows. The "Strangers in Our Own Land" episode begins with land commissioner Manu arriving at Honolulu airport after a trip to the mainland. As he gets into a taxi, someone pushes a briefcase through his window. Astute viewers who have noted that the taxi is an old 1960 Ford, and therefore an expendable prop, are not surprised when the briefcase explodes, destroying the cab and killing poor Manu.

Steve McGarrett, head of Hawaii 5–0, the criminal investigation division of the mythical Hawaii State Police, arrives on scene with screeching tires and asks his standard question—"Whatta we got, Danno?"—of Danny Williams, his second-in-command. Williams briefs him. A witness, tourist Grace Willis, comes forward and says she just happened to have filmed the bomber with her 8 mm movie camera. He's quickly identified as local boy Tommy Kapali, but there's no motive. However, Kapali left the Army on a "section eight" discharge and he was a bomb disposal expert in Vietnam, so he has the technical skills necessary for the crime. This is one example of 5–0's many references to the Vietnam war, something unusual in contemporary entertainment television, but natural within the context of the program due to physical proximity to Pearl Harbor.

McGarrett's suspicions are aroused by the odd behavior of Benny Kalua, a friend of Manu, who surprises McGarrett by saying that he's happy that Manu is dead because Manu supported the despoilers of the Hawaiian environment, building skyscrapers that blot out the view of the sky and the mountains. He recites the aphorism that serves as the episode's title, thus linking the "Hawaiian way of life" with nature and pointing out how endangered both have become.

McGarrett tracks down Tommy's last known address through a land developer who's building a housing tract. Along with the address McGarrett gets a lecture about economic development and the betterment of the "child-like" native Hawaiians, statements that McGarrett disagrees with and which are clearly designed for viewers to also disagree with. But when the 5–0 team arrives with guns drawn at Tommy's ramshackle house, they find he's committed suicide by hanging. McGarrett's facial expression signals this as a tragedy.

A closer look at Willis's film reveals that although Tommy appears in it, it was shot hours before the bombing and is being used to implicate him. When the officers can't locate Willis, who had provided a false name and address, the investigation comes to a halt. But then the case breaks when Leilani, Benny's daughter, reveals that Tommy was her boyfriend and names her father as Manu's murderer.

The officers rush off to arrest Benny. He's kidnapped the nasty land developer and is about to bury him alive with a huge bulldozer. McGarrett shoots Benny, but instead of surrendering, Benny drives the bulldozer into a storage building full of dynamite, which colorfully blows up. The theme of the episode is underscored when detective Zulu sadly repeats the Hawaiian aphorism that "someday we'll be strangers in our own land" as the camera lingers on a sign that promises the development of 400 new low-cost homes. The crime has been solved, but the destruction of the environment continues, and the episode comes to its downbeat ending.

Usually McGarrett was a stalwart law-and-order man, opposed to hippies, drugs, protestors, and all other anti-establishment forces of the Vietnam era, but even he could sympathize with the environmentalists who were trying to save Hawaii from the effects of over-development. McGarrett did his duty, but perhaps more reluctantly than usual. Since the program was shot on location, the audience could sympathize with his attitude.

Hawaii 5-0 offered a law-and-order view of the world with Jack Lord and James MacArthur as state policemen. The series was shot mostly on location, and the scenery was definitely part of the appeal of the program. Courtesy of Photofest.

At the beginning of the time period a subgenre that focused on young detectives developed, no doubt in an attempt to lure younger viewers to the networks, a strategy designed to make advertisers happy, which would in turn make networks happy as money rolled in. ABC became the home of the young detectives as the network made itself into the place of youth-oriented, hip programs. The network, through the Warner Bros. film studio, developed a set of programs that were similar in content, beginning with the most successful of the lot, the Hollywood-based *77 Sunset Strip*, which ran 1958–1964. Of course, this practice is similar to today's *Law & Order* and *CSI* franchises. But Warner Bros. not only borrowed stars and formats, it even had different series sharing the same script. Only the names and locale changed.

77 Sunset Strip is nowadays more notable for flopping over into the realm of popular music and the resulting contract dispute between one of its stars and Warner Bros. than for its somewhat umbrella-like format in which most episodes centered on just one of the principal actors (Efram Zimbalist, Jr., Roger Smith, Edd Byrnes and Richard Long, all of whom played detectives) instead of all of them.

77 SUNSET STRIP

After a prologue that introduces the plot, the opening sequence shows viewers an aerial photo of a film studio, the Warner Bros. logo is superimposed on top of it, and a portentous announcement that the program is a WB production is made. A static shot of the 77 Sunset Strip building marquee and a single chorus of the monotonous, finger-snapping theme song follows. A brief shot of traffic serves as a reminder that sunny, exotic, affluent, urban California is far from the heartland of 1960 America.

Handsome private investigators Stuart Bailey, Jeff Spence, and Rex Randolph are looking into "The Valley Caper," the blackmailing of movie star Abby Adams by her ex-husband Jimmy Cook. But the plot is secondary to the milieu of Hollywood at the start of the swinging 1960s, with its emphasis on movie studio glamour and the good life of the West Coast.

Trend-setting language is important in *77 Sunset Strip*. For example, Kookie, who parks cars at the restaurant next door, is a hipster, too late in historical time to be a beatnik but too early to be a hippie. He speaks in a cool slang patois that's incomprehensible to squares like us. Kookie comes into the office and says to Rex, "Hey dad, your wheels need a Saturday night. You got the sixties?" Rex replies, "Splash away! And hit me on the ding-dong when you reach the top." Jeff, sitting at his desk, is confused, so Rex translates, explaining to him, and us, that the topic of discussion is a car wash. Kookie simply wants the keys to Rex's car, and Rex has asked Kookie to phone him when he's finished.

Cars, in fact, form a significant part of the background to the episode. California has long been known as the most car-loving state, and the seemingly endless miles of freeways and eternal sunshine evoke images of long drives in convertibles. The episode showcases Ford's brand-new 1960 models, which the company had supplied to Warner Bros. Rex drives a shiny Mercury convertible (it looks red even in black and white), Cook drives a shiny black Mercury hardtop while his henchmen tool around in an equally shiny and black Ford sedan, and Stuart and Jeff ride to the rescue in a shiny Thunderbird convertible.

In the climax of the blackmail story, Rex has Abby's studio plant a false story in the newspaper that she's gotten a $20,000 bonus. He plans to use the money as bait to capture Cook. Abby and Rex go to her house to set the trap, but he's already there when they arrive and he holds them hostage. As they wait for the money, Kookie innocently shows up with Rex's convertible, the car wash by now complete. Rex pretends to not recognize Kookie, gives him a nickel tip and says, oddly, "You're a fine broth of a boy and I don't want to spoil you." Kookie reports this cryptic comment to Stu and Jeff, and as they translate it to "too many cooks spoil the broth" for Kookie's benefit—Kookie needs as much help with square English as we need with his hip version—they realize that Rex is telling them that Cook is in the house. They speed off to the rescue, knights in shining T-bird. They confront Cook and after a brief fistfight knock him unconscious.

The case over, Rex briefly explains to Kookie how it has been wrapped up. He humorously gives Kookie another nickel as a tip. Kookie responds by getting out his famous comb and running it through his equally famous pompadour, thus evoking in viewers' minds the hit song "Kookie, Kookie, Lend Me Your Comb."

To many, the series portrayed the essence of "coolness": stylish clothes, snazzy cars, the hip jargon. The detective stories were less important than projecting the image of an enviable lifestyle.

In a parallel to what was happening with the westerns *Cheyenne* and *Colt .45*, Byrnes attempted to break his contract after his novelty song duet with popular singer Connie Stevens, "Kookie, Kookie, Lend Me Your Comb" became a hit. Byrnes eventually returned to the program, and his character was promoted from parking lot attendant to detective, for greater prominence in the series. Stevens was herself a regular cast member of the similar *Hawaiian Eye* at the time, playing Cricket Blake.

77 Sunset Strip was followed by three more ABC series that focused on handsome young detectives in quasi-exotic locales, but none was as successful as the original. *Bourbon Street Beat*, set in New Orleans, aired in the 1959–1960 season; the aforementioned *Hawaiian Eye* (1959–1963) was set, of course, in Hawaii (and as such was a thematic precursor to CBS's *Hawaii 5-O*); and *Surfside Six*, set in Miami, ran from 1960 to 1962. Because all of the programs were produced to a formula by Warner Bros., characters appeared in crossover roles, with, for example, Detective Ken Madison (Van Williams) of *Bourbon Street Beat* taking the lead role in *Surfside Six* after *Bourbon Street* was canceled. Efram Zimbalist, Jr. made the transition from young, hip PI Stuart Bailey in *77 Sunset Strip* to his antithesis, the uphold-the-power-structure Inspector Lewis Erskine in *The F.B.I.* as the 1960s developed.

By the end of the 1960s, the young detectives were, naturally, becoming rather more hippie-like. A good example is *The Mod Squad* (ABC, 1968–1973), a program based loosely upon the activities of a youthful drugs squad within the Los Angeles County Sheriff's Department during the 1950s and updated to contemporary times. Unlike many detective programs, which tended to be all white and all male, *Mod Squad* was a model of diversity for the time, with its three main characters, the white male Pete Cochran (Michael Cole), the white female Julie Barnes (Peggy Lipton) and the black male Linc Hayes (Clarence Williams III), all working as equals.

Other minorities were only occasionally seen as detectives or private investigators. Burt Reynolds played a Native American investigator in *Hawk* (ABC, 1966). The title character was an Iroquois who worked as an investigator for the District Attorney of New York City. Asian detectives were few and far between, existing only on *Hawaii 5-0*, and even then in supporting roles, while African-American detectives were all but invisible until later in the 1970s. And there was a handicapped police officer. Raymond Burr's character in *Ironside* (NBC, 1967–1975) was in a wheelchair, but he and his trusty staff solved crimes in a highly effective manner.

Reenactment programs, in which episodes were dramatizations of actual police cases, continued to be of interest to viewers, although the programs were not great in number during the time period. The primary entry in the subgenre was long-lived, though. *The F.B.I.* (ABC, 1965–1975), a program produced with the approval and cooperation of J. Edgar Hoover and which shared his right-wing worldview, spanned a time period of significant social unrest in the United States and perhaps comforted viewers with the thought that the buttoned-down, immaculately groomed agents of "the Bureau" always got their man, whether he was a bank robber or a member of the international communist conspiracy.

The fight for law and order in disorderly times was helped by the revival of the 1950s staple *Dragnet*, retitled *Dragnet '67* throughout its run on NBC (1967–1970) but still with its usual no-nonsense, just-the-facts investigatory style of LAPD detective Joe Friday, still played by program creator Jack Webb and still a sergeant after all those years.

Private investigator programs continued throughout the 1960s, and like earlier PIs, some were based on literary figures, such as *Philip Marlowe* (ABC, 1959–1960), a TV version of the Raymond Chandler detective. Others were unique to television, for example, *Mannix* (CBS, 1967–1975), a program described as "one of the most violent detective shows of its time"[6]—and its time was one of considerable prime-time television violence, it should be noted—but also noteworthy for its inclusion of an African-American woman character (Gail Fischer) as an employee of the title character Joe Mannix (Mike Connors) at a time when television was still largely white. She was still his secretary, though.

The occasional historical detective drama was seen during this time, as well. The ultra-violent *The Untouchables* (ABC, 1959–1963) was one of the first prime-time programs to spark public outrage over violence. It told a fictionalized version of the story of Elliot Ness (Robert Stack) and his band of incorruptible G-men in Depression-era Chicago, a setting that allowed for

The Untouchables, starring Robert Stack as a G-man against the gangs, was considered one of the most violent shows on TV. Criticism of it led to Congressional hearings and a temporary toning down of gunfire in prime-time. Courtesy of Photofest.

exciting scenes in which Tommy guns were fired by bootleggers from passing 1930s sedans. A less successful precursor to *The Untouchables* was *The Lawless Years* (NBC, 1959–1960), which covered the same period of time but was set in New York City. It, too, offered fictionalized versions of real events that had transpired during the 1920s.

A few police-oriented sitcoms came and went during the period. Perhaps the best remembered of them is *Car 54, Where Are You?* (NBC, 1961–1963), about a pair of hapless New York City uniformed patrol officers, Francis Muldoon (Fred Gwynne) and Gunther Toody (Joe E. Ross), who worked from the fictional 53rd precinct in the Bronx. Exterior scenes were shot on the streets of New York, and to prevent public confusion, their patrol car was painted red and white, which registered as black and white on film.[7]

ANIMATION IN PRIME TIME

After long being considered the province of children and being confined to Saturday mornings, animated cartoons made the leap into prime-time programming for adults at the start of the 1960s, an event that parallels the rise of adult westerns a few years earlier. *The Flintstones* (ABC, 1960–1966) was the first and the longest running of the adult animated sitcoms that reached their peak of popularity during the 1961–1962 television season. Thematically *The Flintstones* made fun of contemporary suburbia and simultaneously a variation of Jackie Gleason's famous *The Honeymooners*. It followed the everyday domestic adventures of, as its theme song described them, "a modern Stone Age family" in what appeared to be a 1960s suburb hewn from rock. It certainly touched a chord with viewers: It was one of the top 20 most popular prime-time programs during the 1960–1961 and 1961–1962 television seasons, the only animated series to be ranked so highly.

Although remembered for its apparent primacy, *The Flintstones* was actually the fourth animated program to run during prime-time. Its earliest predecessor was *CBS Cartoon Theatre*, summer 1956, which featured Terrytoons characters, such as Heckle and Jeckle, the crows first seen in theatrical cartoons in 1946. The program was hosted by a young Dick Van Dyke. Two other animated programs preceded *The Flintstones*, as well. *The Boing Boing Show*, featuring Gerald McBoing-Boing, an annoying little boy who communicated only through sound effects, aired on CBS in 1958. ABC premiered *Matty's Funday Funnies* on 30 September 1960, an hour before *The Flintstones* premiered; it would run until December 1962 under the title *Beany and Cecil*, the names of its two principal characters, a beanie-wearing boy and his dragon.

A wave of animated prime-time programs followed *The Flintstones* in short order, but none matched its popularity. *The Bugs Bunny Show*, which premiered on ABC just two weeks after *The Flintstones*, was the first of the first wave. Bugs was very well known to viewers, of course, having first appeared in Warner Bros. theatrical cartoons in the late 1930s.

But *The Bugs Bunny Show*, along with several other programs that premiered in 1961, lasted only until the start of the television season. *Top Cat*, another ABC show dating from September 1961, was about a group of alley cats on Broadway. *The Bullwinkle Show* premiered on NBC, also in September 1961, and is perhaps the best remembered of the lot for its topical Cold War references and sense of general irreverence. *The Alvin Show* began on CBS in October 1961 and followed the highly popular recordings of David Seville, whose "The Chipmunk Song" had reached number 44 on the Billboard charts in 1958. *Calvin and the Colonel*, a now-obscure October 1961 entry on ABC, was similar to *Amos 'n' Andy* but with cartoon animals—Calvin was a bear, The Colonel a fox—voiced by Freeman Gosden and Charles Correll, the originators of *The Amos and Andy Show*, which had run on radio 1928–1960 and on television 1951–1953.

The second wave of prime-time animated programs was smaller but fared little better. *The Jetsons* (ABC, 1962–1963) was a clone of *The Flintstones*, but set in a technologically advanced future that was as referentially 1960s as was the Stone Age. *Jonny Quest* (ABC, 1964–1965) was an action-adventure series. And *The Famous Adventures of Mr. Magoo* (NBC, 1964–1965) followed the misadventures of the myopic senior citizen, uniquely voiced by actor Jim Backus and first seen in theatrical cartoons in 1949. While all three series had relatively short lives in prime-time, all would live for years, and in some cases decades, on Saturday morning television, with *The Jetsons'* 24 episodes running continuously in repeats and syndication for more than 20 years, until additional episodes were made in 1985 and 1987.[8]

However, animation would have only a small role to play in the history of prime-time television after its heyday in the 1960s. Once *The Flintstones* left the air in 1966, only two animated programs showed up on the prime-time schedule. The first was a half-hearted stab at animation in the form of *The New Adventures of Huck Finn* (NBC, 1968–1969). It placed three live actors in an otherwise animated series and was understandably a failure. The other was a minor summer replacement series, *Where's Huddles*, about professional football players. It aired on CBS during the summers of 1970 and 1971, the 10 episodes being shown each year.

The Flintstones remained the longest-lived animated prime-time program until *The Simpsons* debuted on the Fox Network in December 1989. And, like *The Flintstones* before it, *The Simpsons* would spark another wave of animated series and, again, would prove to be much more successful than all the others.

ANTHOLOGIES

The few remaining anthology programs were the remnants of the Golden Age of television broadcasting that was rapidly retreating into the idealized past. Only a handful of the live drama-anthologies that had premiered during the 1950s made it into the 1960s, and those that did survived for only a short time. Most of the major prestige series, with their big budgets and sponsorship by major corporations—*Armstrong Circle Theatre, Goodyear Television Playhouse, The U.S. Steel Hour* and *Playhouse 90*—had disappeared by 1963. *Alfred Hitchcock Presents*, the suspense anthology, continued until 1965 when its 10-year run came to an end, which implies that anthologies with more specialized content were somewhat more popular with viewers, sponsors and networks than the old general anthologies had been.

A handful of new suspense and sci-fi anthologies went on the air. The suspense anthologies were *Thriller* (NBC, 1960–1962), hosted by ageing horror film star Boris Karloff, by then toward the end of his long career, and *Kraft Suspense Theatre* (NBC, 1963–1965). Science fiction was represented by Rod Serling's *The Twilight Zone* (CBS, 1959–1965) and its chief competitor, *The Outer Limits* (ABC, 1963–1965). Occult and supernatural anthologies also existed; for example, *Alcoa Presents* (ABC, 1959–1961) reenacted what were allegedly real-life events. The patriotic Americanism subgenre continued during the Cold War, with *The DuPont Show with June Allyson* (CBS, 1959–1961) expanding on themes first explored in *Cavalcade of America* during the early 1950s, while *The Great Adventure* (CBS, 1963–1965) emphasized stories that were historically accurate representations of events in American history.

THE TWILIGHT ZONE

"The Shelter" episode opens with a boozy surprise birthday party of the sort that typifies 1960s suburban life. Although, with the suburb located firmly inside *The Twilight Zone*, it comes as no great shock when Pauly, the son of the local general practitioner, whose birthday it is, interrupts the proceedings with the news that he's just heard on the radio that Conalrad, the early-warning system, has been activated. And that can only mean one thing—the worst fear of the Cold War, nuclear death, will rain down from the sky.

The partygoers are stricken sober as they learn that the president has declared a state of yellow alert after UFOs were sighted at precisely 11:04 P.M. EST. As the guests flee into the streets, the sound of something whizzing through the air over their heads, Rod Serling, the host of the show, pops out of the shrubbery to say that we're about to see a nightmare that no one hopes will ever actually happen.

Doc, his wife Grace, and Pauly make a beeline for the bomb shelter that the father, like the ant who stored up food for the winter while the grasshopper played, had the foresight to build in his cellar. The other partygoers (grasshoppers all) arrive one by one at Doc's house to plead their cases for entry into his bomb shelter. Jerry's modern home doesn't have a cellar, let alone a bomb shelter. Marty has a three-month-old baby. Doc refuses to let them in, of course, and although he points out the impracticality of all of them hiding in a 10 foot by 10 foot shelter, he takes the time to chide them for throwing barbeques and parties when they should have been digging. But none of them seem quite in the mood to have that rubbed in right then and there, and the situation turns ugly.

Egged on by their wives, arguments break out among the men. Frank wants to break the door down. Marty wants everyone to agree that his family is most deserving of being saved. At this comment, Frank takes note of Marty's swarthy ethnic looks and says "this is what happens when foreigners come here." Marty responds by calling Frank a "garbage-brained idiot." Others discuss how to obtain a battering ram without letting the neighbors know about it. Worse, they begin referring to the shelter as "theirs" and call the people on the neighboring street a mob that doesn't belong on their street, let alone in their shelter.

Without realizing that they *are* the mob, they manage to break down the bomb shelter door—thus making it worthless as a shelter—just as Conalrad announces a false alarm. Air raid sirens sound the all-clear as the couples embrace, the threat of annihilation suddenly past.

But all's not right. Apologies are stammered out. Doc looks shaken, exhausted by the events. The others suggest a block party the following night so they can all get back to normal, but Doc says he doesn't know what normal is anymore. He says he's learned what they all really are, however—"a lot of naked, wild animals" who will "claw their neighbors to death" to stay alive.

As the shock settles in, Rod Serling, off camera, delivers the moral to the story: "No moral. No message. No prophetic tract. Just a simple statement of fact: if civilization is to survive, the human race has to remain civilized." As usual, the *Twilight Zone* had used the little-respected genre of science fiction to critically observe the human condition. In the 1950s, when Serling wrote for TV's Golden Age of Drama, such examination of ordinary mortals under pressure was normal, but in the 1960s, the *Twilight Zone* was one of the few refuges of serious drama, and it had to be carefully disguised as mere entertainment.

On the other hand, the comedy anthology, a form that had not previously been particularly popular, caught on in *That's Life* (ABC, 1968–1969) and its sister program *Love, American Style* (ABC, 1969–1974). One of the last real successes in the anthology format, *Love, American Style* focused, as its title so boldly states, on three or four romance tales per episode and featured a large number of easily recognizable television actors and movie stars—somewhat past their prime—as guest stars.

New anthology series were all but replaced by "umbrella" dramas such as *The Bold Ones* (NBC, 1969–1973), which packaged together episodes of unrelated programs with self-explanatory titles: *The New Doctors, The Lawyers, The Protectors,* and the singular *The Senator.* These existed alongside the seemingly endless supply of Hollywood films and the growing number of made-for-television movies that became necessary once the supply of Hollywood films turned out to be finite. Only a handful of traditional anthology dramas were seen after 1970 as the form all but disappeared from TV.

VARIETY SHOWS

By the late 1960s, if not before, variety shows came to be a reward for success in music or in some other genre of television programs; for example, Jim Nabors went from being a supporting character in *The Andy Griffith Show* to his starring role in *Gomer Pyle, U.S.M.C.* to hosting *The Jim Nabors Hour* (CBS, 1969–1971) before largely disappearing from television, surfacing only on rare occasions, such as his standing appearance on the first *The Carol Burnett Show* of each season.

The variety show epitomized square, middle-class, Midwestern America, and it didn't survive television's makeover into something sophisticated, urban and hip during the 1970s. It's somewhat difficult to today imagine that programs as un-hip as *Jimmy Durante Presents the Lennon Sisters* (ABC, 1969–1970) aired after the counterculture's peak at Woodstock in August 1969, and at the same time as youth-oriented programs such as *The Mod Squad* and *Rowan & Martin's Laugh-In* were growing in popularity.

Three variety programs that were quite successful in their day, and quite typical in form, were *The Perry Como Show, The Andy Williams Show,* and *The Carol Burnett Show,* which together spanned 30 years of prime-time television history.

Among the long-lived musical variety shows from the earlier period of television, *The Perry Como Show* (NBC and CBS, 1948–1963) lasted from the age of standards (a form of music now difficult to describe after 50 years of rock) well into the age of rock and roll, the latter a genre of music that

Como, like Frank Sinatra and others, had once predicted to be no more than a passing fad. The program is of interest as it reflects the structure of television when the medium was new and the people working it in were inventing it as they went along. Under its original title of *The Chesterfield Supper Club*— named after the sponsor's cigarettes, back in the days of the unrestricted advertising of tobacco products—the program was a simulcast of Como's successful NBC radio show, complete with the cast standing at microphones, reading scripts. It evolved over the following months, soon developing the usual sort of sets and props and looking more like a recognizable television program. *The Perry Como Show* also serves as a sort of primer about program length, as it ran in 15-minute time slots up to three times per week—typical scheduling for its time—and later in 30-minute length once a week before stabilizing as a one-hour weekly program in 1955.

The Andy Williams Show was a well-regarded musical variety program built around the easygoing personality of its star, who specialized in the sort of ballads, show tunes, and standards that had been part of television since the end of World War II. *The Andy Williams Show* had a somewhat checkered history, though, airing first as a summer replacement series on ABC in 1958 and CBS in 1959. It then became a regular program, meaning that it *didn't* air during the summer, on NBC (1962–1967), at which time Williams shifted from a weekly series to starring in no more than three network specials per year. It returned again to NBC on a weekly basis during the period 1969–1971, during which time it was updated to include the more contemporary (but still safe) music that would (supposedly) appeal to a younger audience. The lasting claim to fame of *The Andy Williams Show*, however, is that it is the program that first inflicted the Osmond Brothers on a national audience when in 1962 they performed the song "I'm a Ding Dong Daddy from Dumas."[9]

The Carol Burnett Show (CBS, 1967–1979) was one of the last of the traditional comedy variety programs and was quite similar in style and format to its predecessors in 1950s. The show was built around the sketch humor of Burnett and a cast of regular performers that included Vicki Lawrence, Tim Conway, and Harvey Korman, all of whom would go on to greater or lesser (often lesser) success in other programs and in movies: Lawrence later starred in the lowbrow sitcom *Mama's Family*, a spin-off from a continuing sketch on *The Carol Burnett Show*; Conway had a series of short-lived sitcoms and variety shows of his own; and Korman was a costar in several Mel Brooks's films, including the infamous Western parody *Blazing Saddles* and *High Anxiety*, which lampooned Hitchcock films. Their chemistry was obvious to viewers, and it wasn't unusual for them to break down in laughter during the show, something not usually associated with professionalism on stage, but which was seen as part of the charm of the program. Consistent parts of the show from week to week included the answering of questions from the audience, Burnett's signature tugging of her earlobe, and her loud rendition of the Tarzan yell, itself an inevitable request from someone in the audience.

The Dean Martin Show (NBC, 1965–1974) changed formats but maintained its relaxed host and easygoing style. He sang a little, presented a variety of talent, and shared the stage with a group of lovely young ladies, known as The Golddiggers. Mainly, they would giggle as he teased them.

No overview of the variety shows of the 1960s would be complete without mention of *The Smothers Brothers Comedy Hour* (CBS, 1967–1969). The program epitomizes the general tumult of the decade as its stars, the comedy duo Tom and Dick Smothers, continually battled the stuffed-shirt executives in charge of the network. The program was left-wing in its outlook and subjected to censorship that today seems silly; for example, the "controversial" appearances by folk singer Pete Seeger, who had long been blacklisted from television because of his quite liberal views. After being canceled by CBS, the Smothers Brothers went to ABC with the same sort of variety program, but it aired only during the summer of 1970.

MUSIC

By the start of the 1960s most of the musical interlude programs were gone, killed off by rock; a prime-time television schedule that had solidified into fixed genres of variety programs, adventure shows, westerns and sitcoms; and the loss of the 5- to 15-minute program lengths that had been used for music programming. A few attempts were made to provide youth-oriented music shows during prime-time in the 1960s, such as *Shindig* (ABC, 1964–1966) and *Hullabaloo* (NBC, 1965–1966), but for the most part pop music was to be found on the many variety programs that were scattered across the programming week.

The major exception was *Sing Along with Mitch* (NBC, 1961–1964), the last of the music programs to focus on the standards that were in the process of becoming the oldies that appealed to an ageing generation. *Mitch* was Mitch Miller, known to viewers as the good-natured, goateed conductor of a chorus known as Mitch's Sing Along Gang, but in reality the head of recording for Columbia Records who in 1958 had issued albums of standards with their lyrics printed on their dust jackets so that listeners could sing along. It was a reaction against rock n roll, which was hurting Columbia's sales, and it had found an appreciative audience by the time the idea was successfully moved to television. Viewers at home saw the lyrics superimposed on their TV screens as Mitch invited them to "follow the bouncing ball."

NEWS AND DOCUMENTARIES

In 1960, Richard Nixon, who had been vice-president under Dwight Eisenhower for two terms, was running for president and leading in the polls over the lesser-known John F. Kennedy. The candidates agreed to a series of live televised debates, to be seen in prime-time nationwide. For the first debate, on 26 September 1960, Nixon made a critical error that would have not mattered a bit in any previous presidential campaign: he wore a light-colored suit and refused makeup, which on black-and-white TV screens made him look gray, unshaven and more than a bit shifty. Kennedy, in contrast, in dark suit and properly made up, looked young and vital. This points for the first time to the importance of television image for politicians, for while radio listeners believed that Nixon had won the debate, TV viewers thought Kennedy was the victor. Further debates improved Nixon's standing, but not enough. Of the more than 68 million votes cast for president in 1960, Kennedy's margin of victory was a bare 118,550 votes, although his victory in the Electoral College—303 to 219 (with 15 going to Sen. Byrd of Virginia)—was significantly larger.

Radio news could be said to have grown up during World War II, but the defining moment for television news was the Kennedy assassination in 1963. The public learned about the death from tearful anchors. They saw Jack Ruby kill the accused assassin, Lee Harvey Oswald, right before their eyes as it happened. And through the days of mourning, capped by the funeral, people shared the experienced together, glued to their sets, listening to the somber tones of the correspondents. Unfortunately, in 1968, the violent deaths of Senator Robert Kennedy and the Rev. Martin Luther King underlined the role of TV news in keeping viewers informed immediately about national tragedies.

Richard Nixon was elected president in 1968, defeating Hubert H. Humphrey by a tight half-million votes and was reelected in the 1972 18 million vote landslide victory over George S. McGovern. Television news played a significant role in the coverage of the Watergate scandal that led to Nixon's historic resignation from the presidency on August 9, 1974, following the long, convoluted chain of events through daytime coverage of the impeachment hearings, reports on the nightly newscasts and in the requisite prime-time news specials.

One of the most contentious times in American history, the 1960s, saw declining amounts of public affairs programming during prime-time compared to the 1950s, although it must be said that many of the programs were prestigious documentary series and not the 1950s-style talking-head, gray-haired men in gray suits sort of discussion program.

Unlike in the previous decades, though, news programs were more closely connected with the star power of the network anchors who also hosted them. During the 1962 television season, for example, three network documentary programs ran once per week in the late evening 10:30 to 11 P.M. ET time slot. *David Brinkley's Journal* on NBC, *Howard K. Smith—News and Comment* on ABC and *Eyewitness* on CBS, hosted by Walter Cronkite, and later that year by long-time CBS correspondent Charles Collingwood, provided prime-time exposure for the anchors of the network newscasts.

The international events and social changes of the 1960s were fodder for the documentary programs, of course, and episodes were devoted to the deeper coverage of political intrigue, the war in Vietnam, the rise of hippies and women's liberation, drugs, civil rights, and all the other contemporary topics touched briefly upon by network newscasts. Coverage of civil rights was significant, with *ABC News Reports* taking the lead with the five-part "Crucial Summer: The 1963 Civil Rights Crisis" which brought the sights and sounds of the civil rights struggle into American homes. The idea of civil rights was not universally popular, unfortunately, and it was at about this time that WLBT in Jackson, Mississippi, lost its broadcasting license for routinely blocking network newscasts and programs that dealt with civil rights events going on in the Deep South at the time.

It would be remiss to fail to mention that the 1960s also saw the debut of *60 Minutes*, the newsmagazine that is at this writing the longest-running program in all of network television history. Its familiar close-up of a ticking stopwatch on what appears to be a magazine cover was first seen on CBS on 24 September 1968, and since then it has remained not only one of the most highly watched documentary programs but one of the most highly-watched programs of any type, often in the top 10 in terms of numbers of viewers. It regularly drives off its competition, including the then well-regarded *CBS Reports*, which was the network's premiere news/documentary program during 1961–1971 and which had shared its timeslot with the upstart *60 Minutes* during its early days.

MOVIES ON TELEVISION

The complex history of movies on network television took a major turn with the 1961 premiere of *NBC Saturday Night at the Movies* and its dramatic opening sequence in which viewers saw what appeared to be a continuous point-of-view shot as they magically rode a roller coaster along the letters that spelled out the program title. The program was so popular that it remained on the NBC schedule for the next 17 years, finally being replaced in 1978, its two-hour time slot taken by one-hour specials and a short-lived adventure series called *Sword of Justice*, which starred Dack Rambo as one of television's legion of playboy/private investigators.

The appeal of *NBC Saturday Night at the Movies* was twofold: first, NBC was able to run relatively recent Hollywood films—the first was 1953's *How to Marry a Millionaire* with Marilyn Monroe, a film just eight years old at the time—and, second, the program featured, for the first time, color films broadcast in color, designed to both capitalize on the increasing sales of color TV sets and to further promote their sale, and to shift viewer interest away from the black-and-white films on independent stations. The other networks would soon follow suit, scheduling an increasing number of film shows with a baffling array of shifting titles during prime-time.

Saturday Night at the Movies was possible because the relationship between the movie studios and the networks had changed dramatically. By 1960, 40 percent of network TV programs were being produced by the major movie studios themselves, the studios having given up the notion that their survival depended on people *not* watching TV. An agreement was finally reached with the various guilds, also in 1960, to allow the valuable post-1948 movies, many of them made in color, to be shown on television. The networks paid large sums for this privilege: in 1966 ABC spent $20 million for the broadcast rights to 17 20th Century-Fox movies, and the same year CBS paid $52 million for the broadcast rights to 45 MGM movies. Prices continued to escalate, with ABC eventually paying $2 million to Columbia Screen Gems for the right to broadcast two showings of the 1957 British blockbuster *The Bridge on the River Kwai*[10] in 1966, the first of which would draw the tenth-largest audience ever for a movie shown on TV, garnering a rating of 38.3 in a season when *Bonanza*, the top-rated series, had a 31.8 rating.

MADE-FOR-TV MOVIES

The insatiable public demand for movies on television soon outstripped the available supply as Hollywood films were being sold right, left and center to the networks and to local stations in sometimes enormous syndication packages; for example, the three CBS owned-and-operated stations in New York, Chicago and Milwaukee bought the broadcast rights to 725 MGM feature films in 1956.[11] By 1964 it was necessary, for both financial and supply reasons, for the networks to commission their own films, and the resulting made-for-television movies slowly became part of the networks' prime-time schedules.

What would have been the first made-for-TV movie, in 1964, wasn't shown on television at all, being instead diverted for theatrical release. *The Killers* was a very loose adaptation of the eponymous Hemingway short story (which had been made into a Hollywood theatrical film in 1946), and was considered to be too violent for television, coming as it did on the heels of TV violence hearings in Congress. *The Killers* was directed by tough-guy director Don Siegel and was Ronald Reagan's final film, before he was elected governor of California. It contains a perversely entertaining scene in which Reagan, playing an evil mob boss, backhands Angie Dickinson for mouthing off to him, something quite at odds with his grandfatherly image as president.

By default, then, the first "real" made-for-television movie became *See How They Run* (NBC October 1964), which is perhaps the only distinguishing characteristic of the routine movie in which mobsters try to kill children who know too much. It did, however, star a number of people who already were or would become mainstays of television, both in series and made-fors: John Forsythe, Senta Berger, Leslie Nielsen, and George Kennedy.

LAW AND REGULATION

By the 1960s, much of the novelty of television had worn off, and as it became an integral part of everyday life, a vague sense of dissatisfaction, a feeling that the programming was not quite what it should be began to seep into the public consciousness. This feeling led to two events of symbolic importance: FCC chairman Newton Minow made his famous "vast wasteland" speech in 1961, and in the following year the first Congressional hearings into TV violence opened under Sen. Thomas Dodd.

THE "VAST WASTELAND" OF TELEVISION

Disputes over what television ought to be, as opposed to what it is, continue to play a role in how we envision the past and present of television. Programming history is usually conceptualized into comprising an early quality period, the so-called Golden Age of Television, followed by a much longer period during which standards have continued to fall. This debate continues today, at the start of the twenty-first century, with the success of the "lowbrow" Fox, UPN, and WB networks and shows along the lines of the notoriously worm-eating reality program *Fear Factor* and the leer factor of *America's Top Models*.

The debate over quality came to the forefront of public consciousness in 1961, when the chairman of the FCC, Newton Minow, delivered his famous speech at the annual convention of the National Association of Broadcasters, a powerful trade organization. In the speech Minow called television a "vast wasteland," a phrase that still resonates among television workers, scholars, and viewers to this day.

The ratings for the 1960–1961 television season indicate the types of programs that were popular, of course, but that particular season, to which Minow was indirectly referring, doesn't seem out of the ordinary—which may have been his point. Of the 10 most popular programs that season, the top three were westerns (*Gunsmoke*, *Wagon Train*, and *Have Gun, Will Travel*); the rural comedies, *The Andy Griffith Show* and *The Real McCoys*, were in the numbers four and five spots; *Rawhide*, another western, was sixth; *Candid Camera*, one of the first "reality" programs, was in seventh position; *The Untouchables*, a crime drama, and *The Price is Right*, a game show, were tied for eighth; and the vaudeville-like comedy *The Jack Benny Show* was tenth. Proponents of quality programming would be quick to point out the absence of the sort of dramatic anthologies that characterized the Golden Age, and it was to these kinds of programs that Minow seems to have been alluding, or perhaps he was thinking about the lack of variety in formats or the potential for the medium to be creative and challenging.

It's somewhat difficult, more than 40 years after the speech, to see exactly how these programs were consigned to the wasteland, although for fairness sake it should be mentioned that none of the programs was specifically singled out by Minow. By contemporary standards they don't look all that bad, although it is worth noting that five of the top 10 programs were rather violent, given that four were westerns and the other was the Prohibition-era crime drama *The Untouchables*.

VIOLENCE ON TELEVISION

The other symbolic issue of the 1960s also sounds familiar today, as the issue of violence on television is still discussed. Prime-time programming had long contained violence as a part of westerns, police shows and dramatic anthologies, and violence in one form or another was found into many forms of programming, with the eyeball-poking antics of The Three Stooges and the screeching of car tires being defined as violent by some. The possible effects on viewers, especially children, of exposure to violence were of academic, governmental and parental concern.

Two early academic studies on the effects of televised violence on children were ambiguous, although they spurred literally thousands of additional studies during the following decades. The researchers Himmelwest,

Oppenheim, and Vince published their examination of the issue in the UK in 1958, while Schramm, Lyle and Parker published a similar examination in the United States in 1961. Both studies found that the effects of violence were so variable that it was impossible to say that there was an across-the-board effect of exposure to violence on TV as children were affected in a broad range of ways.

Governmental concern over the amount and effects of televised violence led to several Congressional hearings on the subject. Hearings called by Sen. Estes Kefauver of Tennessee in 1952 into the causes and effects of juvenile delinquency included testimony about the role of television, and hearings in 1954–1955, also presided over by Kefauver, looked into the modeling of behavior by children, something that had been studied in the 1920s in connection with movie attendance and children. In 1961 Sen. Thomas Dodd of Connecticut held hearings specifically to look into television violence and children, but only an inconclusive interim report on the findings of the hearing was issued.

Television programming was undoubtedly violent during the decade between the Kefauver hearing and Minow's speech. For example, an episode of the drama *Bus Stop* (ABC, 1961–1962), titled "A Lion Walks among Us," was singled out as being explicitly violent and sadistic. It starred singer Fabian as a "youthful psychopath bent on murder and mayhem." *Bus Stop* achieved notoriety when the president of ABC admitted to his embarrassment during Dodd's hearing that he didn't let his children watch the program,[12] a statement that privileges the notion that all prime-time TV should be suitable for children—a view with which a considerable number of parents of the era, and still today, would agree.

Another often-cited example is *The Untouchables* (ABC, 1959–1963), a program still criticized as "mindlessly violent" and perhaps the most violent program on television of its time, although it's difficult to imagine how a program about crime-fighting during the violent Depression years could be nonviolent. Nevertheless, the program played fast and loose with historical accuracy (not the first program to have done so, by the way) and resolved most if not all of its dramatic conflicts by having Elliot Ness and his incorruptible G-men machine-gun the bad guys in the name of justice in the same way that episodes of the later *Hawaii 5-0* ended with Steve McGarrett shooting the bad guy with his .38-caliber police special.

The Untouchables probably repelled as many people as it lured with violence, though. It went from being rated as the no. 43 program during its first season to no. 8 in its second season to no. 41 in its third, when it was trounced in its time slot by *Sing Along with Mitch* on NBC, a clear indication that people seeking out vicarious thrills through violence were not the largest part of the audience.

At the risk of oversimplifying, the thousands of studies that have been done on the effects of television violence on children can be summarized by the scientific cliché "results are inconclusive." A half-century of continuing research has shown that exposure to violence on television sometimes affects some children, but the type and degree of effect depend on the personality of the child and the totality of circumstances surrounding viewing. This debate continues today, of course, although much of the controversy over the content of television has shifted to the issue of sexual content and its appropriateness at times of day when children might be watching.

CONCLUSION

Television's reaction to the swinging 1960s (to again use the cliché) was to change from a medium that catered to a mass audience of families who watched TV together, basking in the warm glow of their small sets, to something that specifically targeted a young, affluent, urban audience with attention-getting, color programs that featured growing amounts of violence, sexual innuendo and an overall "hipness" that was earlier missing. The comfortable, ordered world of *Leave It to Beaver* was gone, replaced by the chaos of *Rowan & Martin's Laugh-In*, and the westerns that had been firmly lodged in the nineteenth century were phased out in favor of contemporary urban detective dramas.

The apparent growing amount of violence on television, something long feared by parents, became the focus of Congressional investigations. FCC chairman Newton Minow's comment that television was "a vast wasteland" still resonates with many today. But despite the protests, network prime-time programming remained profitable and popular with the audiences, routinely attracting over 90 percent of the homes having television sets

CHAPTER 6

Controversy in Prime-Time (1970–1984)

*R*elevancy, the catchword of the 1970s, was in the forefront of the minds of program producers and networks during the early part of the period. Programs had to be "real" and to deal with "issues," and even sitcoms, such as *All in the Family,* routinely incorporated the hot topics of the day with references to race relations, impotency, and the generation gap, just to name a few. But relevancy went out the window after a few years, replaced by the easy retro escapism of *Happy Days* and *Laverne and Shirley,* innuendo-laden "jiggle" programs such as *Charlie's Angels* and *Three's Company,* and prime-time soap operas that followed the rich and super-rich through the early Reagan years. Along the way a number of sitcoms that focused on independent, self-sufficient, and single young women in the workplace attained significant popularity.

Dramatic changes in the television industry began with the rise of cable toward the end of the period. As the number of cable networks increased, fueled by the spread of the availability of cable in homes, the size of the audience for prime-time network programs began a decline that continues today. Cable networks like MTV drove popular music off the programming schedules of the traditional, over-the-air television networks, and easy-to-use and increasingly inexpensive VCRs allowed programs to be time-shifted and commercials to be virtually ignored.

LAW, REGULATION, AND TECHNOLOGY

The general social upheaval of the 1960s was reflected in a number of related regulatory events that affected prime-time television during the 1970s and into the 1980s.

Violence on Television

Continuing concern over the real or imagined influence that televised violence was having on children resulted in a number of investigations. In 1969, following the assassinations of Martin Luther King and Bobby Kennedy, Sen. John Pastore of Rhode Island asked the Surgeon General to create a panel for further research into the effects of television violence on children. The panel was convened, but it was compromised when the television networks were given power over the selection of researchers and promptly banned those who they considered to be anti-television or likely to find a causal link between the viewing of violence and violent behavior. A watered-down report was issued in 1972 that again found that some children were sometimes badly affected by TV violence, the same philosophically unsatisfactory conclusion to which studies in the 1950s had come.

However, these unsatisfactory results coincided with, or gave impetus to, the rise of citizens' actions groups, part of the wave of social activism that had begun during the 1960s and that gained strength during the 1970s. Led by Action for Children's Television (ACT), activist groups took on causes that focused on, among other things, violence and racial, ethnic, and sex-role stereotyping during prime-time. The FCC chair was able to convince the networks to "voluntarily" tone down violence and other adult themes before 9 P.M. EST. As such, the fall 1975 television season briefly instituted "family viewing time," which was almost immediately challenged in court by producers, led by Norman Lear, who saw the agreement as a violation of FCC procedures and the First Amendment. Since there were no written guidelines, writers just had to guess what was acceptable. If controversial programs like *Barney Miller, M*A*S*H,* and *Maude* had to change from their usual time slot, the producers feared they would lose audience. The alternative was to tone down the programs, but would the viewers still like the child-proof versions? After the case bounced around for several years, family viewing time formally came to an end in 1976. But the networks were convinced it was a failure its first year after the overall decline in ratings for the 8 to 9 P.M. period.

Activism spilled over into the community of program creators in other forms as well. An actors' strike in 1980 and a writers' strike in 1981 both delayed the premiere of new programs until well past the traditional start of the new season in early fall, with some new programs not appearing until January, instead of the usual September.

Prime-Time Access Rule

The other major issue of the time period involved the somewhat arcane world of the Prime Time Access Rule. PTAR went into effect 1970 as an attempt to encourage local TV stations to produce programming that was relevant to the communities they served, instead of relying on homogenous network programs seen everywhere by everyone. The rule removed from network control one hour of prime-time, leaving the networks with the three hours from 8 P.M. to 11 P.M., except on Sundays when the traditional 7 P.M. start was allowed.

The PTAR was both a noble experiment and a failure. Local stations, mindful of the costs of producing their own shows and usually without network quality talent on staff, simply bought relatively inexpensive syndicated shows or obtained them for free through barter, and sat back to collect revenue from the sale of local advertising time. Thus, the promise of home-grown programming that reflected the interests of the local audience, and that made them better people by their viewing, went largely unrealized.

At the same time, the FCC also passed the financial interest/syndication rule (known as fin/syn) that said the networks could not syndicate television programs in the United States and could own only a few prime-time shows. The purpose was to lessen the power of the networks in negotiations with program producers, but of course it didn't succeed. There were only three possible customers for TV series—the networks.

Video Cassette Recorders

But all of the regulatory issues of the day must be considered in light of the most significant technological change to perhaps ever occur in television, the advent of the video cassette recorder (VCR). Fabulously expensive when it first came on the market—the original Sony VCRs of the mid-1970s cost about $1,200 and only worked when connected to a Sony monitor, which cost another $1,200—prices fell as demand increased. In a relatively short period of time, VCRs changed the way people watch television. Programs could be time-shifted (recorded for later viewing at a more convenient time), and commercials zipped (sped through) or zapped (not recorded), a major change in which it is viewers who determine what and when to watch, not the television networks or their local affiliates.

SITCOMS

Happy Family Sitcoms

During the 1970s and 1980s, the racial composition of prime-time tele-vision had changed to the extent that the traditional, intact nuclear fam-ily was usually found in Norman Lear–produced family sitcoms that had predominately African-American casts and which aired for long periods of time. Both *Good Times* (CBS, 1974–1979), a spin-off from *Maude*, and *The Jeffersons* (CBS, 1975–1985), a spin-off from *All in the Family*, were based on intact nuclear families, as was, of course, the highly regarded Marcy Carsey/ Tom Werner–produced *The Cosby Show* (NBC, 1984–1992). The intact fam-ily structure of these programs flew in the face of the conventional view of African-American families as being fragmented, crime ridden, poverty-stricken, fatherless and headed by unemployed women.

Interestingly, *Good Times* had a good bit of family evolution in it, which perhaps is a better reflection of the real world than is found in many series. First, James Evans, the father of the family died—actor John Amos had left the series—and the program centered on widow and main character Florida (Esther Rolle) and her children, J.J. (Jimmie Walker), Thelma (BernNadette Stanis), and Michael (Ralph Carter). Later in its run, it had an entirely parentless family at its center, when Rolle, upset over the stereotypical portrayal of young black men in the person of J.J., left the series for the 1977–1978 season. It again became a widow-with-children sitcom when the producers made J.J. a more "respectable" character and she returned to the fold.

Bill Cosby had been one of the most recognizable African-Americans on television since the 1960s and his costarring role, with Robert Culp, in the espionage thriller *I Spy* (NBC, 1965–1968). He had starred in the eponymous sitcom *The Bill Cosby Show* (NBC, 1969–1971) and in an earnest flop, *Cos* (ABC, September–November 1976), a variety show aimed at 2- to 12-year-olds at a time when there were few children's programs in prime-time and when the variety show as a form was dying. *The Cosby Show* was a significant success for him and is the program that perhaps defines his career. He later tried to repeat his success with *Cosby* (CBS, 1996–2000), a situation comedy about an unemployed grouch and a patient wife, but it lacked the sparkle of its predecessor.

The Cosby Show, produced by Marcy Carsey and Tom Werner, was a deliberately progressive program and a counterpart to the usual sitcom portrayal of African-American families. For one thing, the Huxtables were affluent—father Cliff was an obstetrician and mother Claire (Phylicia Rashad) an attorney—which was a good thing as they lived in a brownstone in New York City with their five children, Sondra (Sabrina La Beuf), Denise (Lisa Bonet), Theodore (Malcolm-Jamal Walker), Vanessa (Tempestt Bledsoe), and Rudy (Keshia Knight Pulliam). For another, they seemed to actually like each other, and the program's humor was much gentler than the insult-and-response humor employed in many other sitcoms, both those with predominately white and those with predominantly black casts. Interestingly, it was this positive portrayal of the lives of African-Americans that made its critics brand *The Cosby Show* as being unrealistic and "not black enough."[1] But the program mirrored the happy family sitcoms of the 1950s, complete with an emphasis on everyday domestic concerns and was similar in theme to the stand-up comedy of Cosby himself.

The program struck a chord with large numbers of people. Its premiere episode garnered a 21.6 rating and an impressive 39 share; it was the number-three rated program in its first season and would go on to be the number one program for each of the next five seasons. Among African-American viewers, it was especially effective. An African-American student

As in most sitcoms, the family in *The Cosby Show* spent most of their lives in the living room or kitchen, but very little time watching TV. The cast included Sabrina Le Beauf, Malcolm-Jamal Warner, Bill Cosby, Keshia Knight Pulliam, Tempestt Bledsoe, Lisa Bonet, and Phylicia Rashad. Courtesy of Photofest.

of the author of this section wrote in an essay that he watched reruns of *The Cosby Show* daily and wished that he was part of the family.

At the other end of the humor spectrum from *The Cosby Show* was *The Jeffersons*. Although both programs centered on affluent African-American families in New York City, *The Jeffersons* traded in insult-based humor and clashes within the family were played for laughs.

The Jeffersons was produced by Normal Lear and was a spin-off of Lear's phenomenally successful *All in the Family*. Its main character, George Jefferson (Sherman Hemsley), had been Archie Bunker's next-door neighbor and shared many of Archie's personality traits in that he too was a not particularly intelligent, loudmouthed bigot. Like the Huxtables, the Jeffersons represented an affluent, intact family unit: George owned a chain of dry cleaners and lived in a luxurious high-rise apartment with wife Louise (Isabelle Sanford) and son Lionel (played by the unrelated Mike Evans and Damon Evans over the years), a college student.

But the program, unlike *The Cosby Show*, dealt with racial issues. *The Jeffersons* is notable for having the first interracial couple to appear as regular characters in a prime-time sitcom, Tom and Helen Willis (Franklin Cover and Roxie Roker). The relationship between Lionel and Jenny Willis, the daughter of Tom and Helen, was a thorn in the side of George Jefferson. As the series developed, they married and had a child of their own, but, unlike in the Huxtable family, separated and then divorced.

Diff'rent Strokes (NBC, 1978–1986) reverted to the wealthy bachelor with inherited children variation of the happy family formula, something that had explored during the 1950s by *Bachelor Father* and by *Family Affair* in the 1960s. But *Diff'rent Strokes* created a new racial/economic variation of its own, with its poor, African-American children living in a swanky penthouse with their new, white "father," who had promised their mother, his housekeeper, on her deathbed that he'd care for the boys, ages 8 and 12. Like *Family Affair*, *Diff'rent Strokes* has come to be well-known for cast-related tragedies after the series left the air: the multiple arrests of Todd Bridges, who had played Willis Jackson, the older of the boys, and the fatal drug overdose of Dana Plato, who had played Kimberly Drummond.

The classic all-American, all-white situation comedy survived. Perhaps the best example was *Family Ties* (NBC, 1982–1989). The parents were survivors of the hippie generation, but the children were definitely from the 1980s. Michael J. Fox as Alex Keaton was the teenage embodiment of the Reagan-era entrepreneur.

Changes in family structure that began on a fairly large scale during the 1960s were reflected in *The Brady Bunch* (ABC, 1969–1974), which dealt with a blended family of six children, headed by a widowed mother (Florence Henderson) and a widower father (Robert Reed) who had married. The program played extensively in reruns during the 1990s, and it was not unusual at the time for college undergraduates to describe the Brady household as the kind of home they wished they'd grown up in.

On a similar theme was *Kate & Allie* (CBS, 1984–1989). Although it didn't have a traditional blended family (note how fast the nontraditional becomes traditional on television) it featured two divorced mothers (Susan St. James and Jane Curtin) with three children between them and who functioned as a de facto blended family. The suggestion of lesbianism that had unfairly haunted *Cagney and Lacy* just a few years before was not attached to *Kate & Allie*, as both were portrayed as heterosexuals who actively dated men.

Domestic servant variants also continued into the 1980s in two programs. *Who's the Boss?* (ABC, 1984–1992) was about a "male governess" and carried at least a portion of its humor from the wacky, gender-reversing notion of a hunky man working as a domestic (cue laugh track here). The program came to focus on the relationship between Tony Micelli (Tony Danza), the domestic, and Angela Bower (Judith Light), his employer, as it evolved into a blended family sitcom—each had a child—with their marriage. *Charles in Charge* (CBS, 1984–1985 and first-run syndication 1987–1990) was an almost identical idea, but with a younger protagonist. In it, 19-year-old college student Charles (Scott Baio) became the "governor" to a family with three children, with the inevitable comedic results.

The mixing of generic elements common in prime-time television continued during the 1970s and 1980s, and hybrid forms of programming were developed, not always successfully. Worthy of brief mention is the overly complex blend of single parent and domestic servant sitcoms, with some cultural clashes thrown in for good measure, *Mr. T. and Tina*, which lasted just six episodes on ABC in 1976. In the series a Japanese man—played by that most prominent of Japanese-American actors, Pat Morita—with two children and other relatives in tow adapted, or rather failed to adapt, to life in Chicago and an American nanny/housekeeper. Its failure indicates that a sitcom that tries to overlap three fairly distinct types of program is spread too thin and becomes confusing, in this case perhaps to the point of inducing headache.

Divorce in Sitcoms

Divorce finally reared its head on prime-time sitcoms in the 1970s. Programs in which divorced characters played leading roles were typified by *Fay* (NBC, 1975–1976), a sitcom about an attractive (of course) divorcée in her 40s, Fay Stewart (Lee Grant), who dealt with dating, postdivorce sex, her family and her new job as a secretary, the most clichéd woman's career on television.

One Day at a Time (CBS, 1976–1984) featured a lead character, Ann Romano Royer (Bonnie Franklin), a divorcée who became a widow in her second marriage and who later married for a third time. The series featured two younger actresses who were becoming quite well known at the time. Mackenzie Phillips, who played Ann's daughter Julie, missed a season as she was in rehab for a drug problem, and Valerie Bertinelli, who played Ann's other daughter Barbara, went on to star in a number of made-for-television movies and series of her own.

Inverted Family Sitcoms

Inverted family sitcoms—which deal with unhappy families (who nonetheless remain families and attempt to work out their problems within the bosom of the family unit without resorting to divorce)—began with the new sitcom structure of *All in Family* in 1971. Other, similar programs about relatively unhappy families dealing with various personal and societal problems included *Maude* (CBS, 1972–1978), a spin-off of *All in the Family*, and *Mama's Family* (NBC, 1983–1985 and first-run syndication, 1986–1990). The latter was a spin-off of skits performed years previously on the long-lived *The Carol Burnett Show*; it dealt with a blue-collar family somewhere in the Midwest whose bickering and anger were played for laughs.

The dysfunctional families at the heart of 1970s family-oriented sitcoms were part of the age of tele-liberalism. *All in the Family* (CBS, 1971–1983) promoted producer Norman Lear's left-wing worldview by deliberately setting up the audience to see the prejudiced Archie Bunker as an idiot. Apparently, the tactic didn't always work as it is widely believed that significant numbers of the prejudiced found Archie's regressive views curiously refreshing, and that "Archie Bunker for President" bumper stickers could be found plastered on their cars at the time.

Whatever its interpretation by its audience, *All in the Family* was undoubtedly a hit, and the program generated considerable controversy—another catchword of the 1970s—in its dialogue and plots. The main characters are familiar to all: Archie Bunker (Carroll O'Connor) was saddled with a blue collar job; a wife, Edith (Jean Stapleton), he referred to as "dingbat"; and a daughter (Sally Struthers) who had not only married a liberal college student (Rob Reiner) but had moved him into the family home, where his liberalism

All in the Family introduced America to a new type of TV family. Carroll O'Connor was Archie Bunker, a man who was politically incorrect and proud of it, and Jean Stapleton played his long-suffering wife, Edith. Courtesy of Photofest.

clashed continually with Archie's conservatism. Archie called him "meat-head"—it was not a term of endearment. The program traded in racism and stereotypes, "taboo" subjects such as impotency and miscarriage, and anything else that could be branded controversial, including the unheard-of-to-that-time sound of a toilet flushing. After a somewhat slow start in the ratings during its first season, *All in the Family* became the number-one program for the next five seasons in a row, during which time its rating was 30 or above.

The opposite of Archie in political viewpoint was *Maude* (CBS, 1972–1978). But she shared his ability to tackle tough topics in a loud, blunt fashion. One of the most controversial shows was about her decision to have an abortion. Bea Arthur played the wife, mother, and advocate.

Workplace Sitcoms

Several workplace comedies blended nuclear family and work family life. For example, *The New Dick Van Dyke Show* (CBS, 1971–1974) was in some ways an update of the old *Dick Van Dyke Show* from the 1960s. Dick Preston, a talk show host, was the central character, instead of Rob Petrie, the television writer, and the wife was now Jenny (Hope Lange) instead of Laura (Mary Tyler Moore).

Others of the type focused almost entirely on relationships within the workplace, such as *Alice* (CBS, 1976–1985), about a widowed singer-waitress in Phoenix and based in theme on the dramatic 1974 film *Alice Doesn't Live Here Anymore*, and the Boston bar-based *Cheers* (NBC, 1982–1993). Both programs are notable in their own right. *Alice* serves as an example of the genre-shifting that takes place as a dramatic film becomes a quite different television sitcom.

One of the reasons for the appeal of workplace sitcoms is that they allow a collection of oddball characters, none of whom are heroic or even commendable, to hang out together and share their tilted views of the universe. Frequently, they have little in common except their shared time; without the workplace, these people would never see each other, but nevertheless they bond together. In *WKRP in Cincinnati* (CBS, 1978–1982), the workplace was a struggling radio station. The mismatched crew included a program director (Gary Sandy), a bumbling station manager (Gordon Jump), an attractive secretary (Loni Anderson), an eccentric newsman (Richard Sanders), and hip DJs (Tim Reid, Howard Hesseman). In *Night Court* (NBC, 1984–1992), the judge (Harry Anderson) oversaw a courtroom that featured a wide array of whimsical characters.

Cheers proved that a TV series could take a group of losers who hung out in a bar and make them into lovable characters. Ted Danson, as the bartender, set the tone. He was a skirt-chasing, former alcoholic with few redeeming qualities except his charm. And the other inhabitants of this world were equally flawed and equally appealing.

A predecessor to *Cheers* was *Taxi* (ABC, NBC, 1978–1983). The characters worked for a small cab company in New York City. The mood of the boss (Danny DeVito) ranged from unpleasant to downright mean. He enjoyed reminding his employees that they were failures, but they never truly bought his message. The cast included Judd Hirsch, Tony Danza, Marilu Henner, Christopher Lloyd, and Andy Kaufman.

Welcome Back, Kotter (NBC, 1969–1972) dealt with the schoolroom. Gabe Kaplan played a man who returned to his old high school as a teacher and was assigned a class of potential dropouts including John Travolta. He used humor to win them over.

In fact, workplace sitcoms during the 1970s and 1980s include some of the longest-lived programs in prime-time history. Various incarnations of Bob Newhart's buttoned-down comic persona were found for 14 years as Chicago psychiatrist Dr. Bob Hartley in *The Bob Newhart Show* (CBS, 1972–1978) and as Vermont innkeeper Dick Loudon in *Newhart* (CBS, 1982–1990). *Newhart's* final episode ended with a surreal scene in which Bob Hartley (*not* Dick Loudon) awoke suddenly to tell his wife (Suzanne Pleshette from the older series) that he's had a strange dream about running an inn—an example of intertextuality run amok and something quite sophisticated by network sitcom standards. *The Bob Newhart Show* also had a special place in the hearts of college students during the 1980s for its role in a drinking game played during reruns of the series. The game was simple: All one did was drink every time someone on the show said "Hi Bob," which was frequent.

In a sense, *The Facts of Life* (NBC, 1979–1988) could be classified as a workplace sitcom. True, the main characters were children, but they were in a boarding school under the supervision of a character played by Charlotte Rae. They came from a variety of backgrounds—wealthy (Lisa Whelchel) to poor (Nancy McKeon). They looked different from each other—plump (Mindy Cohn) to African-American (Kim Fields). But they formed a family of sorts and worked together.

Ethnic Sitcoms

The married-couples-without-children subgenre continued through the 1970s, by which time it too began to grow offshoots. One offshoot was the ethnic comedy, which included *Bridget Loves Bernie* (CBS, 1972–1973), a sitcom about newlyweds Bernie Steinberg (David Birney) and Bridget Fitzgerald (Meredith Baxter) who were respectively Jewish and Catholic. It was cancelled despite high ratings—it was the number-five program of the season with a rating of 24.2—after religious organizations, both Jewish and Christian, complained about its portrayal of what were then called mixed marriages.

One of the few programs starring a Hispanic was *Chico and the Man* (NBC, 1974–1978). Freddie Prinze played a happy-go-lucky guy with a charming personality who worked for a curmudgeon (Jack Albertson). When Prinze committed suicide, his character was replaced by a young boy (Isaac Ruiz), but the chemistry was never as effective, and the show was soon canceled. *Mork & Mindy* (ABC, 1978–1982) wasn't really ethnic, but dealt with the hijinks that ensued when a space alien joined an earthbound father and daughter. The main source of laughter was the high energy comedy of star Robin Williams.

"Britcoms"

The long-term influence that British programming has had on American prime-time came in the form of sitcoms, many of which ran for years. The era of British-originated sitcoms (occasionally called "Britcoms") during the 1970s began with producer Norman Lear's *All in the Family,* which was based on the United Kingdom sitcom *Till Death Do Us Part.* Likewise, Lear's *Sanford and Son* (NBC, 1972–1977) was based on *Steptoe and Son.* And the now fairly obscure *Lotsa Luck* (NBC, 1973–1975) was based on the series *On the Busses.*

Producer Don Taffner's *Three's Company* (ABC, 1977–1984) was an Americanized *Man About the House,* and its short-lived spin-off *The Ropers* (ABC, 1979–1980) was based on *George & Mildred,* which was itself a spin-off in the United Kingdom from *Man About the House*—a unique case in the world of British-American programming. Taffner was also responsible for Americanizing *Keep It in the Family* into *Too Close for Comfort* (ABC, 1980–1983).[2]

Independent Woman Sitcoms

By the 1970s, network television had come to recognize the inescapable fact that large numbers of women had permanently entered the workplace, which had been dominated by men ever since millions of soldiers came home at the end of World War II and women were forced back to the domestic sphere of housework and child care. This change in the employment status of women was related, of course, to the women's movement itself, as well as to a stagnated national economy, and as a result producers developed comedies that centered on the lives of independent (i.e., unmarried, but sometimes widowed or divorced) women, usually young and always pretty, as they moved about the previously masculine world of work. Social support for these women came not from their families, but from their coworkers, which allows the programs to be characterized as workplace sitcoms as well.

The Mary Tyler Moore Show (CBS, 1970–1977) was the longest-lived of the type. Like much programming, it can trace its roots back in history, in this case to Connie Brooks (Eve Arden) in *Our Miss Brooks* (CBS, 1952–1956), which had begun on radio, and to its more recent precursor, *That Girl* (ABC, 1966–1971) and the character Ann Marie, played by Marlo Thomas. The character of Connie Brooks has been described as the first independent woman in radio,[3] and she naturally became the first independent woman in television when the program moved to TV with Arden still in the title role.

Mary Tyler Moore's character in *The Mary Tyler Moore Show*, Mary Richards, was an updated, 1970s version of Laura Petrie from *The Dick Van Dyke Show*. Where Laura had been the typical sort of stay-at-home suburban wife found everywhere on television during the 1960s, Mary was the embodiment of the new, independent, single, urban woman of the 1970s: at the end of a romance of several years, and with no offer of marriage, she moved to Minneapolis and a career as a TV news producer. The program struck an obvious chord with viewers, lasting for seven seasons, figuring in the top 20 programs for several of them and winning a number of Emmy awards. It is frequently thought of as being feminist in nature, but is really quite traditional in that Mary's career came about because she didn't get married.

Moore's television career has been limited, however, by the success of the program, as she was firmly associated with the character of Mary Richards in the minds of viewers, who seemed unwilling to accept her as a different character. She followed *The Mary Tyler Moore Show* with a comedy-variety program called, simply, *Mary*, which flopped, airing just three episodes during fall 1978. Next came a second comedy-variety program, *The Mary Tyler Moore Hour*, but it lasted only from March to June 1979. Another workplace comedy, which confusingly reverted to the title *Mary*, followed in turn, but met with little additional success in its one-season run between December 1985 and April 1986; her character was a tabloid newspaper columnist. A final attempt was made with *Annie McGuire*, a blended family sitcom set in Manhattan, but like the others it lasted only a short time, from October through December 1988.

The Mary Tyler Moore Show is also notable for spinning off a drama instead of the usual case in which one sitcom begets another. *Lou Grant* (CBS, 1977–1982) took its title character from being Mary's boss at the TV station to being the city editor of a Los Angeles newspaper. The program was one of the longest-running of many newspaper-based dramas over the years and is thought of today as having been canceled because of star Edward Asner's well-known leftist political views about the role the United States was playing at the time in Central American politics. CBS, naturally,

The Mary Tyler Moore Show followed the classic
formula of combining work and home as
settings, providing two sources of laughter. At
the TV station, the crew was played by Betty
White, Mary Tyler Moore, Georgia Engel, Gavin
MacLeod, Ed Asner, and Ted Knight. Courtesy
of Photofest.

said that declining ratings were behind the cancellation, but ratings data
shows that *Lou Grant* was the 27th most popular of 75 shows running during
prime-time in 1981.

The Doris Day Show (CBS, 1968–1973) was an obvious vehicle for its
eponymous star, who had been a popular singer just after World War II and
is today remembered for roles in gentle sex farce films, such as *Pillow Talk*
(1959), which helped cement her "professional virgin" image. The program

was a rare foray into television for her, and it rapidly evolved through several iterations in four seasons. It began as a blend of the happy family and rural sitcom subgenres, with Day as a young widow with children who moved from the big city in search of the usual sort of better life in the country, and ended as an urban, office-based independent woman/workplace sitcom with Day as a single magazine writer.

The mother (Shirley Jones) of *The Partridge Family* (ABC, 1970–1974) dealt with the dilemma of keeping the family together while she worked by organizing her brood of children (including David Cassidy and Susan Dey) into a rock band. To many teens in the audience, it seemed like the ideal solution.

Julia (NBC, 1968–1971) was one of the first programs to break network color barriers in its casting of an African-American woman, Diahann Carroll, in the lead role of a sitcom, this at a time when minorities were routinely relegated to secondary roles in prime-time programs. Moreover, the program was quite popular, albeit for a short time. It ranked as the seventh most popular show in its first season, before falling to the number 28 position in its second and out of the top 30 in its third and last season. The content of *Julia* was routine—young widow Julia Baker has humorous interactions while working as a nurse for crusty old Dr. Chegley (Lloyd Nolan)—although topical as her husband had been killed in Vietnam, an early prime-time reference to the war.

Nostalgic Sitcoms

The mid-1970s were a time of nostalgia for the 1950s, a seemingly simpler time when issues were more black and white, given the winding down of the war in Vietnam and the resignations of Vice-President Agnew and President Nixon. The sense of nostalgia was reflected in the box office success of the George Lucas–directed film *American Graffiti* (1973). Although the movie was set in 1962—sort of a transitional year between the 1950s and the "real" 1960s that revolved around protests, hippies, and liberated women—it sparked an interest in all things 1950s, including a revival of 1950s rock music and television programs set during the decade.

The two major 1950s-themed programs were the sitcoms *Happy Days* (ABC, 1974–1984) and its spin-off *Laverne & Shirley* (1976–1983). *Happy Days* was built around the domestic adventures of the Cunningham family, and focused on the activities of son Richie (Ron Howard, who had also starred in *American Graffiti*, but had been part of prime-time since his days as Opie on *The Andy Griffith Show*) and his greaser friend Fonzie (Henry Winkler), who wore the famous black leather biker jacket that was later displayed in the Smithsonian Institution. *Laverne & Shirley* was a slapstick sitcom about two working-class young women, Laverne DeFazio (Penny Marshall) and Shirley Feeny (Cindy Williams), who had first appeared as dates for Richie and Fonzie in an episode of *Happy Days*. Both programs were situated in Milwaukee, a somewhat unusual location for network sitcoms, which tend to take place either in New York City or California.

The programs were immensely popular. *Laverne & Shirley*'s premiere episode on January 27, 1976 pulled a 35.1 rating, the highest first-episode rating in a decade, and was averaging roughly the same size audience as was watching *All in the Family*, which was by then a well-established and top-rated program. By the 1977–1978 season, *Laverne & Shirley* and *Happy Days* sat atop the ratings in first and second place, respectively, with ratings of 31.6 and 31.4,[4] although they both fell out of the top 10 by the following season.

All long-running series undergo changes in their casts, as well as in the focus of the program itself, and the two sitcoms were no different. The focus of *Happy Days* eventually shifted from Richie to the Fonz, who was so popular that the American Library Association reported a 500 percent increase in applications for library cards from children ages 9 to 14 after an episode in which Fonzie got his card.[5] Howard, meanwhile, left the program in 1980 and only returned on occasion as a guest star as the characters aged through high school, college, and the start of careers. *Laverne & Shirley* changed as well. It began as a sitcom "about" working-class life—the characters worked in a brewery—but was retooled into a form that concentrated on slapstick comedy and the *Odd Couple*-like personality clashes of Shirley and Laverne. These personality clashes were reflected in the production of the program, as well, as disputes between Williams and Marshall got considerable coverage in the entertainment-oriented press, and culminated with Williams quitting the series in 1982; the show, of course, could not go on for long without her.

Military-Themed Sitcoms

The mother of all military-themed sitcoms was *M*A*S*H* (CBS, 1972–1983), with an impressive 11-year run. Based on a darkly humorous novel and film of the same title, and centering on the activities of the 4077th Mobile Army Surgical Hospital, the sitcom was ostensibly about the Korean War, but really more relevant to contemporary societal concerns about the Vietnam War, civil rights, and other 1970s-era issues. It was deeply liberal in plot, dialogue, and personal appearance; characters, especially the long-haired Capt. "Hawkeye"

Pearce (Alan Alda), reflected 1970s, and later 1980s, sensibilities—he was sympathetic to the plight of gays and minorities, for example—and not the views of military personnel, or even mainstream American civilians, during the early 1950s, when the program was set. So compelling was *M*A*S*H* that its hugely publicized, two-and-a-half hour finale on February 28, 1983, drew a 60 rating that comprised some 77 percent of television viewers that night , the largest audience for any individual television program to date.[6]

DRAMA

Happy Family Dramas

By the 1970s, the happy family sitcom had spun off the happy family drama variant. Usually one hour in length, happy family dramas included *Little House on the Prairie* (NBC, 1974–1983)—,a program that was somewhat similar to a western, in that it was set at about the right time, the 1870s, although not quite geographically far enough west in Minnesota. The program, of course, centered on the interactions of the loving Ingalls family: parents Charles and Caroline (Michael Landon and Karen Grassle) and the older daughters Laura (Melissa Gilbert) and Mary (Melissa Sue Anderson). They dealt with everyday concerns in a wholesome sort of way, and the series itself was based on the series of autobiographically based novels written by Laura Ingalls Wilder early in the twentieth century.

The variations on a theme that characterizes so much of television continued, naturally, in the happy family dramas. *Eight Is Enough* (ABC, 1977–1981), for example, played off the widowed father variant, in this case caused by the death of actress Diana Hyland after the completion of just four episodes. The character Tom Bradford (Dick Van Patten), suddenly a widower, remarried as the series progressed and turned into a blended family happy family drama. Van Patten, by the way, had a lengthy career in prime-time television, beginning with his role as the son in one of the earliest of the happy family sitcoms, *Mama* (CBS, 1949–1956).

Perhaps the best known of the genre was *The Waltons* (CBS, 1972–1981), the story of a rural family trying to survive the depression. Although the premise sounds grim, the warmth and humor of the family helped them survive and kept the audience entertained and even a little nostalgic for the hard times. The characters in *Family* (ABC, 1976–1980) weren't always happy, but the superior acting (Sada Thompson, James Broderick, Meredith Baxter-Birney, Gary Frank, Kristy McNichol) and writing raised the level of suffering and joy from the simple soap opera.

Adventure Dramas

The period 1970–1985 provides a contrast between programs that came and went quickly, and those that lasted for surprisingly long lengths of time. Two programs that reflected the immense popularity of the 1981 Hollywood blockbuster film *Raiders of the Lost Ark* premiered in September 1982, but each lasted less than a year. *Bring 'em Back Alive* survived on CBS only until the following June and *Tales of the Gold Monkey* on ABC for an additional month, evidence that no matter how popular a blockbuster movie, a necessarily low-budget TV knockoff won't draw a large audience.

But the period also saw some of the longest-lived adventure programs in television history during a renewal of the genre in the 1980s. *The Dukes of Hazzard*, a difficult-to-pigeonhole program that was somewhere between a semi-serious adventure/drama and an hour-long sitcom about Southern good ole boys (and girls), ran on CBS (1979–1985). *The Fall Guy* followed the adventures of a stuntman/bounty hunter (Lee Majors) for almost five years on ABC (1981–1986). And *MacGyver,* a program about an incredibly resourceful hero (Richard Dean Anderson) who could make complicated technological devices from everyday components, ran for a commendable seven years on ABC (1985–1992) before entering the eternal afterlife of syndication and pop cultural references in *The Simpsons.*

Rescue Dramas

Adventure programs, as a genre, share a boundary with what have been called "rescue" programs, all of which center on teams of professionals, such as firefighters, paramedics and park rangers, whose job it is to physically rescue people in distress. Programs of this type share characteristics with police shows because of obvious similarities between the work of police departments and rescue agencies, as well as similarities in the way uniformed personnel look and act within hierarchal service organizations. The physical setting of the programs also allow opportunities for exciting shots of fire trucks with flashing lights and screaming sirens, which are certain to get viewers' attention.

The most popular rescue program was *Emergency* (NBC, 1972–1977), which followed the adventures of a paramedic squad within the Los Angeles County Fire Department. Its executive producer was Jack Webb and it utilized the semidocumentary style that Webb had created for *Dragnet* back in the 1950s. *Emergency* also incorporated elements of the medical drama. In each case the paramedics contacted the hospital by

In some of the action-adventure series, the cars seemed to deserve top billing with the heroes. Tom Wopat and John Schneider starred as *The Dukes of Hazzard*, but the General Lee was almost as important. Courtesy of Photofest.

radio and were invariably told to start a drip with Ringer's Lactate before transporting the person they'd just rescued.

At about the same time as *Emergency* was on the air, several less successful attempts at imitation were tried. *Sierra* (NBC, 1974) followed the activities of National Park Service rangers. *240-Robert* (ABC, 1979) had many similarities to *Emergency,* including being set in Los Angeles County, although with the minor difference that the paramedics were attached to the sheriff's department, not the fire department. Both *Sierra* and *240-Robert* aired for three months. The Los Angeles Fire Department again figured in *Code Red* (ABC, 1981–1982), in which veteran actor Lorne Greene played an arson investigator who headed a team that included his two sons.

Science Fiction

By the period 1970–1985, the bloom was off the rose of television sci-fi. Audience interest shifted to blockbuster Hollywood films such as *Star Wars,* in part because big screens and bigger budgets generate much more spectacular special effects than can be done in television. Although a number of prime-time sci-fi programs were attempted, none really developed an audience of a size large enough to ensure a continuing place on the TV schedule. Most programs lasted a year or less; the most popular, the tongue-in-cheek *Buck Rogers in the 25th Century* (NBC, 1979–1981), a parody of the film serials of the 1930s, continued for a bit less than two years, during which time it overlapped the 1980 British film *Flash Gordon,* also a parody of the old serials of the same period.

The sci-fi program with the most notoriety from the period was *Battlestar Galactica,* which was heavily publicized for not only its reputed $1 million per episode budget but for a lawsuit brought by the producers of *Star Wars* over the program's too-close similarities to the film. *Battlestar* thus had two incarnations on network television, airing on ABC (September 1978–August 1979) and again, in reworked, less *Star Wars*–like form, January–August 1980. Despite the publicity, it soon lost viewers. Lorne Greene, a television icon after 14 years on *Bonanza,* was cast against type as Adama, the commander of the enormous, miles-long spaceship of the title. An updated version of *Battlestar Galactica* popped up on cable's Sci-Fi Network in summer 2005.

Related in theme to science fiction were programs that focused on the adventures of comic-book style superheroes and which enjoyed brief popularity during the 1970s and to a lesser extent in the 1980s. That these programs existed during the period that saw the resignation of President Nixon, the "malaise" years of the Carter administration and the rise of the optimistic Reagan years is perhaps not coincidental, and the programs' easy escapism from an increasingly angst-producing world may have been a great part of their appeal.

The cycle of superhero programs, which had had some brief popularity with the syndicated *The Adventures of Superman* in the 1950s and with *Batman* and *The Green Hornet* on ABC during the 1960s, began in earnest with *The Six Million Dollar Man* (ABC, 1974–1978). It was, as all Baby Boomers know, the story of Col. Steve Austin (Lee Majors), an astronaut who was rebuilt by the government's shadowy Office of Scientific Information into a sort of living cyborg following the crash of the moon-landing craft he was testing. Austin soon did battle with OSI's evil, but higher budgeted, $7 million man (a race driver gone bad), then was joined by Jaime Sommers (Lindsay Wagner), who was reconstructed after a skydiving accident, and later by a teenager with bionic legs. These events were themselves followed by the inevitable spin-off, the less popular *The Bionic Woman* (ABC, 1976–1977 and NBC, 1977–1978), which also extended biomechanical engineering to dogs, in the form of Max, the bionic German Shepherd.

Then, just as bionics was fading from television screens, *Wonder Woman* appeared. Based on comic books of the World War II era, the program during its run on ABC (1976–1977) was true to that time, but it was updated to the easier-to-produce contemporary era when the series moved to CBS (1977–199) and was retitled *The New Adventures of Wonder Woman*. Lynda Carter starred in the title role as the proto-feminist super-heroine, whose chief armaments were a belt and bracelets made of the mysterious element "feminum." The Macintosh apple-jawed Lyle Waggoner, who had earlier appeared on *The Carol Burnett Show*, was the male lead. The series was preceded by two made-for-TV movie series pilots, *Wonder Woman* (ABC, 1974) and *The New Original Wonder Woman* (ABC, 1975).

Lynda Carter as Wonder Woman played the ultimate feminist. She could fight evil fearlessly and toss men around like matchsticks. Of course, she did get a little help from super weapons sometimes. Courtesy of Photofest.

Wonder Woman was followed in short order by other comic book-style superheroes. *The Man from Atlantis* (NBC, 1977–1978) briefly followed the adventures of Mark Harris (Patrick Duffy in his pre-*Dallas* incarnation), a gilled and web-fingered survivor of the lost island. More successful was *The Incredible Hulk* (CBS, 1978–1982). Based on the popular Marvel comics character, the program followed the adventures of reluctant superhero David Banner (he had the less macho first name Bruce in the comic books), who had been accidentally irradiated. Instead of dying of radiation poisoning, Banner developed super powers in the fashion of comic books and 1950s sci-fi films. Unfortunately his super powers were somewhat beyond his control, for at usually inopportune moments he would metamorphose into an immensely muscular and green-skinned, well, hulk. The program's two stars shared the lead role, Bill Bixby as the runty Banner and bodybuilder Lou Ferrigno as his alter ego, the Hulk.

The end of the superhero cycle was marked with the departure of the Hulk and the appearance of an even less human variant. Where Wonder Woman was visibly quite human, the Hulk at least humanoid, and Austin and Sommers blends of human and machine, *Knight Rider* (NBC, 1982–1986) was all machine: a computerized, crime fighting, talking Pontiac Firebird Trans-Am, piloted by undercover operative Michael Knight (David Hasselhof). Perhaps intended as a children's program, *Knight Rider* had a significant number of adult viewers, who made it popular enough for it to spin off a syndicated series after its network run and two made-for-TV movies during the 1990s.

Legal Dramas

By the 1970–1985 period, legal dramas were developing in the same pattern seen among all the other categories of dramas. A large number of legal series were developed and aired, but few caught on and none came close to the success *Perry Mason* had during the 1950s and 1960s. Both CBS and ABC continued their attempts to attract younger viewers with legal shows that followed young attorneys: *Storefront Lawyers* (aka *Men at Law*) on CBS and ABC's unambiguously titled *The Young Lawyers* both aired from September 1970 to March 1971. Even CBS itself was unable to recapture the magic of *Perry Mason*, and *The New Perry Mason*, with none of the original's cast, seems in retrospect to have been an idea that never should have been tried. It lasted five months during 1973–1974. In fact, only two legal dramas of the period aired for more than a season, the topical *Owen Marshall, Counselor at Law* (ABC, 1971–1974) and *Petrocelli* (NBC, 1974–1976), a contemporary clash-of-culture/legal drama about a Harvard-educated lawyer working in cowboy country out west.

Sports Dramas

Dramas about sports are conspicuously missing from the prime-time television schedule. One exception was *The White Shadow* (CBS, 1978–1981) starring Ken Howard as a former professional basketball player who takes on the challenge of coaching a team at an inner-city high school. But the plots were usually more about the players' personal lives than about the games. Another exception was *The Bay City Blues*, an obscure program about a minor league baseball team, the Bay City Bluebirds. Described as being more depressing than an example of the gritty realism so popular during the 1980s, it lasted just four episodes on NBC during October and November 1983. The program was produced by Steven Bochco in the pseudo cinéma vérité style of his successful *Hill Street Blues*, but five additional episodes that had been made were never seen.[7]

Why certain types of programs don't catch on with audiences is difficult to assess as many factors contribute to a program's success or failure (e.g. the personality of actors, the writing and editing of episodes, the viewers' preexisting expectations of what constitutes a drama). If nothing else, *The Bay City Blues* can been seen as evidence to support the network program-mers' notion that the ideal audience for prime-time television is women who, if one may use the sort of stereotypical thinking that programmers rely one, don't really care for sports all that much, at least not fictional sports in a television environment that offers plenty of the real thing.

Medical Dramas

In the early- to mid-1970s, the *Dr. Kildare-Ben Casey* competitive pattern repeated itself in the pairing of *Marcus Welby, M.D.* and *Medical Center* on ABC and CBS, respectively, which premiered just one day apart in 1969 and aired through 1976. Both programs were part of the "relevancy" trend in programming that brought contemporary themes and references into the plots of dramas and sitcoms alike.

Marcus Welby, M.D. centered on the dramatic older-younger pairing of the title character (Robert Young of *Father Knows Best* in the 1950s) and Dr. Steven Kiley (James Brolin). Together they dealt with the gamut of illnesses, including such topical concerns as addiction to drugs and faith healing in the place of orthodox medicine. The program soon became the first ABC show to be rated as a number-one program for a full season, with an average rating of 29.1 during the 1970–1971 season. Youth and experience also featured in *Medical Center,* in this case in the persons of the experienced Dr. Paul Lochner (James Daly), chief of staff at large university hospital, and the youthful Dr. Joe Gannon (Chad Everett), director of student health services.

The networks, as usual, scheduled a large number of medical dramas but with little success. Viewers were uninterested, for example, in seeing Patrick McGoohan (the former *Danger Man*) as *Rafferty,* a short-tempered, ex-U.S. Army physician trying to adapt to life in the civilian world on CBS in 1977, and even less in a program bearing the wonderfully tabloid-like title *Doctors' Private Lives,* seen only during April 1979 on ABC.

Out of at least eight medical dramas that premiered during the 1970–1985 period, only one, *St. Elsewhere,* could be described as a hit of any sort. It ran on NBC from 1982 to 1988 and was the sort of drama usually described as "gritty" and "realistic," and was visually and conceptually related to the police drama *Hill Street Blues.* Both were produced by Steven Bochco, and both had elements of prime-time soap operas in their focus on the personal lives of characters. *St. Elsewhere* ended its run in an odd, postmodern-ish sort of fashion. Its final episode suggested that the entire program had existed only in the mind of the autistic son of one of the main characters.

Soap Operas

True success for the soap opera genre came right at the end of the 1970s and continued into the early 1990s with the "big four" programs—*Dallas, Knots Landing,* and *Falcon Crest,* all on CBS, and *Dynasty* on ABC. If the conventional view of the 1980s is correct, if it was in fact a decade of Reaganism that celebrated the rich and powerful and made heroes of the captains of industry, then the big soaps reflected the zeitgeist almost perfectly.

The domestic popularity of *Dallas* is difficult to underestimate. Its most popular episode, the famous revelation that it was Kristen who had shot J.R. in the previous season's famous cliffhanger ending—the motive, in true soap fashion, was that he was about to frame her for prostitution after learning that she was pregnant with his child—was seen by 80 percent of those watching television on the night of November 21, 1980, making it one of the most-viewed programs in history and one of those rare nights when the United States all but came to a halt. *Dallas* was a significant international hit, as well, being seen in about 90 countries at its peak, which immediately raised questions in the minds of scholars about how overseas audiences perceived the United States: did they see it as a land of immense wealth, expensive cars, mansions, heavy drinking and adultery, all of which

The 1980s were seen as a time of corporate and private greed. *Dallas* seemed a perfect reflection of the era or at least of its myth. The stars included Patrick Duffy, Larry Hagman, Barbara Bel Geddes, and Jim Davis. Courtesy of Photofest.

were portrayed as the everyday elements of life in the most popular soap opera of the time? Whatever the answers to those questions, *Dallas* was quite popular everywhere, except Japan, where the program was an expensive failure for Television Asahi.[8]

The plots of the prime-time soaps of the 1980s are nearly impossible to summarize in brief form. The programs, like their daytime counterparts, evolved during their long runs: actors came and went and returned, not always as the same people they had been earlier; characters did likewise; marriages, affairs, pregnancies, divorces and remarriages took place; identities were mistaken; amnesia stole memories; business empires were built and collapsed; the rich became poor before becoming rich again; scandals tore families asunder; and murders, rapes, and kidnappings were routinely committed, for which the guilty parties were not always punished. And, just when it seemed that too much had happened too fast, entire seasons could be written off as dreams, as happened at the start of the 1986–1987 season of *Dallas* when it was revealed that the entire previous season, and everything that had happened during it, was but a dream of Pam Ewing

(Victoria Principal) who awoke to find that her husband, Bobby (Patrick Duffy), wasn't dead after all, but merely in the shower.

The settings of the big prime-time soaps were in the heady world of the biggest of big businesses. *Dallas* (CBS, 1978–1991) was of course centered on the Texas oil industry and dealt with the incredibly complex business and family life of the Ewings, with the evil J.R. (Larry Hagman) at its head. *Dynasty* (ABC, 1981–1989) reflected the *Dallas* theme of oil as the lubricant for the hyper-rich, and in it Blake Carrington (John Forsythe) and his glamorous-but-unhappy wife Krystle (Linda Evans) presided in soft focus over high society Denver. *Falcon Crest* (CBS, 1981–1990) did more of the same, but set the double-dealing and back-stabbing in the wine country of California, whereas *Knots Landing* (CBS, 1979–1993), the most successful of the lot in terms of time on the air, moved a branch of the Ewings, Gary (Ted Shackleford) and wife Valerie (Joan Van Ark), onto a suburban cul-de-sac in southern California. The wonderfully named Abby Cunningham Ewing Summer (Donna Mills) was a malevolent presence on *Knots Landing* in shaggy blonde hair and raccoon-like black mascara. Mills was often featured in contemporary magazines, and always shown in full character makeup, so that the image of the actress and the character blended together to some degree.

A subgenre that never really went anywhere was the military-themed soap opera. Despite massively increased spending on the military and the public relations efforts to improve the image of the uniformed services during the Reagan administration, viewers did not flock to *Emerald Point N.A.S.* (CBS, 1983–1984), set on a naval air station, or *For Love and Honor* (NBC, 1983), which dealt with life, love and lust among the Army's paratroopers, two of whom, unlike in the highly gendered real army, were women.

WESTERNS

By the 1970s, westerns had all but disappeared, replaced by the urban-oriented detective programs that perhaps better reflected the real world lives and interests of thoroughly urbanized contemporary viewers, especially the younger ones the networks were courting, for whom westerns would have been the programming of their parents and childhood, and as such seriously uncool. Although *Bonanza* and *Gunsmoke* continued on into the mid-1970s, only a few new westerns were attempted at the time, and most of them were variations on time-tested, if not timeworn, themes.

NBC had the greatest success, with three series that lasted for more than a season or two, but none of them were traditional westerns: *McCloud*

(1970–1977) was a contemporary western set in New York City; *Little House on the Prairie* (1974–1983) was a "heart-warming" Michael Landon–produced family drama in which its setting in 1870s Minnesota was neither exactly western nor of more importance than its overt advocacy of traditional family values; and *Father Murphy* (1981–1984), a spin-off of *Little House,* which was produced as well by Landon and featured the same sort of wholesome (perhaps "treacly") family-oriented entertainment.

The other western of note in this period was the decidedly nongeneric *Kung Fu* (ABC, 1972–1975). This famous program followed the adventures of a Chinese-American Shaolin monk (David Carradine) as he traveled the west dispensing hippie-influenced Buddhist philosophy and sharp kicks to the head, and was part of the martial arts craze of the time that was fueled by the films of Bruce Lee, who had been turned down for the lead role in the program in favor of the non-Asian Carradine.

A few twentieth-century westerns cropped up again in the 1970s, although with little success. *Nichols* (NBC, 1971–1972) coexisted with *Bearcats* (CBS, 1971). Both programs were remarkably similar in that they were set at about the time that Arizona, the last of the wild west territories, became a state in 1912 and the Old West was symbolically turning into a New West that was more civilized and urban. For example, the heroes of *Bearcats* traveled in a Stutz Bearcat automobile instead of on horseback, a clear symbolic link between the Old and New West and a visual motif used in western films set around the turn of the twentieth century. The programs ran back-to-back on NBC at 8 P.M. and CBS at 9 P.M. on Thursdays so viewers could presumably enjoy both.

Modern sheriff's deputies—in programs that were crosses between the older cowboy programs set in the nineteenth century and the contemporary detective dramas that were enjoying increased popularity—maintained law and order in the New West in the one-hour shows *Cade's County* (CBS, 1971–1972) and *Nakia* (ABC, 1974). The former centered on the activities of Sheriff Sam Cade (Glenn Ford) of Madrid County, California. The latter program's protagonist was an urban New Mexico detective of Native American descent, Nakia Parker (but, as is typical of network television, played by Robert Forster, who was not); although set in the West, the program took place in a city that reflected the lives of those whom the networks and advertisers most wished to reach.

Hec Ramsey was simultaneously an early twentieth-century western, a sort of mystery-western hybrid and an example of the long-form western variant. It was a two-hour program, one of the rotating elements of the "umbrella" series *The NBC Monday Mystery Movie,* and focused on a former gunfighter

(Richard Boone of 1950s *Have Gun, Will Travel* fame) turned forensic investigator in circa 1900 Oklahoma. *McCloud,* another long-form variant, brought the central character, a New Mexico deputy, to New York City during the 1970s; its memorable opening title sequence showed Sam McCloud (Dennis Weaver, who had played Chester on *Gunsmoke),* in cowboy hat and boots, astride his horse and towering over a herd of yellow taxis in metropolitan New York. It too was part of NBC's *Sunday* and Wednesday *Mystery Movie* series, and episodes ran 90 minutes or two hours. Like many other television westerns, it was thematically related to a movie, in this case the 1968 Clint Eastwood film *Coogan's Bluff* in which Eastwood updated his nineteenth-century cowboy persona and, like McCloud, moved him east to twentieth-century Manhattan.

Although no western sitcoms aired during the 1970s, the form was tried again in the 1980s but to no greater success. Viewers didn't care that *Best of the West* (ABC, 1981–1982) was a mockery of TV westerns, and *Zorro and Son* (CBS, April–June 1983, was, of course, an update of the original series and again produced by Disney, as had been the original during 1957–1959. Both failed to make enough of an impression to stay on the programming schedule for long.

Other western variations were simply dead ends. The cowboy ideal had been transplanted overseas to Kenya in the aptly titled *Cowboy in Africa* (ABC, 1967–1968) and, somewhat confusingly, across the Pacific to a ranch on the "the big island" of Hawaii in the aptly titled *Big Hawaii* (NBC, 1977). Perhaps the juxtaposition of the ruralism of *Big Hawaii* and the urbanized world of *Hawaii 5-0* created too much dissonance in the minds of viewers, and the program was canceled after just three months.

And perhaps fortunately, the western science-fiction genre went no further than the headache-inducing *The Secret Empire* (NBC, 1979), in which cowboys discovered a civilization of space aliens living beneath 1880s Cheyenne, Wyoming. Each episode was 20 minutes in length as the program was one-third of the series *Cliff Hangers,* an unsuccessful attempt by the network to revive movie-style serials with cliffhanger endings.

None of the late westerns lasted for long. The western era, like the frontier days before it, had come to an end on television. The lone hero striding down Main Street of a dusty town while wearing his six-shooter and cowboy boots had been replaced by a team of urban, modern detectives.

DETECTIVES

A boom of new detective programs began in 1972, an element of the perception of a rising crime rate and continued unrest in American society that had led, in part, to the reelection of President Richard Nixon on a law-and-order platform that year.

Television detectives during the 1970s were often recognizable by their physical looks and eccentricities—a genre convention that came to characterize detective dramas. Most of them didn't fit the stereotype of the detective as young, handsome, and physically fit, as was Magnum. *Cannon* was a large man in a large Lincoln Continental in Los Angeles. *McCloud* was a cowboy hat-wearing, horse-mounted New Mexico deputy marshal on duty in New York City. *Columbo* was a disheveled genius with a rumpled raincoat and an equally rumpled Peugeot 403 convertible. *Kojak* was bald and licked lollipops. *Quincy* was a medical examiner. And *Barnaby Jones* was, well, old. In *Vega$*, the location was the gimmick.

Many of the programs were titled using the name, or just the surname, of the main character, something that rapidly became a characteristic of the genre. Over the years and across the networks viewers could find male detectives in *McCloud, Cannon, Columbo, Barnaby Jones, Kojak, Magnum P.I., T.J. Hooker, Simon & Simon,* and *Hunter;* women detectives in *Amy Prentiss, Mrs. Columbo,* and *Cagney & Lacey;* and husband-and-wife detective teams in *McMillan and Wife* and *Hart to Hart.* It's worth noting that despite the advancements made by women in the workplace and in politics during the era, several of the program titles continued to define their protagonists as adjuncts of their husbands.

Programs centering on women detectives blossomed to some degree during the 1970s and 1980s as the women's movement began to appear permanent in the eyes of the networks. ABC, the network that carried huge amounts of police-related programming, had an early entry in the now little-known *Honey West* (1965–1966), the first woman private investigator on television (Anne Francis) and the only one with overtones of James Bond. She carried, for example, a radio transmitter disguised as a tube of lipstick, although she was saddled with a spectacularly sexist name that didn't sound all that inappropriate at the time. She was followed, eventually, by *Get Christy Love* (ABC, 1974–1975), a short-lived series but the first, and thus far only, program to follow the exploits of a (beautiful) African-American woman detective (Teresa Graves), and by *Amy Prentiss* (NBC, 1974–1975), a beautiful (of course) thirtysomething widow and chief of detectives (Jessica Walter) in San Francisco. During the same television season, Angie Dickinson starred in the longest-lived example of the woman detective subgenre, *Police Woman* (NBC, 1974–1978), which focused on a (beautiful) undercover officer with the Los Angles Police Department.

Cagney & Lacey (CBS, 1982–1983 and 1984–1988) brought the conventions of the to-that-time exclusively male buddy relationship to television

Sharon Gless and Tyne Daly were Cagney and Lacey
(portrayed in the drama of the same name), two tough
New York City cops, but they shared laughter and tears in
the ladies' room, where they could find privacy. The
message was: Women can be successful in a man's world,
but it's not easy. Courtesy of Photofest.

with its portrayal of female detectives (Sharon Gless and Tyne Daly) who
were both partners and close friends, although the program itself had a
tumultuous history. Several changes to its cast were made as it progressed
from pilot made-for-TV movie in 1981 to regularly scheduled series—three
actresses played the role of Cagney—its feminist orientation was watered
down, it was canceled for a season and at one point a CBS executive gave an
infamous interview in which he said that the title characters were perceived
by the network to be lesbians.

A minor variation on the women detectives theme was the female private investigator program. Prominent among them was *Murder, She Wrote* (CBS, 1984–1996), a program unusual for drawing a decidedly older audience than many police programs, in part because of the age of its star, Angela Lansbury, who was an ancient (in television terms) 59 years old at the time the program began and 71 when it ended production. Her character, Jessica Fletcher, a crime-solving crime novelist, had some similarities to Miss Marple, the famous elderly amateur detective created by Agatha Christie and who had been seen in British movies and on television in the UK. Lansbury was, of course, instantly recognizable to older viewers for her film roles, which included *National Velvet* (1944) and *The Manchurian Candidate* (1962), and extensive television work in dramatic anthologies during the 1950s.

Significantly more male than female private investigators graced prime-time during this time period, of course. The mustachioed *Magnum, P.I.* (Tom Selleck) carried out his investigations in affluent Hawaii on CBS, (1980–1988); the program not only utilized the old *Hawaii 5-0* production facilities that the network had built in order to economize, but also inherited the 5-0 time slot and even included dialogue that made reference to 5-0, a relatively early example of intertextuality—the notion that TV programs make references to other TV programs and to the pop culture in general—in mainstream programming. Magnum was a Navy veteran, too, just as Steve McGarrett had been in 5-0. In an interesting change in the perception of masculinity, Magnum, who was thought of as epitomizing rugged masculinity in the 1980s, is now often derided for looking "too Village People" with his bushy moustache and colorful Hawaiian shirts. At the other end of the spectrum from the glamorous private eye was *Harry-O* (ABC, 1974–1976) played by David Janssen as a world weary detective whose car spent so much time in the shop that he usually traveled by bus.

A sub subgenre of rich PIs also developed. *Hart to Hart* (ABC, 1979–1984) is a typical example, in this case following the adventures of a handsome self-made millionaire (Robert Wagner) and his beautiful freelance journalist wife (Stefanie Powers). The crimes they solved were of the high-class variety and occurred among the jet set, rather the opposite end of the spectrum from its contemporary program, the gritty *Hill Street Blues*. The setting of *Hart to Hart* in the world of the hyper-affluent is as much a reflection of 1980s culture as were the prime-time soap operas *Dallas* and *Dynasty*.

Just as *Get Christy Love* focused on an African-American woman, two programs followed African-American men private investigators, with both premiering in the same month. CBS had *Shaft*, a sanitized version of the famous blaxploitation film about the New York City private eye with a sexy

The star of *Magnum, P.I.*, Tom Selleck certainly
looked the part of a glamorous detective, and the
character he played drove a sporty car and lived
in a stylish bachelor pad, but they were borrowed.
Even more unusual, the hero sometimes had
trouble winning the girls. Courtesy of Photofest.

style, and NBC's *Tenafly* was a more conventional drama about a PI in Los
Angeles. Both programs went on the air in October 1973, both left at the
end of summer 1974, and both were rotating elements of, respectively, the
Tuesday Night CBS Movie and NBC *Wednesday/Tuesday Mystery Movie*.

Young detectives programs also continued during the period 1970–1985,
with perhaps *Starsky and Hutch* (ABC, 1975–1979) being remembered as the
quintessential period young detective entry and as well-remembered for its
famous red-and-white Ford Torino as for its plots or characters, chiefly Det.

Dave Starsky (Paul Michael Glaser), Det. Ken "Hutch" Hutchinson (David Soul) and their snitch, Huggy Bear (Antonio Fargas). *The Streets of San Francisco* (ABC, 1972–1977) was an example of the more traditional police show. An older, wiser detective (Karl Malden) was paired with a newcomer (Michael Douglas).

Rarer than detective programs were the uniformed officer programs, which nonetheless formed a significant subgenre among the large number of police programs that aired during the 1970s. *Adam 12* (NBC, 1968–1975) was a long-lived uniformed officer show that followed two Los Angeles Police Department officers (Martin Milner and Kent McCord) on routine patrol in their black-and-white marked unit. The program, done in the semidocumentary style of *Dragnet*, was produced by Jack Webb and like the right-wing *Dragnet*, its villains tended to be hippies. It was followed by a variation on the same theme, *CHiPs*, which centered on the motorcycle unit of the California Highway Patrol on (NBC, 1977–1983), and was more lighthearted than had been the humorless *Adam 12*. While both programs prominently featured police cars and motorcycles, focus shifted to the black vans and heavy firepower of *S.W.A.T.* (ABC, 1975–1976), a violent program about officers of the Special Weapons and Tactics unit of an unspecified Southern California city. Real-life SWAT teams are said to have been a response to increasing crime in urban areas, and as such it's no surprise that they would appear on television soon after they deployed in real life.

Police sitcoms continued during the 1970–1985 period, as well. Most, like the earlier incarnations, failed to develop audiences, and lasted only for short periods of time. Typical of the short-lived police sitcom was the dreadful *Holmes and YoYo* (ABC, 1976), in which the stock character bumbling detective was teamed with a life-like robotic partner, which resulted in predictable sorts of hilarity. Much more successful, though, was *Barney Miller* (ABC, 1975–1982), the longest-lived police sitcom in prime-time history. Much of the success of the program can be traced to the interaction between its main characters—Capt. Barney Miller (Hal Linden), Det. Phil Fish (Abe Vigoda) and Det. Nick Yemana (Jack Soo)—and their individual, strongly written personalities. Like many programs, *Barney Miller* saw its share of cast changes during its run. Vigoda left the series early in the 1977–1978 season for his spin-off sitcom *Fish* (ABC, 1977–1978), and Soo died in January 1979. His passing was noted with a special farewell episode the following May.

But the two most significant detective programs of the era were noted largely for their visual style: the "gritty and realistic" uniformed officers of *Hill Street Blues* (NBC, 1981–1987) and their polar opposites in many ways, the

The detectives of *Miami Vice*, played by Philip Michael Thomas and Don Johnson, were seen as the ultimate in hip and cool. The colors, the architecture, the music, and the lifestyles of the drug lords were all part of the style created by producer Michael Mann and inspired by the city. Courtesy of Photofest.

über-stylish detectives of *Miami Vice* (NBC, 1984–1989). The programs were produced, respectively, by Steven Bochco, the most successful developer of yuppie-attracting programming, and Michael Mann, who is said to have taken up the challenge of Brandon Tartikoff, then head of programming at NBC, to develop a series around Tartikoff's two-word story concept "MTV cops."

The two programs could not have been more different in the way they looked and felt to viewers. The anonymous urban-blighted city in which *Hill Street* took place and the livery of the patrol cars was authentic except for the phrase "Metro Police" written on their doors—contrasted in every way with the sunny, colorful urban sprawl of *Miami Vice*. Even the detectives looked different. Sonny Crockett (Don Johnson) and Ricardo Tubbs (Philip Michael

Thomas) created a real-world fashion of t-shirts and pastel suits, worn with the sleeves of the jackets rolled up to expose their manly forearms; Capt. Frank Furillo (Daniel J. Travanti) wore the traditional suits that befitted his rank, while the more junior plainclothesmen, such as Lt. Henry Goldblume (Joe Spano) made do with wrinkly white shirts and polyester neckties. Fashion continued its downhill trend through the ranks of *Hill Street*, ending with the paramilitary uniforms of Lt. Howard Hunter (James B. Sikking), commander of the precinct SWAT team, and the Goodwill-castoffs of Det. Mick Belker (Bruce Weiz), an unkempt undercover officer prone to calling the people he arrested by the colorful nicknames "dirtbag" and "dog-breath."

ANTHOLOGIES

For all intents and purposes, dramatic anthologies no longer existed during the 1970–1985 time period. Focus at the networks for long-form programs had fully switched to Hollywood films and made-for-television movies. Only a handful of anthologies were tried and none lasted for more than three years. NBC attempted two supernatural-themed programs, the Rod Serling produced *Night Gallery* 1970–1973, a sort of updating of *The Twilight Zone* for the 1970s, and the much less successful *Ghost Story*, aka *Circle of Fear*, (1972–1973).

The comedy anthology format was revived, again by ABC, in *The Love Boat* (1977–1985). Similar to the earlier *Love, American Style*, the focus of *The Love Boat* was on romance, but set this time aboard a cruise ship, and it too featured large numbers of easily recognizable guest stars from film and television. The humor was often broad and sometimes verged on the silly, something typical of sitcoms of the time period; for example, the actor Gavin MacLeod played both Merrill Stubing, the balding captain of the love boat, and his womanizing, toupée-wearing brother, Marshall.

Fantasy Island (ABC, 1978–1984) used the same structure—a cast of regulars, a recurring setting, a flock of recognizable guest stars, and storylines that lasted only one episode. The difference was that the program took place on a tropical island where dreams came true—but not always in the way the dreamer had hoped. The host was Mr. Roarke (Ricardo Montalban), with Herve Villechaize and later Christopher Hewitt as his assistant.

Two rather more unclassifiable anthologies had short appearances on the network schedule during the 1970s, and both should not be confused with reality programs despite titles that sound like nonfiction. *What Really Happened to the Class of '65?* (NBC, 1977–1978) looked at the lives of a high school graduating class of 1965 a dozen years after the fact; it was based on a book of the same title. *Lottery* (ABC, 1983–1984) was a program about everyday folks who are the recipients of a $1 million prize and how the money affects them. (Yes, it does sound a lot like *The Millionaire,* the series from the 1950s.)

The final network attempts at anthologies all began during the 1985–1986 television season. *Amazing Stories* (NBC, 1985–1987) was a throwback, at least in title, to the pulp magazines of the 1930s. Its 30-minute stories were directed by some of the biggest names in Hollywood, such as Steven Spielberg, who also produced the program, Clint Eastwood and Martin Scorsese. *The George Burns Comedy Week* (CBS, 1985) was hosted by the ancient George Burns, but the program was not a great success, and CBS had little better luck with its 1985–1986 revival of *The Twilight Zone.*

MUSIC PROGRAMS

Virtually no prime-time programming specifically focused on popular music on any of the three networks after 1970. Pop music artists appeared on the few remaining variety programs, while the networks made only sporadic attempts at doing anything harder; for example, *Dick Clark Presents the Rock and Roll Years* (ABC, 1973–1974), a collection of archival material from the 1950s, 1960s, and 1970s, was less than a success, despite its attempt to capitalize on the wave of nostalgia that followed *American Graffiti* and *Happy Days.* One exception was *The Sonny and Cher Comedy Hour* (CBS, 1971–1977), which included both music and comic elements like most variety shows. He was short and funny, the perfect foil for her insults. The program ended when the marriage between the two stars ended. And *The Flip Wilson Show* (NBC, 1970–1974) also emphasized the comedy and downplayed the music. He was most famous for his glittery character, Geraldine, who was brash and mouthy.

Instead, music programming moved to late nights, with programs such as *The Midnight Special* (NBC, 1973–1981), which had considerable success after *The Tonight Show* on Fridays. However, in 1981 the music environment on television was forever changed when MTV made its debut on cable and set about providing round-the-clock music videos, something the networks couldn't match. And while MTV's first video, "Video Killed the Radio Stars," didn't quite presage the future, the cable network did drive youth-oriented pop music almost entirely off the prime-time network television schedule.

Country Music/Variety Shows

A second wave of countrified music and humor variety programs came along at the turn of the 1970s, all but replacing the musical variety shows that had long traded on the nonrock genre of music known as standards. They were part of a revival and expansion of country music that included musicians such as Ray Charles recording country albums.

The Glen Campbell Goodtime Hour (CBS, 1969–1972) featured the popular singer, who would today be called a crossover artist for his appeal to both country and pop music fans. *Hee Haw* (CBS, 1969–1971), with its combination of well-known country musicians, flamboyantly hick jokes and busty young women, became a major success in first-run syndication after it left the network, staying in production until 1993. A bit more toward the hardcore end of the country spectrum was *The Jerry Reed When You're Hot You're Hot Hour* (CBS summer 1972), hosted by Jerry Reed and titled after his song. The appeal of country music was such that even one of Frank Sinatra's urban Rat Pack of the 1950s got in on the act, via *Dean Martin Presents Music Country* (NBC, summer 1973), a replacement for Dino's long-running variety program, *The Dean Martin Show* (NBC, 1965–1974).

A handful of country variety programs continued into the 1980s. The two best known, *Barbara Mandrell & The Mandrell Sisters* (NBC, 1980–1982) and *Nashville Palace* (NBC, 1981–1982), which originated from Opryland, emphasized the mainstream country music that's come to be called the Nashville sound. The former program concentrated, of course, on Barbara, Louise, and Irlene Mandrell; Barbara was a major star with a significant following at the time. The latter show featured country music and country comedy from a number of performers and guests.

But, as had happened with rock music and MTV, country largely moved out of prime-time network programming and into cable-delivered music videos and niche programs with the independent debuts of Country Music Television (CMT) and The Nashville Network in 1983.

SPORTS

In 1970, *Monday Night Football* came to ABC. Producer Roone Arledge realized that if professional football moved into a traditional family entertainment night, the program would have to appeal at least somewhat to women. To add to the fun, he used "Dandy" Don Meredith and Howard Cosell to provide color analysis. The banter between the cowboy and the New York City lawyer was frequently more interesting than the game.

Arledge also brought his magic touch to the Olympics. In 1964, 1968, 1972, and 1976, ABC covered the events in a style that lured viewers into watching sports they didn't even know existed. The human side of the athletes was portrayed; drama was added; the production was lavish, with cameras everywhere. The most famous was the 1972 Olympics in Munich. Israeli athletes were held hostage and killed. ABC turned its sports reporters into news reporters and covered the tense situation thoroughly.

But sports have always been a part of prime-time. Wrestling and boxing still appear on the networks and have a long history of attracting audiences and stirring up controversy. Special events like the World Series, Super Bowl, and Olympics are now used by programmers not only to sell advertising, but also to promote their own shows.

T AND A

Given that prime-time network television exists in something of a time lag behind changes in American culture—slang, for example, is far out of date by the time it's heard on TV—it should come as no surprise that the vaunted sexual revolution of the late 1960s didn't really arrive on TV until the mid-1970s, the period of time that gave birth to what has come to be known, rather rudely, as "T and A" (tits and ass) programs in which leering at the bodies of actresses was as important a part of the program as was following its plot, if not more so.

This is not to say, of course, that what quaintly used to be called the physical attributes of women were not part of programming before the 1970s. Like the movies, television has always favored a pretty face and curvy figure, and early programs such as *Girl about Town* (NBC, 1948–1949) were built around the youthful good looks of young women, in this case singer Kyle MacDonnell, as she gallivanted around New York City. A number of fashion programs were also to be found—among them the simultaneous *Fashions on Parade* on DuMont and *The Fashion Story* on ABC (1948–1949)—that highlighted not only the latest in urban couture but, unavoidably, the bodies of the models inside the couture as well.

Other programs were more overtly focused on the bodies of their stars. Dagmar (aka Jennie Lewis, but born Virginia Ruth Egnor), one of many busty blondes in contemporary movies and television, was as well known for her chest as for anything else; legend has it that the breast-shaped protuberances on the front bumpers of Cadillacs in the 1950s were called "dagmars" by stylists. Although her television career was rather brief—and tended to be during late nights, which raises the question of whether she was considered too hot for prime-time—her looks resulted in her role as a regular performer on the combination variety/talk show *Broadway Open House* (NBC, 1950–1951). She later hosted the late-night *Dagmar's Canteen*, a variety program catering to Korean War era military personnel, on NBC in 1952, and still later was a panelist during the 1955–1956 season on the long running quiz/panel program *Masquerade Party* (NBC, CBS, and ABC, 1952–1960).

Both Ginger and Mary Anne were the object of the sexual desires of male viewers of the sitcom *Gilligan's Island* (CBS, 1964–1967). So influential on the libido of young men were they that the magazine *Men's Health* in the late 1990s polled its Baby Boomer readers about their lasting preferences for the sophisticated sexual allure of Ginger or the girl-next-door sexiness of Mary Anne (Mary Anne won). Toward the end of the 1960s, *Rowan & Martin's Laugh-In* (NBC, 1968–1973) prominently featured go-go dancers in bikinis, among them Goldie Hawn, who went on to a movie career in which at least some of her appeal was based on her slim good looks and perennially youthful appearance.

The 1977–1978 prime-time season has been called "the season of sex," and it was during that season that sexual innuendo was found across the board at ABC, the network with the greatest appeal to the tastes of the valuable younger demographics. Its sitcom *Soap* (1977–1981), a satire of soap operas, had swirling about it a virtual storm of the sort of network-fueled controversy that draws in curious viewers. ABC called *Soap*'s sexual themes a major breakthrough in television comedy (a much overused term) and as a result the network received 32,000 letters about the show before it ever aired, all but nine of which were in opposition to it.[9] But the program had enough of an audience to last for four seasons and, if for no other reason, is memorable as having one of the first openly gay characters in prime-time, Jodie Dallas (played by the then virtually unknown Billy Crystal).

Charlie's Angels (ABC, 1976–1981) was part and parcel of the mostly heterosexual season of sex. Ostensibly an action-adventure program about three female private investigators who worked for the unseen Charlie (viewers only heard his voice), the program's focus was on the bodies of its stars—Kate Jackson, Jaclyn Smith, and Farrah Fawcett-Majors—who frequently appeared in minimal dress. Their investigations inevitably required them to work undercover (perhaps "uncovered" is a better term) near swimming pools and in bikinis.

The promotion of its stars, particularly Fawcett-Majors, is as well remembered as the program itself. She became a household name, if not image, with the release of a poster of her in a crimson maillot, with visibly erect nipples and flashing the by-then famous smile that showed all 32 teeth. The poster led to a mass marketing campaign that splashed Fawcett-Majors's image seemingly everywhere, which in turn prompted her to attempt to break her contract with the show in favor of a career on the big screen.

Lawsuits followed, of course, at the end of which she agreed to make a number of guest appearances on the program. Her absence from the show required new Angels to come aboard, and the program eventually cycled through six actresses in the three main roles during its five years on the prime-time schedule. Fawcett-Majors' film career never really developed, although she still appears on television some 30 years after she left *Charlie's Angels*, albeit in odd reality programs that reflect her diminished celebrity and under the name Farrah Fawcett, having shed the hyphenated Majors after her divorce from actor Lee Majors of *The Six Million Dollar Man*.

ABC continued its "jiggle" programming in the form of the sitcom *Three's Company* (1977–1984). The premise of the show was the sort that made sense in the skewed world of sitcoms: Jack Tripper (John Ritter) could live platonically with roommates Chrissy Snow (Suzanne Somers) and Janet Wood (Joyce DeWitt) only if he pretended to be gay. The humor, such as it was, centered on innuendo and double-entendres, and Somers, in the same vein as Farrah Fawcett-Majors, was promoted as a major network sex symbol.

There were other parallels between the careers of Somers and Fawcett-Majors, as well. Somers had her own widely distributed poster, on which she wore a black one-piece swimsuit while bending over at the waist. Her growing—but as it turned out, temporary—fame saw her leave the program after four of its seven seasons, although rather than quitting, as Fawcett-Majors had done, she was slowly written out of the show when her salary demands weren't met by the producers. And, like Fawcett-Majors, Somers's career would go into decline after her disappearance from regularly scheduled prime-time programming. She gained some amount of fame by promoting the Thighmaster exerciser during the 1990s and can currently be found hawking cosmetics on cable shopping channels.

At its prime, though, *Three's Company* was of such cultural interest that it was featured on the cover of *Newsweek* magazine in February 1978, and it no doubt generated repeat viewings of the film *American Graffiti*, which had featured Somers in fleeting shots as the Thunderbird-driving mystery woman and object of the desires of young Richard Dreyfuss.

DOCUMENTARIES AND PUBLIC AFFAIRS

By the 1970s, the number of documentary and public affairs programs had dropped off significantly. Advertisers by this time had again become powerful and they shied away from sponsoring hard-hitting investigative-style news programs. And both ABC and NBC had learned the difficulty of trying to compete with *60 Minutes:* Programs at both networks that tried to ape the successful *60 Minutes* magazine format routinely died early deaths in the ratings, although ABC's *20/20*, which first aired in June 1978, was the most successful of the clones and still airs at this writing.

Connoisseurs of newsmagazines point out, however, that *20/20* was more tabloid-like and more sensational than the staid *60 Minutes*. *20/20* was anchored by television news mainstays Hugh Downs, who had been part of the *Today* show for years, and Barbara Walters, and correspondents included the mustachioed investigative reporter Geraldo Rivera who went on to become as much a media celebrity as the people he interviewed. He is perhaps as well known for his later career, during which his nose was broken in a fight that broke out during a discussion he was leading, and for revealing on live television that the contents of 1930s gangster Al Capone's "secret vault" consisted mostly of dirt, as he is for any of his actual reporting.

60 Minutes also proved to be significant outside the narrow limits of television history, as the program was at the heart of two important legal cases that helped shape the rules under which journalists operate. In 1973 the program had aired a report that said that a Col. Anthony Herbert had made false allegations that Americans had committed atrocities during the Vietnam War. Herbert brought a libel suit that named *60 Minutes* anchor Mike Wallace and producer Barry Llando, and in the course of the proceedings the U.S. Supreme Court ruled that in some circumstances journalists could be compelled in libel cases to explain their thought processes, something that had never before happened.

Gen. William Westmoreland, who had command of U.S. forces between 1965 and 1968, during the height of the Vietnam War, filed a libel suit against CBS in 1983 over a *60 Minutes* report that he said defamed him. The report claimed that he was part of a conspiracy that understated the strength of the North Vietnamese Army. The legal issue was whether or not the researcher who gathered the information upon which the allegation was made could be considered to be a journalist or not.

Then, as would be the case time and again, the growing power of cable became a factor in the decline of documentary-style programming on the traditional, over-the-air television networks that over the years had come to an increased reliance on fiction prime-time programming. CNN began airing informational and documentary programming in 1980, and the earliest of the nationally distributed cable networks, such as The History Channel and The Learning Channel, featured enormous amounts of documentary and informational programming in a form that would in time come to be called "infotainment."

MOVIES ON TELEVISION

The broadcast of movies on television reached its peak in 1973, when the big three networks programmed 19.5 hours of movies per week, of which some 6.5 hours were dedicated to made-for-television movies. ABC and NBC took the lead in the production and broadcast of made-for-television movies, with CBS lagging somewhat behind. During 1973, the peak year for made-for-television movies in terms of time devoted to them, NBC ran made-fors in both its *Sunday* and *Wednesday Mystery Movie*s series, while ABC did the same in its competing *Tuesday* and *Wednesday Movie of the Week* series. CBS completed the overlapping pattern of competition in its made-for-TV *Tuesday Night CBS Movie*.

As a whole, the television movie schedule during 1973 was a combination of theatrical films and made-for-television movie series and was indicative of the importance of movies to contemporary viewers. The *ABC Sunday Night Movie* went head-to-head with the *NBC Mystery Movie*, the *NBC Monday Night Movie* was counterprogrammed against *Monday Night Football on ABC*—a strategy that began in 1970 and continued through 1996—and the *ABC Tuesday Movie of the Week* overlapped its final hour with the first hour of the *Tuesday Night CBS Movie*, forcing viewers to choose one or the other in those pre-VCR days. The *ABC Wednesday Movie of the Week* aired opposite the *NBC Mystery Movie on Wednesdays*. The end of the week offered less direct competition as the *CBS Thursday Night Movie* and the *CBS Friday Night Movie* were opposed by sitcoms and dramas. The networks returned to their overlapping strategy on Saturdays, though, when the *NBC Saturday Night Movie* started 30 minutes after the start of the *ABC Suspense Movie*.

However, viewers' tastes seemed to have changed during the 1970s, in part because of VCRs and easily rented movies on videocassette, which not only eliminated pesky commercial interruptions but had the added benefit of allowing movies not suitable for television to be viewed, including pornographic films. After their 1973 peak, the number of hours of movies on the networks trickled away, falling to 10 or 12 hours per week during the 1980s as VCRs spread into more and more homes.

But at its height, the demand for movies on television was such that by 1971 NBC began packaging 90-minute episodes of mystery programs under the umbrella title *NBC Mystery Movie*. During that season, episodes of *Columbo*, *McCloud*, and *McMillan and Wife* rotated through the Wednesday 8:30 P.M. to 10:00 P.M. slot. Each of the programs was produced in 90-minute format instead of the more usual 60-minute length for dramas, and in effect they bridged dramas and made-for-television movies, at least in terms of length of time.

During the 1970s, the made-for-television movie genre came into its own, becoming the equivalent of the B films of the Hollywood studio era—that is, low budget, churned out in large number, and covering a vast array of topics. Although space doesn't permit a detailed examination of the hundreds of television movies made during the 1970s, the following should give a feel for the range of topics the movies covered.

A number of made-for-TV movies were pilots for proposed series, both those that failed and those that succeeded. As such, they bridged all the television genres that viewers had become familiar with. *Human Feelings* (NBC, October 1978) is an example of a failed pilot, in this case a sitcom, complete with laugh track, which starred Nancy Walker as God. *Starsky and Hutch,* on the other hand, successfully made the transition from made-for-TV movie in April 1975 to ABC series.

Historical recreations were made; for example *The Disappearance of Aimee* (NBC, November 1976), which dealt with the 1926 disappearance of evangelist Aimee Semple McPhearson, with Faye Dunaway in the lead role. *Billy: Portrait of a Street Kid* (CBS, September 1977) was a topical drama about an inner-city boy trying to get himself off the mean streets; it was based on the book *Peoples* by Robert C. S. Downs and starred LeVar Burton (of *Roots* fame) and veteran actor Ossie Davis. Crime, of course, was a major subject, and among the dozens, if not hundreds, of crime movies is *Linda* (ABC, November 1973), in which an unfaithful wife (Stella Stevens) not only kills her lover's wife, but tries to frame her own husband for the murder. It is with little exaggeration that one can say that every other topic deemed suitable for television, and some that were questionable, was the subject of a made-for-TV movie at some time during the 1970s.

Like the Hollywood B-films before them, made-for-TV movies were frequently exploitative. Young Linda Blair, fresh off the success of *The Exorcist,* starred in the infamous *Born Innocent* (NBC, September 1974), a movie in which her character, a runaway chucked into a reformatory, was sexually assaulted by the other girls with the handle of a mop. The network was sued as the result of a copycat real-life incident, but a court in 1978 found that as NBC had not incited the assault, the movie, however tasteless, was protected under the First Amendment. The scene was excised from later showings of the movie, though. Blair's follow up to *Born Innocent* was the self-explanatory *Sarah T.—Portrait of a Teenaged Alcoholic* (NBC, February 1975), a movie similar in content, but with the genders reversed, to the other major teenage alcoholic tale of *The Boy Who Drank Too Much* (CBS, February 1980) with Scott Baio of *Happy Days.* The depths of exploitation were perhaps reached by *Intimate Agony* (ABC, March 1983), about doctors coping with a herpes outbreak in a resort community. It was originally, and notoriously, titled *Lovesick: The Herpes Story.*

Some of the exploitative made-for-TV movies of the era had considerable success. *Little Ladies of the Night,* which focused on a teenaged prostitute played by Linda Purl, drew 53 percent of the viewing audience when it aired on ABC in January 1977. *Dallas Cowboys Cheerleaders* (ABC, January 1979) was a fictionalized behind-the-scenes tale of a reporter (Jane Seymour) who dons the skimpy uniform while working undercover to research an exposé. The cheerleaders played themselves, much T and A was on display, and it was, not surprisingly, the highest-rated made-for-TV movie of the 1978–1979 season.

To be fair, though, other made-for-TV movies were more serious in nature, and several came close to the kind of "quality" television usually associated with the Golden Age of the 1950s. The thoughtful, though sentimental, *Brian's Song* (ABC, November 1971) dealt with the terminal illness of Chicago Bears football player Brian Piccolo and was one of the 10 most popular movies of any type shown on television at the time, drawing an audience that comprised 48 percent of everyone watching TV the night it was on. The audience was so large that when the movie became a theatrical release, it failed because so many people had already seen it.[10] The success of *Brian's Song* sparked a raft of inferior imitators—as is typical of any success in TV—as a large grouping of movies known generically as "disease of the week" movies were made during the 1980s. That *Brian's Song* was still playing in 2005 on cable, 34 years after it was first shown, is an indication of either the movie's enduring status or, more cynically, the insatiable need of cable for programming.

The producers of made-for-TV movies didn't shrink from the examination of various topics, although the line between exploitation and serious examination is sometimes faintly drawn, as many movies combined elements of both. *The Day After* (NBC, November 1983), for example, was a critically acclaimed examination of the horrors that could be expected after a nuclear attack, while *The Burning Bed* (NBC, October 1984) dramatized a real-life case in which a woman had immolated her abusive husband. Both movies drew huge audiences. *The Day After*—the second most highly rated movie shown on television, after the 1976 showing of *Gone with the Wind*—was seen by 62 percent of the viewing audience, an estimated 100 million people, and *The Burning Bed,* number 17 on the list of highest-rated movies on TV, by 52 percent. Viewers tuned in to see Farrah Fawcett in a role quite different from her portrayal of the glamorous Jill Monroe in *Charlie's Angels,* and part of the voyeuristic, guilty thrill, no doubt, was to look on as Fawcett was menaced and brutalized.

The constant demand for programming, when combined with network conservatism and the desire to stick with a sure thing, and with a certain amount of audience nostalgia, inevitably led to the production of made-for-television movies based on series that had been popular in years, or even decades, past. As a result, cast reunion movies, in which as many as possible of the original cast members of a program were brought together, were made and aired to often surprisingly high ratings. Sitcoms figured prominently in this category, with, for example, *Still the Beaver* reuniting the cast of *Leave It to Beaver* in March 1983 and becoming the pilot for *The New Leave It to Beaver,* which eventually ran on the Disney Channel and cable superstation WTBS during 1985–1989. Other reunions failed to turn into new series, as exemplified by the three *Gilligan's Island* reunion movies, the last of which carried the largely self-explanatory title *The Harlem Globetrotters on Gilligan's Island* in May 1981. What the title failed to mention, however, is that the inevitable basketball game pits the Globetrotters and the castaways against a team of evil robots controlled by a mad scientist. One can only ask "why?"

The most popular of the reunion movies, both in terms of ratings and sheer number, are the 26 *Perry Mason* made-for-TV movies. Beginning with *Perry Mason Returns* (NBC, December 1985), the top-rated made-for-television movie of the 1985–1986 season, the movies reunited Raymond Burr and Barbara Hale in their roles as attorney Mason and ever-faithful legal secretary Della Street from the series of 1957–1966. The movies are a rare example of a successful revival of a program from the past, and perhaps more would have been made had Burr not died in 1993. The last movie in the series aired in November that year.

MINISERIES

The miniseries was a phenomenon of the 1970s, and combined elements of soap operas, long-form television programs and made-for-TV movies. They represented a rare, and expensive, departure from the norm for network programmers in that their form did not follow the usual 30-minute or one-hour episodes, and all the episodes aired close together in time instead of being spread out across a full season. However, they had one distinct advantage—if the miniseries tanked in the ratings, at least it was over and done with in a hurry.

By far the most successful of all the miniseries was *Roots*, which transcended the popularity of even the highly rated television blockbusters and became a full-fledged cultural phenomenon. It was based on the Alex Haley novel of the same title, and aired in four two-hour segments and four one-hour segments, 12 hours in total, but broadcast all in one week, January 23–30, 1977, on ABC. It told the intertwined stories of Haley's ancestors and the slave trade from eighteenth-century Gambia through the end of the American Civil War, focusing much of its attention on Kunte Kinte (played as a child by LeVar Burton and as an adult by John Amos), the Haley ancestor who had been enslaved and transported to America, and his immediate descendants.

After starting slowly, its audience rapidly grew as newspaper editorials, educational programs, and word of mouth publicized it, and its concluding episode had the largest audience of any dramatic program in television history, an estimated 100 million viewers or nearly half the population of the United States. *Roots* was nominated for a record 37 Emmy Awards and won seven for the members of its enormous cast, which included, of course, a large number of prominent African-American actors, and its huge production crew.

The original *Roots* was followed by the less popular *Roots: The Next Generations*, a 14-hour miniseries than aired over seven days on ABC in February 1979, and which continued the story begun in *Roots* into the civil rights era of the 1960s. Both were produced by David L. Wolper, who had made a name for himself as the premier producer of docudramas, which are characterized by their mixture of fact and fiction into a plausible, realistic whole.[11]

The other major miniseries of the time was *North and South*, a six-episode, 12-hour dramatization of the hugely popular John Jakes novel that had the same title. It was another David L. Wolper production and aired, again, on ABC in early November 1985. It told the story of the lives of two families in the two decades before the Civil War and, like *Roots*, had a huge cast, which in this case included famous guest stars in relatively minor roles, including Elizabeth Taylor in a rare TV appearance and 1950s musicals' mainstay Gene Kelly. *North and South Book II* followed the original in May 1986, a rare same-season sequel, filmed immediately after *North and South*, which picked up the story as the Civil War got underway. Like the original, it was shown in six two-hour episodes. It was based on the Jakes novel *Love and War*, the sequel to the novel *North and South*.

CONCLUSION

Programming again changed during the 1970s and 1980s. A new class of sitcoms, featuring independent, liberated women in the work environment pushed aside the older family-friendly sitcoms. But at the same time, "jiggle" programs, in which the bodies of young actresses were the focus, existed and drew significant attention. Perhaps the liberation of women was complicated after all. Programmers tried to make their shows relevant to attract audiences, but up-to-date issues tended to be controversial and repel advertisers.

The power of the networks came into question during the 1970s and 1980s, and efforts to corral them were made. The PTAR took a half-hour of prime-time away from the networks and turned it over to TV stations, which promptly filled the time with cheap syndicated game shows and network reruns. The plan had been for them to produce shows of interest to their local audiences, but it didn't work out that way. More investigations into the link between watching television violence and violent behavior were made, but the same old conclusion—that violence affects some people some of the time in some way—was arrived at again.

By the end of the time period, cable was spreading across the country. People who had previously been counted as viewers of the Big Three networks began to watch an increasing number of cable networks that were more specifically targeted to niche audiences with particular, and sometimes narrow, interests. Moreover, viewers were watching programs they'd taped on VCRs, which were soon to be found in almost every American home. Could the networks develop a strategy to hold onto their old customers and attract the younger viewers?

CHAPTER 7

Changes in Competition (1985–1995)

The heroes of the 1980s were frequently captains of corporations. They led their companies into mega-mergers and earned stockholders impressive profits on an annual basis. Companies' frantic effort to expand into as many fields as possible and to grow profits quickly spread into the television business.

NETWORKS

The first to succumb was ABC in 1985. A relatively small company, Capital Cities Communications, owned several television stations. It took over the network and introduced a new regime of cutting costs, emphasizing profit, and laying off employees seen as unnecessary. Next in line was NBC, owned by RCA, a telecommunications company. It was purchased by General Electric in 1986. The peacock network underwent the "lean and mean" treatment.

Finally, CBS looked over its shoulder and saw Ted Turner approaching. He attempted to buy the network, but its board of directors felt that he was unacceptable as the head of a major broadcast network. He had done well as a station owner, taking WTBS in Atlanta from an independent station to the first national "superstation" on cable and had started up several cable networks including CNN, but his brash style didn't appeal to the people who saw themselves as leaders of the elite network.

They responded by borrowing money from the company of hotel magnate, Lawrence Tisch, to buy up CBS shares and keep them out of Turner's hands. The strategy worked in that Turner didn't get the network—but Tisch did and in 1986 became the new leader of CBS. Again, he introduced new measures to trim staff and expenses. The department in all three networks that most bitterly resented the changes was news. Covering major events around the world was an expensive business, but the networks had traditionally looked at the cost as necessary for building prestige and serving in the public interest, as required by the Communications Act of 1934. Now, news was told to be a profit center. The result was fewer reporters, especially on the international scene, and more justification for each dollar spent.

Of course, the penny-pinching also affected programming, but the costs of the producers were going up, and they were naturally reluctant to accept lower prices. Writers went on strike in 1988, hoping to get some of the profits from videocassettes and international sales, and succeeded in most of their demands. But then the networks cut back on the number of original episodes they were willing to buy and were quicker to cancel series that failed to win ratings immediately. The major effect of all these developments was an unwillingness to experiment with more expensive genres like science fiction and an increase in cheaper genres like reality shows and news magazines.

It might have seemed logical for the three broadcast networks to join the corporate fashion for vertical integration, in which one company controlled all of the steps involved in manufacturing, distributing, and selling a product. The networks already distributed programming and owned a few stations for displaying it, called O&Os (for owned and operated). But the Federal Communications Commission at that time limited the number of stations that any one entity could own. In 1985, the FCC had raised the limit from 7 VHF stations to 12.

As for the production of programs, the major film studios were still dominant, with a few independent studios as exceptions. The FCC and the Justice Department said the networks could own only a small percentage of the programs in prime-time. Furthermore, the networks were restrained by the FCC's financial interest/syndication rule ("fin/syn") from participating in syndication in the United States. Since selling reruns to stations was the most profitable aspect of programming, the networks had little motive to produce programs. After all, they could buy a series for less than the cost of making it, because the studios were hoping to make their profits in syndication. The average one-hour show cost $1.2 million to produce, and the networks paid $800,000 for it except if they were renewing a contract for a hit series, a situation in which the producer had more leverage and could command more money.

The three broadcast networks for decades had been run as profitable businesses with a tradition of noblesse oblige inspired by government regulation. Now they had new ownership with new expectations of making profits and public service was a lower priority. Then, to add more confusion to the scene, a new competitor arrived. Fourth networks had appeared before—DuMont in the 1950s, United in the 1960s, Paramount in the 1970s, and Metromedia in the early 1980s—but they had all failed within days, except for DuMont. Since the FCC had assigned to most cities only three VHF channels, only three national networks could survive. The alternative was to rely on UHF, but its signal was more difficult for television antennas to receive, and picture quality was poor, with grainy images and ghosts. But by 1985, cable had spread nationwide, and TV sets connected to cable received VHF and UHF signals equally well.

Rupert Murdoch, the media baron from Australia, saw an opportunity. He bought a studio, 20th Century Fox, to help produce programs. (Because of the FCC's interpretation of the rules, his fledgling network would not be subject to the same regulatory restrictions as the traditional Big Three.) He purchased a bundle of television stations in major cities across the United States. Then, he lined up affiliates from independent stations in other cities. That was an important step in creating a network—making sure he had enough affiliates to bring in the number of viewers needed to ensure large advertising revenues.

The next step was creating programming. He hired a former film studio executive, Barry Diller, to head up his new network. The Fox strategy was to offer series that appealed to a young audience, ages 18 to 34 years, the people, executives believed, who were most likely to experiment with a new network. And to attract that audience, programs with an edge were needed, but who would make them?

In the eyes of a network, two of the most desirable qualities of a producer are the ability to stay on schedule and within budget. The logical assumption is that experience is the best teacher of these skills. Fox wanted successful producers on their team, but the other networks were competing for the same pool of talented, experienced people. As incentives, the new network encouraged creativity and promised less interference. Furthermore, Fox was willing to make commitments for more episodes; a show would be given a chance for the audience to find it on the schedule. The older networks would sometimes commit to only six episodes, then cancel.[1]

The first programming deal was struck with Disney for a half-hour sitcom, *Down and Out in Beverly Hills* (April–September 1987), based on a film of the same name. In the early days, the network frequently settled for a written or verbal proposal or a scene from the show acted on a stage since it couldn't afford to pay for a pilot.

Next the network went to film director/producer, James Brooks, who had been a driving force behind *Taxi*, a critically acclaimed sitcom on ABC. He developed *The Tracey Ullman Show* (1987–1990), a comedy-variety half-hour hosted by the British comedienne. One element of the program was a short cartoon about a family named the Simpsons, which was spun off into a successful series that from time to time pokes fun at both the Fox network and Murdoch himself.

Another early commitment was to Michael Moye and Ron Leavitt, formerly of *The Jeffersons*. They teamed with Embassy Communication to produce a series that was originally titled *Not the Cosby Show* in its formative period, but came to be called *Married . . . with Children*.

Fox decided to go after Stephen Cannell, who had been behind *The A-Team*. The Prime-Time Access Rule permitted the traditional networks to offer only children's programming and news from 7 P.M. to 8 P.M. EST on Sundays. It made sense for Fox to counterprogram with a show aimed at teens and young adults. *21 Jump Street* (1987–1990), starring Johnny Depp as a detective on undercover duty in urban high schools, was the result.[2]

The network's strategy of attracting young people with creatively interesting series sometimes worked, but ingrained viewing patterns change slowly. The network took a stab at instant success with *Monday Night Football*. Fox offered $384 million to the National Football League, and ABC countered with a deal that was equally lucrative. The team owners, worried that some of the Fox affiliates had a weak signal, decided to stay with ABC, where they had been since 1970.

Fox debuted with a late-night show starring Joan Rivers and followed up with two nights of prime-time programming in 1987, Sunday from 7 P.M. to 10 P.M. ET and later Saturday from 8 P.M. to 10 P.M. Many of the shows failed miserably—for example, viewers found not much funny in the sitcom *Women in Prison*—as did their replacements. But fortunately, Murdoch had deep pockets and an iron will. He expanded the number of nights Fox was on the air, adding Mondays, 1989; Thursdays and Fridays, 1990; Wednesdays, 1992 and Tuesdays, 1993, all during the valuable prime-time hours of 8 P.M. to 10 P.M.

The addition of a new network had an interesting effect on the relationship between other affiliated TV stations and their networks. Fox continued to buy stations, including some that had previously been affiliated with other networks. The Big Three found that they had to compete with the newcomer by offering their own affiliates more compensatory money and better affiliation contracts. And when a group of CBS's more important affiliates were sold to Fox, the old network lost ratings and the new one gained.

In the early 1980s, thanks to cable, independent stations (i.e., with no network affiliations) had increased in numbers "from 120 in 1980 to nearly 300 in 1988"[3] and were seeing their ratings increase. They were nibbling away at the ratings and revenues of the traditional stations by offering movies, sports, and an endless supply of reruns. When the Fox network debuted, many of these stations became affiliates of it, and as Fox expanded the number of nights it offered programming, these stations found themselves looking more like network affiliates than independent stations.

The 1985–1995 period was a time of growth and retrenchment. Networks faced more competition and were required to make greater profits. The producers faced equal pressures to be profitable. The effect on programming was the creation of some successful series, some interesting experiments, and the usual number of failures.

SITCOMS

Critics and industry observers declared the death of the situation comedy in the early 1980s. Old favorites seemed to lose their audiences, and new shows suffered a high rate of mortality. But a new sitcom, *The Cosby Show*, premiered in 1984 and proved everybody wrong. The situation comedies that followed included some of the best-written and best-acted of the all-time favorite sitcoms.

Family

The tradition of the family sitcom was upheld by *Growing Pains* (ABC, 1985–1992). Dad (Alan Thicke) was a psychiatrist and Mom (Joanna Kerns) was a TV reporter, but they shared the usual quips with their kids and survived the usual dilemmas, and when the children aged, a new baby was added to the household.

Home Improvement (ABC, 1991–1999) starred stand-up comedian Tim Allen as the father of three sons with a wife (Patricia Richardson) who frequently ran out of patience with her household of boys. It was clearly a descendant of the traditional 1950s-style sitcoms with a patient Mom, cutely aggravating children, and a lovable but doltish husband. It was also one of several programs over the years to be about television, as Allen's character, Tim Taylor, was the host of a TV home-improvement show.

Perhaps the purest of the family sitcoms was *The Wonder Years* (ABC, 1988–1993). The characters, both adult and children, seemed to have more depth than found in most series. The gentle plots dealt with the foibles and joys of family life and sometimes presented an ambiguous world where good and evil could not always be easily separated by the child, Kevin

The concept of many modern sitcoms began as routines by stand-up comedians. Tim Allen created a bumbling, well meaning man whose love of tools was never understood by his wife. For *Home Improvement*, he and Richard Karn (on the left) were hosts of a do-it-yourself program. Courtesy of Photofest.

Arnold (Fred Savage), who narrated the program from the viewpoint of a reminiscing adult.

A familiar variation was *Fresh Prince of Bel Air* (NBC, 1990–1996), the story of a street-smart teenaged boy (Will Smith) taken in by his wealthy West Coast relatives. Smith went on to a career in music and film. *Family Matters* (ABC, 1989–1998) began with the usual setup of dad, mom, kids, and in-laws. But a minor character won the attention of the audience: Steve Urkel (Jaleel White), a friend of the family. He was a scrawny kid with huge eyeglasses and old-man trousers hiked up to just under his armpits. Later episodes focused on Urkel and the father of the family. Margaret Cho introduced viewers to the problems of an *All-American Girl* (ABC, 1994–1995) trying to deal with her parents who maintained many of the traditions of Korea. And there was the variation of happy family plus space alien in *Alf* (NBC, 1986–1990). Mom, Dad and the kids had to deal with a sarcastic, hairy creature from outer space.

The single father remained a standard character in prime-time. In *Full House* (ABC, 1987–1995), a widower raised his three girls with the help of his brother-in-law and a good friend. The baby of the family was played by twins Mary Kate and Ashley Olsen, who grew up to be teen idols. The father in *The Nanny* received help from Fran Fine (Fran Drescher); she was working class, Jewish, and with a loud nasal whine, but she won the family's gentile hearts. And the divorced mother became a sitcom character. In *Grace under Fire* (ABC, 1993–1998), Brett Butler played a woman trying to deal with earning a living and raising her children, while recovering from an unhappy marriage.

Frasier (NBC, September 1994–2004) was an example of the combination of the workplace comedy with the family comedy. Kelsey Grammar played Frasier Crane, who had left his friends from *Cheers* in Boston and moved back to Seattle. He shared a home with his grumpy Dad and a rivalry with his fussy brother, Niles (David Hyde Pierce). But Frasier also had a call-in show at a radio station, which served as a platform for a rich assortment of oddball characters. (Frasier Crane is the longest-lived character in prime-time history, having been on the air continuously since his introduction on *Cheers*.)

In *Mad about You* (NBC, September 1992–August 1999), the family was small, just a husband and wife (Paul Reiser and Helen Hunt), but there were in-laws and coworkers and neighbors and a dog who created problems when the couple's lives became too bland. The setting was New York City, and critics liked the urban, modern quality of the marriage, with its combination of quirkiness and passion.

The Darker Side of Sitcoms

But other family comedies of the period had a darker edge to them. In *Roseanne* (ABC, 1988–1997), the wife freely criticized her children and husband with spiteful words and an impatient tone, and the audience was expected to sympathize with her. Throughout most of the series, she was a working mom mired in a blue-collar world, and her economic situation fueled her anger. Like Bill Cosby, Roseanne Barr had been a stand-up comic, and she brought her style and sense of humor to her series.

ROSEANNE

In 1988, Marcy Carsey and Tom Werner were riding high. Their production team had the most successful sitcom of the 1980s, *The Cosby Show*. They decided to try the same formula again: Take a successful stand-up comedian and give him a family, somewhat similar to his own, and build a series around them. Only, their new project used a female, Roseanne Barr (as she was known then).

Usually the producer of a series is also the originator of the concept, the writer of the pilot and the first few episodes, at least, and the person who makes sure the program maintains its creative vision. But Carsey and Werner had less of a hands-on style. Their stars were allowed a high degree of creative input into their shows, which, therefore, reflected more of their personality and interests. The result, in this case, was a set of pitched battles between the star and the creative staff, mostly won by Roseanne.

Roseanne debuted on ABC in 1988. The setting was Landford, Illinois, and the suburban house indicated the direction of the series: the decorations were tacky (Was that an act of defiance by the characters or did they genuinely appreciate the kitsch?) The cast consisted of talented professionals, who knew how to deliver the funny lines, while keeping their characters believable.

The show was rated in the top five for its first six years on the air. This success was despite the differences between it and the traditional sitcom. The show dealt with a blue-collar family. Most of the inhabitants of the comedy world are professionals. (A few exceptions have been successful—for example, *The Honeymooners, Alice, The Life of Riley, All in the Family, Sanford and Son*.) And *Roseanne* quite clearly had a female star, one of the few to lead a successful series since Lucille Ball.

Perhaps, the most noticeable difference was the tone of the series. In the television world, adults may get upset temporarily with their mildly annoying, but always well-meaning children and spouses. But in the conclusion, order is restored, and the family relationships are returned to their normal warmth and placidity. Apologies are proffered and accepted.

In *Roseanne*, the mom expressed anger, ranging from mild sarcasm to outright screaming, directed at her children and her husband. In the first season of the show, the actress played her role with an "I'm only kidding" attitude. But as she got more control over the series, Roseanne's character became more openly bitter at her family's lack of respect and consideration for her. The family loved each other, but, as in real life, that emotion was challenged daily by everybody's faults and flaws.

Roseanne, the character, was also angry about her economic status. She held a succession of low-paying, unskilled jobs. Eventually, she managed to scrape together the money to buy a diner, but financial insecurity was a constant reality for her family. The husband's motorcycle shop went bankrupt, and he was back to finding construction jobs whenever possible. Her dream was to be a writer, but her family and her economic status seemed to stifle every chance she had to succeed. She looked honestly at all of their lives and realized that none of the family had a chance at achieving their dreams for a better life.

The last year of the series had a surreal tone. Roseanne won a lottery prize of $108 million dollars; she went on *The Jerry Springer Show;* she heard a proposal for making her life into a TV sitcom. The final episode revealed that the past season had been merely a script written by the character, Roseanne. Perhaps the most interesting aspect is that the newly rich mom spent her money on the extravagant extras of life, not on good deeds and charities. Her experience as self-proclaimed "white trash" had not led her to be less selfish or more giving than the elite she had always despised.

Roseanne paved the way for other sitcoms to challenge the world of the almost-perfect family by describing the blue-collar lives of a family with honesty, sympathy, and humor usually, but anger, mockery, and disappointment were aspects of the portrayal also.

The writers of *Married . . . with Children* (Fox, 1987–1997) ridiculed all the family members equally—husband, wife, children—but reserved for shoe salesman Al Bundy (Ed O'Neill) his own ring in lower-class suburban hell, a punishment he seemed to richly deserve. He was as unpleasant a character as any sitcom has ever seen, yet somehow audience members identified with him or at least his fate. And *Malcolm in the Middle* (Fox, 2000–present) offered an equally funny, equally dysfunctional family. Mom

In *Roseanne*, the family lived in a house that seemed real. The furniture was more comfortable than stylish, and the decoration leaned toward the tacky. As played by Sara Gilbert, Michael Fishman, Alicia Goranson, John Goodman, and Roseanne, the family wasn't always warm and lovable, but it seemed authentic at times too. Courtesy of Photofest.

(Jane Kaczmarek) battled with her four sons, who were often in open warfare with each other, while dad (Bryan Cranston) looked on in the benign but confused manner of sitcom fathers. But at times, they pulled together as a family to make the lives of outsiders miserable. (The addition of a baby may offset the fact that the child actors are rapidly outgrowing their roles.) The success of these programs indicates that the audience was ready for a challenge to the ideal of the warm, fuzzy, almost perfect family.

The Pseudo-Family

Families on sitcoms don't always come packaged with a mother, father, and cute kids. Some families are created among friends and coworkers. As the perception spread in the 1980s that the traditional family was being replaced by single parents and divorced couples, the audience seemed to enjoy the reassurance offered on television that not only could substitute families be created, but that they would provide as much love and comfort and security, as well as exasperation, as a real family.

The Golden Girls (NBC, 1985–1992) focused on four characters, played by Rue McClanahan, Bea Arthur, Betty White, and Estelle Getty, who were past middle age chronologically, but who feuded with each other and discussed sexual matters like teenagers. They created their own family while living together in retirement, and even young adults could identify with them.

THE GOLDEN GIRLS

Since the 1970s, television networks have concentrated on providing programming for people 18 to 49 years old. Their logic is that this age group buys more of the products that TV commercials sell. The broadcast networks reach a mass audience, and most of the advertisers are selling products like toothpaste, fast food, and detergents, products that are purchased frequently by everybody. Families with young children are most likely to need these items and therefore to be the best customers. Also, advertisers believe that younger consumers are more likely to try new products and older consumers have already chosen favorites and won't experiment, no matter how winning the commercial is.

Because of the desire for this audience, CBS canceled its popular comedies in the 1970s, shows like *Green Acres, Mayberry R.F.D.,* and *Petticoat Junction.* Their ratings were fine, but the viewers were, on the average, too old. Programs like *Hill Street Blues,* with small ratings, could pull in higher advertising revenues than a hit like *Murder She Wrote* because of the ages of their audiences. This trend led the networks to believe that their programming staff and the producers and writers had to be under 30 to create programming appealing to the young viewers. Even creative people with impressive credentials had a hard time selling their talent if they were much over 30. And, of course, the stars had to be young to attract the desired audience.

But one show proved to be the exception. *The Golden Girls* was about four female friends who shared a house, and all of them were over 50. It took courage for NBC to put the program on the air, but it was a success with both young and old, ranking in the top 10 for its first six years.

The creator of the series was Susan Harris, who had been a writer on *Maude,* a show about a middle-aged woman who was highly opinionated and definitely liberated. She later developed *Soap,* a prime-time soap opera that was comic and controversial. For *The Golden Girls,* her partners were Paul Witt and Tony Thomas.

Until that series, older women had been portrayed as the mean old witch, the sugary sweet grandma, or the doddering fool. They were seen as unattractive, uninteresting, and asexual. They led narrow lives, making cookies, dusting the living room, and going to funerals for fun. But these women had a touch of glamour in their style, and they most certainly had not lost interest in having sexual relations with men.

But what made these women truly different from most of their peers on television wasn't their age or their honest interest in sex; it was the full, rich, well-rounded quality of their lives. They had jobs, which were not just casually mentioned, but part of their lives. They were involved in social causes; they participated in local theater and fundraisers; they took classes in topics like yoga and foreign language. All generations of their families were intertwined in their lives. These characters were more truly alive at this stage of life than almost any younger inhabitant of a sitcom.

Furthermore, their lives were not irrelevant; they were caught up in social movements, more than most sitcom characters. Topics for discussion on the show included homosexuality, artificial insemination, impotence, interracial marriage, addiction to pills and gambling, as well as medical problems of all sorts.

The series ended with Dorothy getting married and moving out. In the next season, the remaining ladies bought a hotel and lived there; the new series was called *The Golden Palace*, but without the chemistry among the four, the program lacked appeal and was canceled after a year.

The Golden Girls was not only a well-acted, well-written program; it was pure fantasy fulfillment. This is the old age we would all love to have, surrounded by friends, full of energy, still attractive, involved in the world around us, and with a continuing appetite for cheesecake and men. The show was a success not in spite of the age of the leads, but because they were at the right age to live life to the utmost.

Another quartet of sassy women also formed an unofficial family. The characters of *Designing Women* (CBS, 1986–1993) discussed politics, insulted each other, and argued about almost everything. They dealt with the problems of divorce, dating, and single parenthood, but they also supported each other in times of trouble and worked together to accomplish their goals. They were Southern belles who had been transformed—some willingly, some not—into career women, and they enjoyed their status.

Murphy Brown (CBS, 1988–1998) was about a woman who was independent, strong, and feisty. Candice Bergen played the lead character, a network newswomen and a recovering alcoholic. She could drive her coworkers crazy, but they formed a family of sorts, sharing their problems

The Golden Girls performed that almost impossible deed in the
United States: The program made growing older look fun. Even in their
nightgowns, the actresses have a touch of glamour—Betty White, Estelle
Getty, Bea Arthur, and Rue McClanahan. Courtesy of Photofest.

and celebrating their victories together. The program was criticized by Vice
President Dan Quayle, during the 1992 presidential campaign, when an
unmarried Murphy got pregnant and decided to keep the baby. The controversy raised the ratings, and Murphy went ahead with her plans.

Perhaps the most controversial situation comedy of the decade was *Ellen*
(played by Ellen DeGeneres) (ABC, 1994–1998). The title character worked
in a bookstore and had a group of friends, who formed a family of sorts.
In spring 1997, she announced she was a lesbian, and the series, which
had never hit a comfortable stride, faltered. The audience didn't seem quite
ready for a gay lead, or at least this gay lead.

Seinfeld (NBC, 1990–1998) offered an extremely successful variation of
the sitcom formula. He (played by Jerry Seinfeld) and his friends (Julia Louis-
Dreyfus, Jason Alexander, and Michael Richards) lived in New York City and
were basically selfish people. Unlike many of us, though, they felt no guilt
at being self-centered and were only mild embarrassed when their shal-
lowness was exposed. Most of the show's topics dealt with small questions

about the manners and mores of the time, which led to its description as "the show about nothing." After a slow start, the program reached cult status. The audience seemed to identify with characters who weren't villains, but could be considered anti-heroes on a petty scale.

Friends (NBC, 1994–2004) had some of the same elements: the New York City setting and the focus on people who used friendship to create their own family. But these characters were younger, in their 20s when the show began, and were more sympathetic, although each had had irritating qualities. They were played by Courteney Cox, Jennifer Aniston, David Schwimmer, Matthew Perry, Matt LeBlanc, and Lisa Kudrow. It was one of the first shows to center on characters of that age, and a generation identified with it.

Drew Carey created a family from friends and coworkers at a department store in Cleveland on *The Drew Carey Show* (ABC, 1995–2004). The humor

Seinfeld broke some of the rules of sitcoms. The characters were not lovable, and the series didn't have a high concept that could be summarized in an attractive phrase. The program was about four people, played by Michael Richards, Jerry Seinfeld, Julia Louis Dreyfus, and Jason Alexander, who formed more of an alliance than a true friendship. And yet it was definitely funny. Courtesy of Photofest.

could be broad and the insults flew, but the characters created a warm feeling despite all of the chaos. *A Different World* (NBC, 1987–1993), a spin-off from *The Cosby Show*, was set at a college. The major characters bonded so well that they were reluctant to leave after graduation.

VARIETY

The variety show disappeared during this time. *Dolly* (ABC, 1987–1988), hosted by Dolly Parton, tried to lead a comeback, but no single style of music attracted a big enough audience, and programs that combined styles weren't easily tolerated. Country western fans didn't want to hear rap and vice versa. *In Living Color* (Fox 1990–1994) came close to being a variety show. There was music, dancing, but mainly cutting-edge comedy skits. Keenan Ivory Wayans led a team of comics (including members of his talented family and Jim Carrey) until differences with the network caused him to pull out of the show. Some say the variety show lives on in the late-night talk show, where conversation mixes with music, comedy skits, dog acts, and so on.

DRAMA

The period 1985–1995 provided an interesting new direction for drama. Many of the classic formulas survived but were revitalized by novel variations. Some of the experiments led to successful series, while others failed, but the overall effect was greater creativity in themes, visual style, and plot.

Quality Drama

The series that usually gets credited with being the first successful "quality" drama is *Hill Street Blues*. Its techniques were clearly inspired by dramas like *The White Shadow* (CBS, 1978–1981) and *Lou Grant* (CBS, 1977–1982), but also by comedies like *The Mary Tyler Moore Show* (CBS, 1970–1977) and by prime-time soap operas like *Dallas* (CBS, 1978–1991).

Hill Street Blues and many of its successors shared some or most of the following factors:

1. Appeal to an upscale, urban audience, the yuppies. The result was not always great ratings, but the demographic was desired by advertisers.[4] Pay cable channels like HBO were luring away the yuppie audience, and the networks, especially NBC, mired in third place, wanted to win them back.

2. Complex, in-depth characterization. The emphasis was placed on an ensemble cast, rather than on a small cast supplemented with easily recognizable guest stars.

3. A worldview in which the good guy/bad guy paradigm was shifted. The difference between right and wrong became more ambiguous;[5] happy endings weren't guaranteed. Evil was sometimes rewarded rather than punished.

4. Multiple narrative lines. Like soap operas, several plots were woven through each episode.

5. "Arcing" stories. Plot lines were not tied up neatly at the end of every episode. Some lasted for the season, while others continued throughout the history of the show, which made them more serial in nature.

6. Nontraditional visual styles. For example, *Hill Street Blues* looked more like a documentary with long, fluid takes and infrequent cutting from character to character.[6] Quality dramas frequently relied on handheld cameras for a less polished look.

7. Importance of the producer. Producers had long been the creative force behind television series, much as directors are for films, but in quality dramas, the producers became more clearly identified with their series and sometimes evolved into celebrities. Some of the subsequent series produced by Steven Bochco, who created *Hill Street Blues,* were promoted with his name to entice the audience, and he was able to get a contract for 10 new series from ABC with a signing bonus. If the shows were successful, producers could exercise their power in battles with the network over censorship and other issues.

8. A new group of producers. As part of the quality movement, film directors like Steven Spielberg and David Lynch tried producing television programs but found that success wasn't as easily achieved. During this period, some female producers worked their way up the ladder: Marcy Carsey, Terry Louise Fisher, and Susan Harris became influential and developed hit series.

9. Controversial topics. Sex, for example, became more openly discussed and more openly portrayed,[7] although innuendo still predominated. Political issues were raised, frequently from a liberal point of view.

10. Overlapping dialogue. The audience was forced to listen carefully since characters used a more natural style of speaking, interrupting one another and stepping on the ends of others' sentences.

11. A willingness to experiment with visual techniques, genres, dialogue, plotting, and themes.

The quality programs didn't follow the usual safe formulas; therefore, the networks that aired them appear to have been motivated by a desire for a better image (to be perceived as hip, modern, creative) or by desperation. Frequently, the number-three network in the ratings was the most willing to experiment. A side effect was that the topics, images, and language of these programs drew controversy, and the networks had a juggling act on their hands—to encourage creative freedom, avoid the consequences of outraged citizens and politicians, and still benefit from the publicity generated by the controversy.

The broadcast networks felt that their rivals, the cable networks, were able to get away with more overtly sexual material than they could. After all, cable content was not as strictly regulated as broadcast content was. (The legal justification for restricting broadcast material was that stations used the public airwaves to send their signals. Cable, at that time, used privately owned wires for transmission of programming and, therefore, received the same First Amendment protection as movies and books.) To some broadcast executives, that greater freedom gave cable an advantage in winning ratings, and they started gradually pushing the edge of the envelope: a gay couple shared a bed in *thirtysomething*; fleeting nudity could be glimpsed on *N.Y.P.D. Blue*; Movies of the Week dealt with topics like incest; language got raunchier.

By the early 1980s, NBC was a struggling network. In 1981, it brought on board a president with a new philosophy of programming, Grant Tinker, former head of the highly respected production company MTM. He advocated giving critically respected programs a chance to find their audience. The usual approach had been to quickly cancel series that did poorly in the ratings, but Tinker was willing to be a little more experimental, a little less formulaic in his choice of programs. He gave producers more creative latitude and interfered less than most of his predecessors. (Of course, even with this attitude, NBC had some lemons on its schedule; e.g., *Mr. Smith*, a sitcom about a talking orangutan with a genius IQ, lasted for just three months in 1983.) Some of Tinker's philosophy rubbed off on his program director, Brandon Tartikoff. When Tinker quit the network, Tartikoff remained and allowed the development of quality TV programming.

Other programs that have been label quality dramas include *St. Elsewhere* (NBC, 1982–1988), *Sisters* (NBC, 1991–1996), *I'll Fly Away* (NBC, 1991–1993), and *Chicago Hope* (CBS, 1994–2000). Comedies are also included in this quality category: *Brooklyn Bridge* (CBS, 1991–1993) and *My So-Called Life* (ABC, 1994–1995), for example. (Other examples of programs that were influenced by the quality approach are included in some of the following categories.)

These series all shared excellent production values; they looked as though they had been made by people who cared about lighting, editing, sets, and camera movement. The acting and writing in each was outstanding. They were all willing to challenge the old formulas and experiment with new approaches. And their topics were not always predictable.

General Dramas

The series included in this category can all be labeled quality programs in some sense. Although they differed from each other in significant ways, they shared some characteristics common to other quality programs. Some critics felt that these programs had major flaws. Some were quirky in an irritating style as logic in characterization and plotting was replaced by randomness. The creators seemed to be more interested in artistic self-indulgence than in telling a story or entertaining an audience.

One of the more extreme examples was *Twin Peaks* (ABC, 1990–1991), the product of David Lynch, whose career as a film director indicated a preference for interesting visuals, weird characters, and plots that were incoherent at times. The TV series displayed this sensibility. At first, audiences were intrigued by the odd and unpredictable episodes about detectives trying to solve a murder in a small Pacific Northwest town, but when it became clear that there was going to be no satisfying resolution to the convoluted main mystery, many lost interest and patience, irritated perhaps by dwarves who talked backwards and the focus on cherry pie.

Moonlighting (ABC, 1985–1989) wasn't quite as eccentric as *Twin Peaks*, but it offered moments that broke all the rules of TV scripts. The concept could be classified as a detective show, a comedy, or a romance or a post-modern combination of all three. Cybill Shepherd and Bruce Willis played detectives, but he seemed more interested in catching her than the bad guys. The producer of the series, Glenn Gordon Caron, had problems getting the program done on time and on budget, and his stars' continual feuding got almost as much attention as the show itself.

One favorite setting of the time involved was the supposedly tranquil small town. In *Picket Fences* (CBS, 1992–1996) odd people and odder crimes marred the peaceful life of a typical Wisconsin family, and in *American Gothic* (CBS, 1995–1996), even more bizarre events, sparked perhaps by the sheriff—or was he Satan?—dogged the innocent citizens of Trinity, South Carolina.

On the surface, *thirtysomething* (ABC, 1987–1991) was a normal family drama, centering on mom (Mel Harris), dad (Ken Olin), a baby, and assorted

MOONLIGHTING

ABC had slipped in the ratings to number three, and its chief programmer decided that the way to come out of the doldrums was to borrow a strategy from NBC, who had risen from number three to number one by offering producers more leeway to be creative and break the rules. To send that signal clearly, ABC decided to offer a chance to Glen Gordon Caron, a producer with minimal experience, mainly on *Remington Steele,* a detective/comedy/romance drama about feuding male and female private eyes.

Sexual tension between men and women in a series was a common device, although more subtle in older shows like *Perry Mason* and *Mannix.* (Did the secretary and the boss have something going on? There was no overt indication, and yet imaginative audience members could draw their own conclusions.) But in the 1980s, the tension bubbled over into the dialogue and plots. *Cheers, Who's the Boss?* and *Scarecrow and Mrs. King* were examples.

Perhaps in the age of sexual explicitness, the implied became tantalizingly interesting. Or maybe as the end of the sexual revolution collided with the age of AIDS, the question became: Could men and women who were attracted to each other say no and mean it? Or with more women in the workplace, could the viewers identify with the awkwardness of temptation among colleagues?

In *Moonlighting,* the tension was especially heightened. The stars were Cybill Shepherd, who played Maddie, and Bruce Willis, who played David. They were highly attractive people with healthy doses of charisma and chemistry (whether fueled by mutual attraction or mutual dislike).

Furthermore, the producer refused to follow the rules of the game. *Moonlighting* received nominations for awards as both a drama and a comedy. Not only did the series fail to establish itself as a definite genre, it broke all of the conventions within episodes. For instance, the characters knew they were on a show. They addressed the audience directly, discussed their ratings, and pondered their lack of success on the Emmies.

Episodes frequently paid homage to a director or a style of filmmaking— film noir, MTV, *Citizen Kane,* Frank Capra, for example. One was shot from the point of view of the baby in Maddie's womb; another was done in the style of a documentary with guest stars like gossip-columnist Rona Barrett and Pierce Brosnan (of *Remington Steele*). In other words, the audience had no idea what to expect in plots or styles, much less in the romance aspect of the series.

But programs with titillation between leads built in as an element faced an inevitable problem: How long could the pair ignore the sexual tension between them before they seemed willfully stupid? What happened when the audience got bored with the lack of progress? How could the writers continue to explain the lack of fulfillment between two unmarried, consenting adults? Finally, the producer allowed Maddie and David to become intimate, and the series seemed to lose its energy.

In real life, Shepherd was pregnant and wanted to work as little as possible, and Willis was getting movie offers. The character of Maddie became pregnant and married a stranger. The staff of the private detective agency starred in several of the episodes, as the leads moved into the background. The audience seemed to lose interest in the show. The producer had broken many rules about what a TV series should look like, but changing the relationship between the main characters was too much for the audience. Like most other series with this gimmick, the viewers waited week after week, year after year for the consummation between the leads—only to be disappointed with the results. The charming flirtation and the sexual tension were replaced by the ordinary drudgery of maintaining a relationship under awkward circumstances. The show was soon canceled.

Like many quality dramas, *Moonlighting* could be annoying. The good news and the bad news was that the audience never knew what to expect. Bruce Willis and Cybill Shepherd played the leads with a classic love/hate relationship. Courtesy of Photofest.

relatives and friends. The program seemed designed to appeal to 1980s yuppies as the upscale characters self-consciously examined their lives, explored their guilt, and whined. Some members of the audience identified with the angst of the characters, and others found them annoying.

China Beach (ABC, 1988–1991) used the familiar format of the war drama and gave it a twist. Instead of soldiers firing guns and throwing hand grenades, the stories were about the women in Vietnam—nurses, entertainers, and Red Cross workers. The result was sort of a soap opera near a combat zone, one of the rare programs to have used Vietnam as a setting.

A gentle version of the quality series was *Northern Exposure* (ABC, 1990–1995). The inhabitants of Cecily, Alaska, lived by their own unique rules in a comedy/drama with a charming eccentricity that appealed to many viewers.

Science Fiction Dramas

Only one program in the science fiction genre was a lasting success in this era. *The X-Files* (Fox, 1993–2002) followed two FBI agents (played by David Duchovny and Gillian Anderson) who investigated paranormal phenomena rather than the usual bank robberies and kidnappings. Their probing into weird happenings led to suspicions that shadowy government conspiracies were at work. The show had a dark look, scary special effects, and a pervasive atmosphere of paranoia that created a loyal group of fans.

Other sci-fi series created a brief splash but couldn't sustain an audience, who perhaps were getting their fill of science fiction in the movie theaters. *Max Headroom* (ABC, August–May 1987) was about a stuttering computer-generated character, who seemed to be the alter ego of a television news reporter (Matt Frewer). *Beauty and the Beast* (CBS, 1987–1990) was a rather obvious concept: attractive young woman (Linda Hamilton) fell in love with lion-faced, underground creature (Ron Perlman) in modern-day New York. *Quantum Leap* (ABC, 1989–1993) had a more complicated premise: Scientist Sam Beckett (Scott Bakula) found himself traveling through different time periods, inhabiting the bodies and inheriting the problems of a wide variety of characters while being guided by The Observer (Dean Stockwell). The survival of *Lois & Clark—The New Adventures of Superman* (ABC, 1993–1997) was based more on the romance between Clark Kent (Dean Cain) and Lois Lane (Teri Hatcher) than on the special effects.

Legal Dramas

One legal drama dominated the time period. *L.A. Law* (NBC, 1986–1994) was a glossy descendant of *Hill Street Blues*. A large ensemble cast tackled crime, social issues, and romantic liaisons, but in a setting, much more pol-ished than the Hill Street precinct house. The series had all the peculiarities and style of a quality drama, but in a more palatable package that focused on affluent Los Angeles during the high-flying 1980s.

Medical Dramas

One medical drama was dominant during the time period. *ER* (NBC, 1994–present) was fast-paced and visually graphic, looking authentic enough to allow viewers to feel that they are seeing real life in an emer-gency room. When not healing patients, the staff, of course, have emotional traumas. The series has survived despite a constant turnover in cast, and the newcomers seem to be able to rapidly gain the audience's loyalty. (The Thursday night audience is especially important to NBC because that's the night movie studios advertise their attractions to the young, urban audi-ence, who'll be deciding then what to watch over the weekend. At one point, the network paid $13 million an episode, far above the usual price for a 60-minute drama.)

A more conventional medical drama was *Trapper John, M.D.* (CBS, 1979–1986). The character of Dr. "Trapper John" MacIntyre (Pernell Roberts) was borrowed in this sort of spin-off from M*A*S*H, but he was now 25 years older and a chief of surgery who had to deal with young hotshot Dr. "Gonzo" Gates (Gregory Harrison) on his staff. And what is widely regarded as one of the worst medical shows of all times, *Nightingales* (NBC, 1989) appeared briefly. The episodes consisted mainly of pretty nurses in skimpy clothes standing in front of steamy mirrors drying their hair and discussing sex in the linen closet. Real nurses protested, and no one stepped up to defend the program, which soon disappeared.

Religion Dramas

Highway to Heaven (NBC, 1984–1989) and *Touched by an Angel* (CBS, 1994–April 2003) were both programs that swam against the cultural current of sex and secularism in most prime-time shows of the time. They both dealt with angels—one played by Michael Landon, the other by Roma Downey—coming to earth to help ordinary people by providing inspiration and an occasional miracle. Both programs were well received by their audiences, who skewed toward an older demographic in an era when attracting 18- to 49-year olds was the Holy Grail of network and advertising executives.

Prime-Time Soaps

The old favorites—*Dallas, Dynasty, Knots Landing,* and *Falcon Crest*—lived on into this time period, but they were eventually replaced by younger, hipper soaps. *Beverly Hills 90210* (Fox, 1990–2000) was aimed clearly at an audience on the lower end of the valuable 18–34 demographic. The story began with a group of high school friends and followed them into adulthood. All of the stars (e.g., Shannen Doherty, Jason Priestly) were physically attractive, wore stylish clothes, and lived in glamorous locations, and like most soap operas, the plots centered on people suffering from the consequences of an overabundance of passion and a lack of judgment. *Melrose Place* (Fox, 1992–1999) was from the same producer, Aaron Spelling, and followed the same formula except that the characters were older—in their 20s at the beginning of the show—and lived in the same apartment complex.

ADVENTURE DRAMAS

Pure adventure shows with little claim to aesthetic values proved they remained as capable of winning audiences in the 1980s as they had in the 1950s. For example, *The A-Team* (NBC, 1983–1987) followed the exploits of a group of colorful Vietnam veterans. Although accused of a crime they didn't commit and forced to escape from prison to prove their innocence (a common error in TV logic), they performed good deeds while clearing their names. The program had a heavy dose of violence, but hardly anyone was ever injured. The characters—Hannibal Smith (George Peppard), B. A. Barracus (Mr. T), Templeton Peck (Dirk Benedict), and Murdock (Dwight Schultz)—were played more for humor than anything else.

SPY DRAMAS

As the paranoia of the Cold War died out, the spy drama seemed to be less relevant. One exception was *Scarecrow and Mrs. King* (CBS, 1983–1987). But unlike its predecessors, there was little emphasis on technology or violence. Instead, romance was the focus. Mrs. King (Kate Jackson), an ordinary housewife, was more interested in wooing the hero, code-named Scarecrow (Bruce Boxleitner) than in fighting the battles of espionage. But she turned out to be quite effective in her own feminine style at outwitting the villains.

Some thought of *The A-Team* as a show with a
high level of violence, but the producer, Stephen
Cannell, defended the program as a comedy and
pointed out that few characters were injured.
The stars were Dirk Benedict, George Peppard,
Mr. T, and Dwight Schultz (in the back).
Courtesy of Photofest.

WESTERNS

The genre continued its long, slow decline. One exception was *Dr. Quinn,
Medicine Woman* (CBS, 1993–1998), which starred Jane Seymour as a female
doctor in 1860s Colorado. She overcame the shortsightedness of the conservative townsfolk, cured their ailments, adopted a few orphans, and fell

in love with Sully (Joe Lando), a hunky, mysterious mountain man. She was definitely not the usual western hero.

DETECTIVES

The detective show continued to thrive during this time period. For example *Spenser: for Hire* (ABC, 1985–1988) was the classic private detective show, based on Robert Parker's books and starring Robert Urich. *Jake and the Fatman* (CBS, 1987–1992) followed the exploits of a team of detectives with William Conrad as the mentor and Joe Penny as his skirt-chasing assistant. And *Walker, Texas Ranger* (CBS, 1993–2001) had Chuck Norris displaying his karate talents in the battle against crime.

But there were some interesting variations of the genre. For example, *Wiseguy* (CBS, 1987–1990) told the tale of undercover agent Vinnie Terranova (Ken Wahl), whose specialty was infiltrating organized crime. Each of his assignments lasted for several episodes and usually involved fascinating criminals, creating compelling story arcs.

Another example of the detective show as an art form was *Homicide: Life on the Street* (NBC, 1993–1999), in which Baltimore detectives pursued murderers in a less-than-pure world. The visual style was derived from cinema verité with location shooting, nervous camerawork, and grungy, claustrophobic interiors.[8] The police were richly drawn and well-rounded characters, not always saints. Criminals sometimes were captured and punished, and sometimes weren't. The intense stories never earned a wide audience but did get much critical praise.

Steven Bochco offered two detective shows, one a success and one an interesting failure. *N.Y.P.D. Blue* (ABC, 1993–2004) initially received publicity for its nude scenes and strong language, but after the shock wore off, viewers became interested in characters like Andy Sipowicz (Dennis Franz), an officer with a tough beat and a tougher attitude and a personal life that seemed more appropriate for a soap opera. He went through a number of partners, both professional and romantic, and the audience stayed fascinated with the series. The acting was low key with lines sometimes muffled rather than clearly enunciated.[9]

Bochco's less successful series was *Cop Rock* (ABC, 1990). While it looked like a standard detective drama, characters frequently broke out into song. The result was interesting to some, but highly annoying to most. Many viewers just couldn't understand why a jury about to pronounce sentence was singing like a choir, with the court clerk playing an organ.

One of the results of quality drama was that the producer became almost as well known as the actors. The stars of *N.Y. P. D. Blue* included Jimmy Smits, Dennis Franz, and James McDaniel. Behind them is executive producer, Steven Bochco. Courtesy of Photofest.

1990 saw the beginning of the *Law & Order* NBC franchise. Its lineup consists of the original, *Law & Order: Special Victims Unit*, *Law & Order: Criminal Intent*, and *Law & Order: Trial by Jury*, which was quickly canceled. In the first half of each episode of the original series, New York City detectives investigate a crime, and in the second half prosecutors take the accused to court. The stories are frequently inspired by headlines of the day, but offered surprising plot twists.

21 Jump Street (Fox, 1987–1990) was aimed at a younger audience. In it, baby-faced detectives, led by Johnny Depp in his early years, went undercover in high schools and solved crimes. The program was one of Fox's first successes and was filmed in Canada to keep production costs low.

On the other end of the age spectrum, CBS—a network that appealed to an older demographic (perhaps because no one else was)—had considerable success with *Diagnosis Murder* (1992–2001). In it, Dick Van Dyke played Dr. Mark Sloan, the crime-fighting chief of internal medicine at a Los Angeles hospital, who was helped in his investigations by his son, police officer, Steve Sloan, played by Barry Van Dyke, the star's real-life son.

Another attempt at quality television was *Crime Story* (NBC, 1986–1988). The serialized story of police in early 1960s Chicago battling organized crime never caught on with the audience, but the logic behind choosing it for the network is interesting. In 1986, Nielsen, the company that measures ratings, introduced a new technique, the Peoplemeter. Traditionally, ratings had been measured either by having people fill out diaries with a list of the programs they viewed or by retrieving data from a box attached to the TV set that recorded what channel was turned on.

The problem with the diaries was that they were not completely accurate. People didn't always immediately write down what they had seen, and memory can be less than perfect. The situation was made even more complicated by the increasing number of television sets in the home, the growing number of channels available over cable and satellite, and the ease of clicking through channels with the remote control.

The old meters mounted atop TV sets were a more accurate reflection of which channels TVs were tuned to, but they failed to indicate who was actually watching, if anyone. Advertisers were especially interested in reaching women aged 18 to 49, the demographic most likely to do the household purchasing. For the new Peoplemeter, each member of the family was assigned a code number and had to punch it into the device when starting and stopping their TV viewing. The goal was to match the demographics of viewers with their programming choices. NBC executives felt that men would be more likely, at least in the beginning, to push the buttons. Therefore, they scheduled *Crime Story,* a program aimed at males, in the hopes that it would attract men to the set and get their numbers recorded.

ANIMATION

If there were a signature series of the era, an appropriate nomination would be *The Simpsons* (Fox 1989–present). The family is dysfunctional, in the manner of many modern TV families, but somehow pleasantly so. The father, Homer, is an Everyman, plagued with all of the problems of life today, everything from unruly children to an unfulfilling job. His son, Bart, while not truly evil, is lacking in most moral values and all known forms of etiquette. The other members of the family—mother Marge, daughters Lisa and Maggie—are marginally more normal. Despite criticisms of the

The Simpsons seems to have become so much a part of our everyday culture that it's hard to believe the family members are only TV characters and even harder to believe they're animated. The only clue is that they never age. Lisa, Marge with Maggie, Homer, and Bart pose before their suburban home. Courtesy of Photofest.

program as flouting traditional family values, many episodes underscore their strength as an intact family. Through all of their surrealistic adventures, they remain together.

REALITY

The scripted reality show blossomed during this time period. In 1988, television writers who specialized in fictional scripts went on strike, causing the delay of the traditional fall premiere of shows. But news/documentaries/ reality writers were an exception. Scripted reality could be produced with little expense as no starring actors, no special effects, and no elaborate sets were required.

America's Most Wanted (Fox 1988–2004) was one of the network's early hits. The program was responsible for the arrests of literally hundreds of criminals after viewers phoned in tips to the show's toll-free phone number. Episodes consisted largely of reenactments of crimes, and the host was John Walsh, who became an anti-crime activist after the kidnapping and murder of his son. *America's Most Wanted* cost about one-third as much to produce as the average half-hour. The network followed up with *Cops* (March 1989–present), which presents actual footage of police in action. *Rescue 911* (CBS, 1989–1996), and *Unsolved Mysteries* (NBC, 1988–1999) were other examples.

NEWS MAGAZINES

Documentaries in the traditional hour and half-hour formats disappeared from network television. They were replaced by news magazines, formatted like *60 Minutes*. Programs like *Dateline* (NBC, 1992–present), and *Primetime Live* (ABC, 1989–present) gave the networks a cheap form of programming, produced, and therefore controlled, by themselves. The topics occasionally included serious news that could be boiled down into a 12-minute segment, but most often consumer information, feature items, crime news, and celebrity gossip dominated the time slot.

MOVIES AND MINISERIES

Hollywood theatrical films lost some of their popularity on network television during the time period. People could view them on cable or rent them, unedited, on videocassette before they hit the broadcast window, and as a result, ratings suffered. Made-for-TV movies remained a good way for networks to fill out their prime-time schedules, but it remained difficult to build a loyal audience around them since topics and actors changed from movie to movie.

As the broadcast networks struggled to compete against the rapidly expanding popularity of cable networks, miniseries seemed like one solution, but an expensive one. ABC lavished money on *War and Remembrance*, a World War II saga, but it failed to win enough viewers to cover its cost and the network lost at least $30 million. The most successful of the miniseries, both in popularity and in aesthetics, was CBS's *Lonesome Dove*, an epic western with warm, multidimensional characters.

CONCLUSION

Throughout this period, the networks had to face new competition from other media. As the FCC lifted its restrictions on cable, the industry spread into major cities. By 1994, more than 60 percent of the households had cable. The good news, from the broadcast networks' viewpoint, was that the video and audio on their television stations could be easily received by their audiences. But the bad news was that new cable networks like HBO, USA, and Turner's superstation in Atlanta could also be seen. These program sources had the potential to steal audiences and advertising revenues. And direct broadcast satellites were authorized, giving viewers a choice among broadcast television, cable, or home satellite.

VCRs were in 80 percent of the households by 1994, which meant that viewers were no longer totally at the mercy of network executives. In their own homes, people could time-shift—record programs and play them back whenever they wished—or watch rented films. Now, programming strategists had to compete not only with their usual rivals, the other networks, but also with the movie rental business and with their own programs recorded earlier. Even more frightening to the programmer, the now ubiquitous remote control meant that a failure to entertain instantly could result in a lost viewer.

From 1985 to 1995 the three traditional networks had to face the challenges of a new competitor, Fox, and the spread of new media—at a time when their new bosses were demanding higher profits. The result was sometimes wonderful innovation, but often it was little more than an attempt to do the same old things in the same old way, only cheaper.

CHAPTER 8

More New Voices
(1996–2005)

By the mid-1990s, the original television networks—ABC, CBS, and NBC, the former Big Three—were under increasing pressure. They had undergone stressful changes in ownership and faced stiff competition from newcomer Fox and from rival media like cable networks and videocassettes. The next decade would see even more modifications in corporate leadership, the addition of new competitors, and increasing challenges from emerging media.

INDUSTRY OWNERSHIP

Additional changes in network leadership were set in motion by the Federal Communications Commission. The regulatory body had put two rules into effect in 1971. The first, the Financial Interest/Syndication Rule (called "fin/syn") limited the three TV networks in the amount of prime-time programming they could own and forbade them from syndicating their reruns in the United States. An exception was news programming, which explains why the networks came to schedule so many news magazines. Since income from syndication could be highly lucrative, many companies were not interested in owning television networks.

The second rule was the Prime-Time Access Rule (PTAR), which allowed stations to accept only three hours of programming from the networks between 7 and 11 P.M. EST, with Sunday as an exception. In the 50 largest cities (and therefore, the 50 most profitable markets), affiliates couldn't even show network reruns during those hours. Since the biggest share of a network's profits came from the stations it owned, the logical conclusion was that these owned-and-operated stations would make more income without the rule.

In 1995 the FCC announced that both rules would be dropped. The day after the announcement Disney said it would buy Capital Cities/ABC, and the day after that Westinghouse announced its decision to purchase CBS. Without the rules in effect, Disney and Westinghouse could own some or all of the prime-time programming on their networks, could produce series through their own studios, and could earn hundreds of millions of dollars from syndication. A television network suddenly seemed like even more of an asset.

The demise of the two rules had another effect. Since all four of the major networks—the Big Three had become the Big Four with the success of Fox—now had the power and the facilities to produce their own prime-time programming and to syndicate it, the other film studios that were heavily invested in the television production business began to worry. How could they sell programs to their new competitors? The response was to form two new television networks in 1995—UPN (United Paramount Network) and WB (Warner Bros.). The owners were important producers of TV programming who feared getting shut out by the Big Four.

In their early years, both new networks targeted the young, urban audience most desired by advertisers. Their first problem was finding affiliates as the vast majority of TV stations were already affiliated with ABC, CBS, NBC, or Fox. The next problem was building ratings through attractive programming. WB eventually found its answer with teen-appeal dramas like the "occult" *Buffy the Vampire Slayer,* the high school angst of *Dawson's Creek,* and the college-girl-in-the-big-city atmosphere of *Felicity.* UPN gambled on a known quantity and built its schedule around *Star Trek: Voyager,* a spin-off of the venerable 1960s *Star Trek,* but not even that franchise worked well enough. UPN had more success with urban sitcoms, many with African-American casts. Programs like *Moesha* and *Malcolm & Eddy* were relatively successful, but perhaps the biggest ratings boost came from the wrestling show *WWF Smackdown,* the latest in a long line of wrestling programs that extended back to the dark ages of 1948.

A seventh network, Pax, was added to the six networks in 1998. Bud Paxton had earned a fortune from a home shopping network, which was carried on cable and on low-power TV stations, many of which he owned. After he sold the cable part of the shopping network, he decided to start a

BUFFY THE VAMPIRE SLAYER

In the early days of radio and television, the goal was to deliver the largest possible audience to advertisers. Later, networks like ABC, then NBC, with lower ratings persuaded the ad agencies that they really wanted 18- to 49-year-old women, who were doing more of the purchasing than any other demographic group. When Fox went on the air, it concentrated on the 18- to 34-year-old women but had its greatest success in the early years with the teen audience. No other broadcast network was striving to reach this group on a nightly basis. They purchased lots of CDs, movie tickets, fast food, sneakers, and so on—but was that enough advertising revenue to sustain a TV network? Even worse, they watched much less TV than most adults.

WB learned a lesson from Fox. The teen audience might not be as desirable as the older viewers, but it was loyal to a network that offered suitable programming. And when the teens became a few years older, they would stay with their network. At least, that's what the WB hoped.

The program that cemented its identity as the teen network was *Buffy the Vampire Slayer*, produced by Joss Whedon, based on a film script he had written. The series became a cult hit, endlessly analyzed, discussed, and celebrated by fans and critics. But even more important, from the network's point of view, it attracted a new audience to the screen. The program that followed it in the first season was *7th Heaven*, very different in tone and style, but appealing to the same audience. A spin-off, *Angel*, did well for the network. In other words, *Buffy* was proving to be a building block for the WB.

What made the show so appealing to the teen audience? Of course, there was the heroine, a teen girl. Like Harry Potter, she learned that she was somebody special, with mystical powers inherited from powerful beings, but most of the world saw her only as ordinary, at best. She developed what every teen girl wanted, a team of friends who come to her aid and provided emotional support, when necessary. And she proved herself to be more powerful than the everyday adults of her world.

The topics of the first three seasons dealt with the normal horrors of high school—the talent show, cheerleaders, career night, homecoming, the candy sale, the principal—but turned them into stories about demons, monsters, and hell. The school was terrorized by a student who became invisible when everybody ignored her. On prom night, Buffy found out that hellhounds had been trained to attack people in formal wear. Graduation turned out to be a pitched battle between students and the mayor. She fell in love—with a sort-of vampire, and consummating the relationship just led to more complications. No show has ever done a better job of portraying the fears and fantasies of a teen girl.

Buffy went on to college, dealt with the death of a parent, and battled the stresses of surviving as an adult. At one point, she even sacrificed her life for the world. The dialogue was smart and funny; the acting was on target; and no matter how bizarre the plots seemed, they always had a core of truth.

When it came time to renew the series on WB, the producer, Joss Whedon, asked for more money, assuming the network would be grateful for the teen audience he had helped to bring to the network. But the executives said that the ratings were good, but not excellent, and they weren't willing to pay the increase. Whedon took his show to UPN, which was struggling to find an audience. It had changed its programming philosophy often enough to confuse potential viewers, but had not yet found quite the right formula. Maybe Buffy would help. Loyal fans continued to enjoy their favorite characters, the quirky dialogue, and the operatic quality of the battle between good and evil. But the ratings never pulled back up to their former level, and the program ended as the star and producer decided it was time to travel other roads.

broadcast network linking the leftover low-power television stations, all of which had limited geographical reach, with other stations he didn't own. As some of these included religious stations, he wanted to have programming that was suitable for families and that reflected traditional Christian values. The Pax schedule (note the association of the name *pax*, the Latin word for peace, with religion) was heavy on reruns and infomercials at first, but later added a little original programming, such as the medical program *Doc* and *Sue Thomas: F.B.Eye*, about a hearing-impaired FBI agent. NBC bought a partial interest in the network but Pax remains in financial trouble and is leaning more and more on infomercials as a source of revenue.

One result of the increase in the number of networks was a greater demand for programming to fill the ever-expanding amount of available time. To add to the problem, as the networks saw it, cable networks were doing more original series. Experienced, successful producers were in short supply. The networks had to settle for people with fewer credentials for creating and supervising a program, which led to some degree of innovation, but to a number of unpolished, expensive failures as well.

The musical chairs game of network ownership continued. Westinghouse, the owner of CBS, had produced some of its own programming, but it didn't own a major studio. So, four years after its purchase of the network, Westinghouse sold CBS to Viacom. Back when fin/syn went into effect, CBS spun off its syndication arm into a new company named Viacom. Viacom then

Sometimes it's easy to envy the relationship between the mother (Lauren Graham) and the daughter (Alexis Bledel) of *Gilmore Girls*. But at other times, their snappy, cute dialogue is too precious and downright irritating. Courtesy of Photofest.

expanded into movie theaters, video rentals, cable networks (Nickelodeon, MTV, VH-1, Showtime, etc.), television production (Paramount), and book publishing (Simon & Schuster).[1] Now, with its purchase of CBS, Viacom had actually absorbed its old parent company.

ABC had teamed with Disney studios, CBS with Viacom's Paramount studios, and Fox, which had not been covered by the two rules, had its own production house. That left NBC to create its own small production company, but in television, as in much of American business, bigger is better. In 2004 NBC bought a majority interest in Vivendi Universal in order to take control of Universal Studios, an important supplier of television programming. By 2005, the networks, except Pax, had the ability to be self-sufficient in programming; a degree of vertical integration had been achieved.

But then the networks discovered that being their own best customers could bring problems. The clearest example was ABC. The network's ratings had been satisfactory, but Disney decided that producing more of its own programs would make financial sense. The problem was that the many of the series had the bland look and sound of assembly line production. An outside supplier would have been forced to do revisions or might have had programs rejected outright, but since these shows were homegrown, they went on the air. As a result, ABC's ratings started to fall. Perhaps the best example of the problem was the scheduling of *Who Wants to Be a Millionaire?* up to five times a week. Although the program was cheap to produce and did well in summer ratings, only its producer would think it could sustain an audience over nightly viewings.

It is foolish of a network to schedule a bad program and wise for it to schedule a good program—no matter what the source. The problem lies with mediocre series, the ones that fall somewhere between great and terrible. The networks were simply too often tempted to say yes to their own products and too often reluctant to cancel them when they failed to perform.

The major studios still turn out successful series, and the networks still buy their products, but now the two frequently share the financial risks of a new show and the benefits of a hit (and network studios sometimes buy from each other). The networks now either own outright or have a percentage in about half of the programs in prime-time. Perhaps the biggest loser in this restructuring has been the independent studio. Many of them have either aligned themselves with a major studio or gone out of business.

One result of this wave of mega-mergers has been the growth of symbiotic relationships between cable and broadcast networks. At one point, they were rivals for viewers and advertisers, but now if owned by the same company, they can be allies. A series like *Law & Order* can be seen on the broadcast network on one night, and only a few nights later, the same episode can be seen on a cable network. (This practice is in contrast to syndication, in which older episodes are sold to cable but not the current-season ones). Sometimes, the double play attracts fans to the original, but producers often worry that the show will be seen so often that it will wear out its welcome with the audience.

Of course, repurposing swings both ways. If a cable network starts a new series, some of the episodes may be run on a brother broadcast network to lure viewers. For example, *Queer Eye for the Straight Guy* is on Bravo, but NBC, owned by the same company, ran a few of the early episodes to introduce the audience to it. Likewise, *Monk*, on the USA Network, received the same treatment on ABC. The owners can also craft deals that benefit their other properties, such as music, books, theme parks, radio, and so on, and appearances by the stars of one program "crossing over" to the other program are not unknown.

Consolidation on the networks' side has given them more of an advantage over their affiliates. For example, the original three networks used to pay stations compensation for carrying their programming and commercials. Now, networks are cutting back or eliminating these payments and even talking about demanding money from the stations. Also, the networks want tighter control of their affiliates' schedules, but the FCC prefers that stations remain responsible for their own programs. For example, when Janet Jackson "accidentally" displayed her nipple during the live Super Bowl half-time show in 2004, CBS-affiliated stations said they were innocent of violating indecency rules because they didn't know what the network was going to air. The FCC fined only the stations owned and operated by CBS, and CBS blamed the whole thing on MTV, which had choreographed the half-time show. The underlying question was: Can networks be trusted to control prime-time programming or should the legal responsibility remain with the affiliate?

LEGAL

Another source of contention between networks and affiliates has been the issue of ownership. The FCC had for years limited any one organization to owning a maximum of 12 VHF stations and to reaching no more that 25 percent of American households with their signals. But the Telecommunications Act of 1996 changed the rules so that while one company could own an unlimited number of television stations, it could not reach more than 35 percent of households. Congress then raised the limit to 39 percent, but the issue remains in the courts. Station owners believe that allowing the networks to own more stations gives them more power in negotiating affiliation contracts, scheduling, and compensation—putting owners at a disadvantage.

Another provision of the Telecommunications Act of 1996, the first major set of laws dealing with broadcasting since the Communications Act of

1934, requires that television set manufacturers provide a V-chip in each of their new products. The networks had to rate their programs for suitability for children in areas like sex, violence and language, and parents could then program their sets to filter out unacceptable programs. Relatively few people have taken advantage of this screening technology, and thus it has had little effect on programming.

Moreover, the Telecommunications Act of 1996 has been interpreted by FCC as saying that larger networks can't combine but can own a smaller network. Two broadcasters have already taken advantage of this new rule: Viacom already owned UPN when it bought CBS, and NBC has purchased Telemundo, one of the two Spanish-language networks in the United States.

SITCOMS

One template seemed to dominate the situation comedies of the period: a sloppy, not-very-smart, emotionally immature man of ordinary (or worse) appearance is married to an attractive, intelligent, sharp-tongued woman, and they and their two (or more or fewer) children spout quips with the timing of stand-up comedians. They, of course, all love each other for some reason. To add to the hilarity and conflict, an assortment of eccentric and/or annoying in-laws and friends drop by for witty interaction.

This formula had long been popular in television. It mirrors ambiguities about the roles of men and women and allows viewers to feel superior at times to the TV family and sympathetic at other times. If given excellent execution or a slight twist, the formula can work well, but any fictional scenario, repeated too often, can lose its charm. By 2005, critics and programmers were again declaring the death of the situation comedy. Few of the newer ones had won the loyalty and devotion of *Friends* or *Seinfeld*.

Family Sitcoms

A number of relatively popular sitcoms recycled the formula. *The King of Queens* (CBS, 1998–present), with Kevin James and Leah Remini, is typical, but with the variation that instead of children, they have to put up with her obnoxious father (Jerry Stiller). *Yes, Dear* (ABC, 2000–present) follows a couple (Anthony Clark and Jean Louisa Kelly) with a small child, who deal with various oddball friends and relatives. *According to Jim* (starring Jim Belushi and Courtney Thorne-Smith) (ABC, 2001–present) is yet another example of the formula. And *8 Simple Rules for Dating My Teenage Daughter* (ABC, 2002–present) began in the typical mold but was forced to change with the unexpected death of its star, John Ritter. The program was reworked so that the television family had to adjust to life without father.

Frequently, the family and the workplace interact as a source of comedy. In *Arrested Development* (Fox, 2003–present), a millionaire's son (Jason Bateman) finds himself running the family business, but in this case, the family is not your typical set of slightly wacky relatives, and the result is somewhat less predictable.

One variation on the theme is to have the family belong to a minority. *My Wife and Kids* (ABC, 2001–present) is about an African-American family headed by Damon Wayans and Tisha Campbell-Martin, and *George Lopez* (also ABC, 2001–present) focuses on the Hispanic family of George Lopez and Constance Marie.

The most successful example of the family sitcom in this period is *Everybody Loves Raymond* (CBS, 1996–2005). The usual characters—husband (Ray Romano), wife (Patricia Heaton), children, interfering parents (Doris Roberts and Peter Boyle), and goofy brother (Brad Garrett)—were there, but the tone was edgier, the insults sharper and funnier. Naturally, a truce was always reached at the end of the episode, but the audience never really felt that a permanent reconciliation was either possible or desirable.

Everybody Loves Raymond was about a family who loved each other dearly but had no skills at showing love. The result was hurt feelings, anger, and always a temporary reconciliation. The cast included Brad Garrett, Ray Romano, Doris Roberts, and Patricia Heaton. Courtesy of Photofest.

The Pseudo Family

The family of convenience survived through the mid 1990s. Usually the workplace was the setting but there were exceptions. For example, *3rd Rock from the Sun* (NBC, 1996–2002) centered on a group of space aliens, led by John Lithgow, who had crash-landed on earth and had to adjust to a new cultural environment and to their new roles in a mock family while maintaining the pretense that they were just ordinary people.

3RD ROCK FROM THE SUN

Coming up with an idea for a television show seems easy. The concepts are usually minor variations of each other, but the difficult aspect is that the series, if successful, should last, at least, for a hundred episodes, the usual minimum number for syndication. No other form of art or entertainment requires the creator to develop ideas with that kind of sustaining power.

How do you use the same characters in the same setting week after week without quickly running out of interesting plots? The situation comedy is especially difficult since the setting is quite limited—the office or the home, usually—and the characters act within the boundaries of ordinary human beings, given an eccentricity or two.

To add to the problem, some series have built-in self-destructing mechanisms. For example, a program that derives most of its humor from small children will have to change as they grow older and lose their cuteness. A program set in a school classroom has to face the problem that sooner or later the kids will get promoted or graduate. There are solutions. The family show can have Mom get pregnant or she can adopt. At school, the kids can fail together or go on to college together. But will the audience be willing to adjust to the new changes? The series risks losing the chemistry that was so successful.

One type of show that faces this dilemma is the "alien" comedy. A creature from outer space lands on earth, makes friends, and then creates havoc with its skewed view of human culture. In series like *Mork & Mindy*, *My Favorite Martian*, and *Alf*, we all enjoy the creature's comments on our rituals and attitudes. Our contradictions and silliness are revealed. Our ideas of the norm are challenged and ridiculed. But at some point, an intelligent alien would have to assimilate and learn our ways. Then what? Usually after the first year or two, the alien loses its charm; the show starts sounding forced.

3rd Rock from the Sun lasted five-and-a-half years. The producers, Bonnie and Terry Turner, created the Coneheads on *Saturday Night Live*, a comedy skit about an alien family who tried to live the All-American life. Their series was about a group of people on a spaceship that crash-landed in the heartland of Ohio. Not only do they have to learn the ways of our citizens, but they also had to adjust to changes in their age, status, and gender.

Their reactions to topics like aging, romance, truthfulness, crime, sports, politics, sex, holidays, jury duty, racism, and plastic surgery were always unpredictable and usually downright wacky. It was fun to get their bizarre take on what seemed so commonplace to us. But by the third year, scripts built on their observations and reactions were fewer. What were the writers to do as the initial impetus behind the series lost its power, when many of the easily available topics had been covered? Shouldn't these characters have caught on by then to earthling ways?

To the viewer, *3rd Rock's* most effective strategy was to have strong comic talent in the primary and secondary roles. John Lithgow as Dick, the leader, in theory, of the aliens, could do physical humor and deliver lines with high energy. The other members of his crew were equally talented. Even Jane Curtin as his "love interest" knew how to project the right reaction to the insanity around her. Furthermore, the show was helped by the different identities of the characters: college professor, high school student, beautiful woman, and eccentric. Each could get involved in a variety of situations and interact with a wide range of people. But still the program was eventually forced to focus more on episodes about relationships that seemed to belong more to the family or work sitcom; the team remained oddball, but not quite as extraterrestrial. They seemed more interested in their own sex lives than in our culture.

Especially, in the fifth season, when a character had an alien baby, the audience must have sensed that finally the creative team had run out of possibilities. They had developed the concept as far as it could go.

Spin City (ABC, 1996–2002) followed a group of people who worked together under the leadership of the deputy mayor of New York City (played originally by Michael J. Fox and later by Charlie Sheen), but who spent most of their time dealing with their interlocking personal lives. *Suddenly Susan* (NBC, 1996–2000), which starred former model Brooke Shields, was set in the magazine publishing industry, and *Becker* (NBC, 1998–2004) is about a crusty neighborhood doctor, played by Ted Danson. One of the more interesting of the pseudo family sitcoms is *Scrubs* (NBC, 2001–present), the story of three medical interns (Zach Braff, Donald Faison, and Sarah Chalke), who share work, friendship, and a rich fantasy life in a hospital.

A group of teenagers (including Topher Grace and Ashton Kutcher) forms a sort of family in *That '70s Show* (Fox, 1998–present), a program set,

They weren't really a family. They weren't even humans. But like most inhabitants of TV sitcoms, the characters from *3rd Rock from the Sun* liked to gather together and discuss the major problems and minor annoyances of life. They were played by Kirsten Johnson, John Lithgow, Joseph Gordon-Levitt, and French Stewart. Courtesy of Photofest.

obviously, in the 1970s. Although the fashions and music are different from today, the problems of being a teen apparently remain much the same as characters deal with parents, romances, and the eternal question of what to do after high school.

Will & Grace (NBC, 1998--present) is about four friends, the two men of whom are openly gay and the two women openly straight. They are the latest in a short line of homosexual lead characters in prime-time televi-sion. *Love, Sidney* (NBC, 1981–1983) centered on artist Sidney Shorr (Tony Randall), who might have been gay, although there was no explicit acknowl-edgement of his sexuality, whatever it was. Later, the title character, played by Ellen DeGeneres, on *Ellen* (ABC, 1994–1998) was revealed to be lesbian in the now-famous "coming out" episode of April 30, 1997. Neither series had won the mainstream audience's loyalty, and both stirred up a degree of controversy. But from the beginning, viewers seemed to accept the orienta-tion of characters of Will (Eric McCormack) and Jack (Sean Hayes) in *Will & Grace*. A good deal of the show's humor is built around making fun of gays, but in a sympathetic style.

A spin-off of *Friends*, *Joey* (NBC, 2004–present) (Matt LeBlanc), tried to maintain the fans' loyalty to one of the original series' characters. Joey moved to California, where his sister and nephew live to form a sort-of family, but the audience hasn't yet warmed to the transplant.

The Divorced Family

As divorce continued to be increasingly accepted in contemporary American society, the relationships of divorced parents, their children and new spouses became fodder for sitcoms. A primarily male version of the divorced family sitcom is *Two and a Half Men* (CBS, 2003–present). After his divorce, a father (Jon Cryer) and son move in to the bachelor brother's (Charlie Sheen) place. *Reba* (with country music star Reba McEntire) (WB, 2001–present) has her children, her ex-husband, and his wife to deal with on a daily basis. *Cybill* (starring Cybill Shepherd) (CBS, 1995–1998) had children and not one, but two ex-husbands, and was perhaps the first prime-time program to center on a multiple divorcée.

The Urban Comedy

African-American actors seldom were chosen to play the lead in action/ adventure show or dramas, but their contribution to the sitcom during the decade has been more substantial. Fox, WB, and UPN have all tried to attract a hip, young, urban audience with comedies about people of color. *The Steve Harvey Show* (WB, 1996–2002) was about a former singer who became a school teacher. The stories involved romance and comedy, and introduced the television audience to Cedric the Entertainer. *Moesha* (UPN, 1996–2001) starred Brandy, the popular singer, and told the story of her family, her boy-friends, and her school experiences. *The Jamie Foxx Show* (WB, 1996–2001) followed his life as an aspiring rap singer. And stand-up comic Bernie Mac plays a version of himself in *The Bernie Mac Show* (Fox, 2001–present), a successful entertainer who ends up taking care of his sister's three children. His persona is not quite as saccharin as most TV daddies, giving the show more sense of realism. Perhaps the biggest contribution of all of these comedies was to introduce new talent to a broader American public.

DRAMA

For some time producers had been reluctant to invest in hour-long dramas, as they were hard to syndicate to television stations, which preferred running 30-minute sitcoms during the lucrative 4 P.M. to 8 P.M. EST timeslot, when the audience is not sitting quietly in front of the set in rapt concentration. But with the advent of cable networks, a new syndication marketplace developed for the drama, and the genre blossomed.

General

Although programmers were reluctant to schedule the more experimental sort of quality drama, they were willing to try variations of familiar themes and techniques with some interesting results. Because some of quality television's innovations had a lasting effect, sometimes it's difficult to draw a line between the dramas of this period and soap operas. They may both have serialized stories and an ensemble cast, but for the purposes of this book, a series is categorized as a drama if its focus remains on one or two characters and if it has a more subdued emotional tone.

For example, *Third Watch* (NBC, 1999–present) combines the action-packed stories of police officers, firefighters, and paramedics with the human drama of their personal lives. The balance between adventure and emotions varies from episode to episode. And *Party of Five* (Fox, 1994–2000) dealt with the problems of a family trying to reorganize their lives after the sudden death of their parents. The oldest son (Matthew Fox) found himself trying to raise his sometimes uncooperative siblings. The story was serial and concentrated on love and heartbreaks, but the focus remained on the family and their problems. Therefore, while these two series share many elements of the soap opera, they were categorized as dramas.

The couple (Sela Ward and Billy Campbell) who were the focus of *Once and Again* (ABC, 1999–2002) found a rocky road to romance with each other. Complications included their careers, their children, and their former spouses. Flashbacks and speeches made to the camera filled in the details about their emotions. One of the more interesting aspects of the program was that although the stars were both over 40 years old—ancient in prime-time standards—and allowed to have a romance, their teenaged children still received much attention in the plots.

One of the most unusual dramatic genres is the political drama. *West Wing* (NBC, 1999–present) is about the president and his staff. Personal lives and political issues intertwine. Another rarity is the period piece. *American Dreams* (NBC, 2002–present) is set in the 1960s and deals with a family's relationships with each other in the context of the political and cultural events of the time. One of the more interesting aspects of the show is its use of present-day performers to imitate singers of the past on *American Bandstand*.

Although many dramas have been set in high schools, few have been successful. An exception was *Boston Public* (Fox, 2002–2005). The program was produced by David Kelley and reflected his style: quirky characters in unusual situations who deal with both the serious and the ridiculous aspects of modern life.

The trend toward attracting a young audience with themes, characters, and settings intensified with the addition of the WB, which tries to attract the same audience as Fox. Three programs stand out. *Felicity* (1998–2002) followed the life of a sweet young girl (Keri Russell) who went to college in the big city and dealt with issues facing those in their late teens and early 20s. *Gilmore Girls* (2000–present) is the story of another sweet young girl (Alexis Bledel) and her young single mother (Lauren Graham), but the tone is much different. These two women don't take themselves quite as seriously as many of the inhabitants of teen shows—and at times seem more like friends than mother and daughter—and their lively, literate banter veers more toward the lighthearted. And *Everwood* (2002–present) is a sort of throwback to 1960s bachelor father and moving-to-the-country-to-start-a-new-life programs. It centers on a formerly urban doctor (Treat Williams) and his children, who have to adjust to small-town living following the death of his wife.

The 1960s battle cry of "don't trust anyone over 30" appears to have been taken to heart in prime-time television. Writers with successful careers complain that producers won't hire them if they're older than 30, producers say the networks won't listen to them if they're over 30, and network programmers all seem to be 30, if not younger. The belief that only young people could create programs for other young people is found across the networks.

Another consequence of the desire to appeal to a younger audience is that the use of popular music has become more prominent. In the past,

In this scene from the finale of *Buffy the Vampire Slayer*, Sarah Michelle Gellar as Buffy prepared her team for their ultimate battle with evil. On the left is Willow (Alyson Hannigan); behind her is Spike (James Marsters); and on the right is Faith (Eliza Dushku), three of her most trusted allies. Courtesy of Photofest.

there had been, maybe, a theme song and some incidental music underlying some scenes to enhance the romance or peril or heartwarming qualities of the script. (This aspect was especially useful if one assumed, as the networks did, that the audience wasn't paying much attention. For example, suspenseful music could lure people back to the set from the kitchen.) But the WB has filled its programs with different songs by different artists every week, and included the lyrics on the audio track. Sometimes the music played under the scene, but often the action all but stopped as the music received the emphasis. Not surprisingly, it usually came from a CD distributed by Warner Bros.' music division.

Occult

The unusual and the downright weird moved into the mainstream of prime-time during the period, part of the desire to reach the young audience, who was seen as being attracted to stories that stretched the imagination. Perhaps teen viewers saw their own world as strange and felt like aliens at times, making them more sympathetic to the characters in these stories.

One of the first successes in the category was *Buffy the Vampire Slayer* (WB and UPN, 1997–2002). When the series began, Buffy (Sarah Michelle Gellar) was a typically shallow teen but was told by her somewhat unorthodox school librarian that she had the potential to be a vampire fighter and needed training. Destiny thus brought romance (including with vampires), heartbreak, friendship, and many battles with a wide variety of supernatural creatures. But even her most extreme problems were recognized by the audience as exaggerations of their own everyday dilemmas, and the program soon reached cult status. *Angel* (1999–2004) was a spin-off of *Buffy* and told the tale of a vampire (David Boreanaz) who was trying to atone for the evil he had done. Similar in its supernatural theme is *Charmed* (WB, 1998–present), the story of three young-adult sisters who are modern-day witches. Their romantic lives get mixed up in their fight against supernatural villains with alarming regularity, and the series is well-known for a feud between stars Shannen Doherty and Alyssa Milano, which ended with Doherty's dismissal from the program.

Science Fiction

Science fiction is a genre that has traditionally not done all that well on television, and like most other forms of programming has been adapted to the interests of the younger audience. The teen years of Superman (Tem Welling) is the premise of *Smallville* (WB, 2001–present). The teen of steel has girl problems, family problems, and school problems, as do most teens, but he also has to learn to develop and control his superpowers and, in his spare time, conquer evil. The emphasis is on emotions, but the science fiction elements add action, special effects, and unpredictable events.

A more traditional example of sci-fi was *Star Trek: Voyager* (UPN, 1995–2001). The program, a clear descendant of the original *Star Trek* (NBC, 1966–1969), followed the journeys of the starship Voyager as it made its 75-year trip back home, under the command of Capt. Kathryn Janeway (Kate Mulgrew), the first woman to hold such a position in the perennial series.

An even more adult-oriented science fiction show is the difficult-to-categorize *Lost* (ABC, 2004–present). Its premise is that an airplane has crashed on a remote island, and the survivors struggle with each other and with dark forces in the jungle. One of the show's appeals is that its format crosses a number of genre boundaries. Like science fiction, the impossible happens regularly; like soap operas, the story has many characters, all with pasts filled with emotional turmoil; like action/adventure stories, danger is everywhere and the characters must fight evil. The series even has overtones of the reality show *Survivor*. The result is programming without a recognizable formula, forcing the audience to guess what is happening and why.

Legal

The quality television effect lingered on in the legal drama. For example, an interesting, but not long-lived, experiment was *Murder One* (ABC, 1995–1997). The entire first season was spent on one case, the sex-and-drugs related murder of a young woman. Producer David Kelley had more success with *The Practice* (ABC, 1997–2004), which followed a team of attorneys led by Bobby Donnell (Dylan McDermott) as they defended a motley crew of clients. The firm's ethical dilemmas and personal interactions were as interesting as the courtroom antics, and there was fleeting nudity in some episodes. But when the network refused to pay the producer his asking price at renewal time, the series metamorphosed into the new, and presumably more cheaply produced, *Boston Legal* (ABC, 2004–present). The plots now center on an attorney (James Spader), who may have his own system of morality, or perhaps he's completely amoral, in a firm of idiosyncratic lawyers and aides.

Perhaps Kelley's most popular creation was *Ally McBeal* (Fox, 1997–2002). The title character (Calista Flockhart), an exceptionally thin young lawyer, worked with clients who ranged from the eccentric to the downright weird, but the courtroom trials were just a backdrop to Ally's personal struggles with her career and her love life. Sometimes, the audience saw the odd images that intruded into her mind when emotions overwhelmed her, like the creepy computer-generated animated baby who danced while she contemplated her ticking biological clock.

Judging Amy (CBS, 1999–2005) looked at family court from the judge's side of the bench. The cases under her consideration sometimes mirrored her own problems with her mother (Tyne Daly), daughter, and brothers. Amy Brenneman was both producer and star of the series.

Medical

E.R. continued to dominate the medical drama genre. One of the few medical dramas to survive for any length of time was *Providence* (NBC, 1999–2002). The story was about a doctor (Melina Kanakaredes) who moved home to Rhode Island to be with her family after her mother dropped dead during her sister's wedding. There were patients to deal with, of course, but the stories mostly centered on the problems of her relatives. Another medical survivor was *Doc* (Pax, 2001–present). A country boy MD, played by country singer Billy Ray Cyrus (of "Achy Breaky Heart" fame), treats folks in the big city in a reversal of the urban-to-rural flow of many prime-time programs.

Grey's Anatomy (ABC, 2005–present) has reintroduced the evergreen storyline about medical interns. Together, they share the long hours and constant pressure of life in the hospital, where a mistake can kill a patient or end a career. Of course, they also share friendship and the enmity that develops along the way. And *House* (Fox, 2004–present) concentrates on the role of doctor as diagnostician. Hugh Laurie plays the irascible, insulting doctor who shares his venom and his wisdom with his colleagues and his suffering patients.

Religion

Programs with religious themes tend to not attract the hip, urban audience desired by advertisers. However, *7th Heaven* (WB, 1996–2006) is an exception, as well as a program that references the happy family programs of the past. Produced by Aaron Spelling, it's the story of Protestant minister Eric Camden (Stephen Collins), his stay-at-home wife (Catherine Hicks), and their children, and it always ends up affirming traditional religious values. Along the way, though, the teen characters are led into temptation, of both the minor and major kinds, and have to deal with the consequences of their actions.

Prime-Time Soaps

In the 1980s, Fox found that teens are attracted to soaps if the setting is glamorous, the young stars are appealing, and the plots are spiced with sexy scenes. With *The O.C.* (2003–present), the network continues that tradition. The series is set firmly in the land of beauty and wealth, Orange County, California. A family (Peter Gallagher, Kelly Rowan, and Adam Brophy) introduces a boy from the wrong side of the tracks (Ben McKenzie) to a new world of affluence and teen angst. Unlike most teen soaps, however, the adults in this series are interesting people, and the plots sometimes have a slight twist that keeps them entertaining, even when the emotions are overwhelming.

The O.C. has the typical ingredients for a teen-aged soap opera—attractive characters engaged in sin, sex, and sunbathing. But the dialogue is occasionally a little lighter than average. These regulars, played by Adam Brody, Benjamin McKenzie, and Peter Gallagher, prove that even the men have to look good. Courtesy of Photofest.

WB has challenged Fox in this category. *Dawson's Creek* (WB, 1998–2003) followed the lives of a group of high school characters into life after graduation. They experimented with careers and universities, but were never able to totally leave behind the loves of their past. The distinguishing characteristic of this drama was its dialogue, which was literate and charming, although perhaps not always typical of what comes out of the mouths of teens.

The prime-time soap for adults also returned, but with a new setting. Instead of concentrating on the lives of the rich and famous, *Desperate Housewives* (ABC, 2004–present) follows four upper-middle-class women, their families, and neighbors through crimes, love affairs, and warm, bonding moments. They live on Wisteria Lane, a quiet street in what appears to be the perfect suburban haven, but as the narrator, who died, says, there are dark secrets behind every door. The program mixes comedy, mystery, sex appeal, and drama to keep the audience wondering what will happen next.

Desperate Housewives tries to answer the questions: How can attractive women who have everything be so unsatisfied? And what happens when your striving for happiness always backfires? Searching for the answers are characters played by Felicity Huffman, Eva Longoria, Teri Hatcher, and Marcia Cross. Courtesy of Photofest.

SPY

The spy genre has turned as stylish on television as it has in films. *24* (Fox, 2001–present) follows a secret agent (Kiefer Sutherland) in real time for 24 hours during a season, with each one-hour episode representing one hour of clock time. Innovative visual techniques and fascinating plots are used to build suspense in a way that's almost addictive for fans. *Alias* (ABC, 2001–present) is also a stylish exploration of the espionage theme but casts a woman, Jennifer Garner, in its lead role. Its plots are less realistic than are *24*'s and have greater emphasis on romance and family issues.

DETECTIVES

The *Law & Order* permutations, distinguished from one another by colons and subtitles, and all produced by Dick Wolf, continued as mainstays of NBC programming as the audience seems to appreciate getting the equivalent of a brand-name product. *Special Victims Unit* (1999–present) deals with sexual crimes, and *Criminal Intent* (2001–present) focuses on a detective (Vincent D'Onofrio) and his deductive style of investigation. However, the less successful *Trial by Jury* (March–August 2005), which concentrated on the legal side of crime-fighting, was quickly canceled when it failed to build the ratings expected of it.

Another popular franchise began with *CSI: Crime Scene Investigation* (CBS, 2000–present), produced by Jerry Bruckheimer. The original series, set in Las Vegas, uses graphic visuals to illustrate its gory crimes. The protagonists, forensic scientists, work out of a well-equipped laboratory, and the audience has responded so well to blunt discussions of maggots, autopsies, and stomach contents that two clones have been added on CBS: *CSI: Miami*, beginning in 2002, and *CSI: NY* in 2004.

The classic detective show with a mild twist remains popular, as does setting the program within the Federal Bureau of Investigation. *Without a Trace* (CBS, 2002–present) follows the FBI in its search for missing persons, and *Numb3rs* (CBS, 2005–present) tells the story of an FBI agent who comes to rely on the skills of his mathematician brother.

JAG (NBC and CBS, 1995–2005) can be classified as a legal drama with military overtones. The two leading characters, Lt. Cmdr. Harm Rabb (David James Elliott) and USMC Maj. Sarah "Mac" MacKenzie (Catherine Bell), were attorneys with the Judge Advocate General Corps of the U.S. Navy, and their cases involved all the usual sorts of crimes but against a colorful backdrop of crisp uniforms, naval aviation, aircraft carriers, and so on. Producer Donald Bellisario created a spin-off, *NCIS* (CBS, 2003–present), about the Naval Criminal Intelligence Service.

The female detective came into her own during this time period. For example, *Crossing Jordan* (NBC, 2001–present) plays off the current interest in forensics and follows a pathologist (Jill Hennessy) who solves crimes in her own not-by-the-book style. *Sue Thomas: F.B.Eye* (Pax, 2002–present) deals with a deaf agent (Deanne Bray) whose talent at reading lips makes her a significant asset in the surveillance of criminals. The police officer (Kathryn Morris) in *Cold Case* (CBS, 2003–present) works with a team of homicide detectives to investigate unsolved crimes from the past. *Profiler* (NBC, 1996–2000) was the story of a female psychologist who used her skills to understand the minds of criminals to aid the FBI. And in *Medium* (NBC, 2005–present), Arizona psychic Allison Dubois (Patricia Arquette) uses her abilities to help the district attorney's office solve difficult crimes.

The mixing of genres continues, as well. *The Pretender* (NBC, 1996–2000) combined elements of science fiction, detective story and soap opera. Lead character Jarod Russell (Michael T. Weiss) escaped from the secret laboratory where he'd been raised and used his extraordinary intelligence to pretend to be other people in an effort to solve crimes. Interwoven with these plot elements was a continuing story about characters, past and present, associated with the lab, including questions about who Russell's parents really were and where exactly they might be.

ANIMATION

As in much of prime-time animation history, the few experiments that were tried in this genre usually met little success. The only program to come close to the popularity of *The Simpsons* was *King of the Hill* (Fox, 1996–present), the comic story of Texan Hank Hill, his eccentric family, and his odd neighbors. They may talk like run-of-the-mill rednecks, but their lives veer off into the preposterous frequently.

QUIZ SHOWS

The quiz show had almost disappeared from prime-time after the scandals of the 1950s. In the summer of 1999, ABC, desperate for ratings, presented two weeks of *Who Wants to Be a Millionaire?* The audience, perhaps bored by summer repeats and the sameness of all the other programming, responded, and the program ran on the prime-time schedule from January 2000 until June 2002. The format was simple: Host Regis Philbin asked contestants questions, and if they answered correctly often enough, they could win big money. *The Weakest Link* (NBC, 2001–2002) was based on a British program, and although it provided a bit of competition to *Millionaire*, it soon moved to Pax and later into first-run syndication.

REALITY

The scripted reality show had been popular in the decade before, but *Survivor* (CBS, 2000–present) brought a variation to prime-time: the unscripted reality show. A group of people were brought to a remote location, given a variety of physical challenges, and allowed to vote on who would be forced to leave. The winner, the one person remaining, got $1 million. Audiences seemed fascinated by watching ordinary people, under pressure

The introduction of unscripted reality shows from Europe brought a new genre to American TV—sometimes with fun, exciting challenges, sometimes with tacky, humiliating stunts. One of the most successful is *Survivor*. In Africa, these team members participate in a stairway to the stars contest. Courtesy of Photofest.

in extraordinary settings, form alliances and then stab each other in the back, metaphorically speaking, when the going gets rough.

Imitations quickly followed, of course. After all, the format was relatively inexpensive to produce, with no actors, no writers, no special effects needed. One of the basic rules of programming is that if a program is cheap, easy to produce, and successful, it will be imitated quickly, if not especially well.

Some of the unscripted reality programs put an emphasis if not on romance, then on sex. Perhaps the most tasteless of the "sexy" unscripted reality programs was *Temptation Island* (Fox 2001–2002). The program kept a close eye on supposedly committed young couples who were brought to a luxurious setting and tempted by seductive men and women. In a similar, voyeuristic vein are *The Bachelor* and *The Bachelorette* (ABC, 2002–present). Both introduce a single person to a variety of potential spouses and allow the audience to sit back and watch the courtships.

Fear Factor (NBC, 2001–present) offered contestants big money to do frightening (jumping off of a building) and disgusting (eating pigs' rectums) stunts. Amazingly, people were willing to participate, and many others willing to watch. One of the classier entries in the genre was *The Amazing Race* (CBS, 2001–present). Here, teams traveled the world to see who would get to the destination first, while overcoming financial, physical, mental, and emotional obstacles.

There are minor variations on the unscripted theme, of course. *Beauty and the Geek* (WB, 2005–present) pairs off hopeless male geeks with gorgeous young women. *Big Brother* (CBS, 2000–present) puts a group of incompatible people in a house, shuts the door, turns on the cameras, and waits for the squabbling and romance to start. For additional money, viewers can tune in for 24-hour-a-day coverage on pay-per-view cable. The format of this program, like some others in the genre, had originally been a hit in Europe before being transplanted to the United States. *The Apprentice* (NBC, 2004–present) with Donald Trump proved that a competition in the corporate boardroom could be as cutthroat and entertaining as one on a remote island. And some of the shows gave the audience the cruel pleasure of knowing more than the contestants. *Joe Millionaire* (Fox, January–February 2003) turned out to really be Joe Blue Collar, but the young women trying to woo him don't know the truth until the final session.

An interesting metamorphosis happened with *Extreme Makeover* (ABC, 2002–present). The original concept followed people through plastic surgery, haircuts, and makeup as they went from ugly ducklings to swans. Critics complained that show overemphasized the role of good looks in creating happiness. But then *Extreme Makeover: Home Edition* (ABC, 2004–present) won viewers with its heartwarming stories of good, honest people who badly needed new homes.

This programming trend has even led to the return of an old favorite, the amateur talent show, which had all but died out by the early 1960s. By far the most successful in the genre is *American Idol: The Search for a Superstar* (Fox, 2002–present). Young singers audition and the number of contestants is whittled down by judges, while the audience vote on finalists, some of whom, like Kelly Clarkson, go on to recording contracts, radio and video airplay, and some degree of presence as pop music–related celebrities.

Doubts about the spontaneity of events in unscripted reality show have been raised on occasion. Certainly, there is much editing of the final product, the situations are contrived, and contestants are aware they're on camera. And the demand of reality show writers for better pay adds to the suspicions. But are scenes and people manipulated to "enhance" reality? Are contests judged fairly or with the ratings in mind? Perhaps only the producers know for sure. But the audience seems willing to put up with some doubt about how real reality is in exchange for seeing programs that are not quite as formulaic as the fiction they've become so accustomed to.

NEWS MAGAZINES

The old favorites survived, thrived, and multiplied. Producing a half hour of news was expensive, but producing an hour didn't cost twice as much. Once the anchors and the reporting team had been hired and the equipment purchased, creating more news programming was relatively cheap; therefore, *60 Minutes*, *Dateline*, and *Primetime Live* expanded the number of nights they were on the air and continued to draw sizable audiences.

MOVIES/MINISERIES

The broadcast networks continued to use Hollywood films to fill blank spots on their schedules, but films could not usually attract a large audience because most people had already seen them, either in theaters, on DVD, or on cable. Nor could films be used to build an audience week after week. Made-for-television movies also held a limited niche in prime-time. Despite the prohibitive cost of limited series—the new term for miniseries—the networks occasionally tried. For example, in 2005 NBC put on the religiously themed *Revelations* at a cost of more than $20 million. Cable networks provided competition, but also a chance for further exposure. *Revelations* also ran on Bravo, the cable network owned by General Electric, parent company of NBC.

The cost of limited series is driven up by the need to make them spectacular enough to attract attention in a media-saturated society, and that means big stars, location shooting, and expensive special effects. ABC's *Dinotopia* and *Threat Matrix* were examples of programs that failed to cover their costs, but producers hope they'll become profitable through sales to broadcasters outside the United States and to domestic cable networks. In 2005, most limited series are made with episodes that are complete unto themselves, which allows the audience to start viewing at any point and still understand what's going on.

TECHNOLOGY

Technological developments continue to reshape the marketplace and challenge network programmers. The audience has more options, and therefore decision making is more complicated for them. All of the changes discussed in this section have the potential to change the industry. But the most difficult questions remain: What does the audience want? What is worth its time and money?

The cable networks continue to be strong competitors. Although more than 50 percent of the audience on many nights is watching cable networks, over-the-air networks still receive substantially more of the advertising revenue. One reason is that the traditional medium is still the only way to easily reach a mass audience easily. Broadcast television still attracts huge numbers of people who make frequent purchases of heavily advertised toothpaste, fast food, and detergents; cable networks continue to do better at attracting viewers with more specialized interests.

VCRs, since their introduction in the 1970s, have allowed the audience to record programs and play them back at their leisure. But a newer technology is rapidly replacing the videocassette: DVDs store much more information on a disc, and the picture quality is superior. The disadvantage is the difficulty of recording one's own disc. For television, one effect has been that an additional stream of revenue can be directed toward some producers. For example, if a series earns a small but loyal audience and is canceled after a short run—as was *Wonderfalls*, which had just four episodes on Fox in 2004—fans may be willing to buy the program on DVD. Series that stir nostalgia also do well. Ordinary, poorly conceived, poorly executed series may not have an eager set of buyers when released on DVD.

Another technology replacing the VCR is the DVR (digital video recorder). These systems, TiVO for example, record the programs that the viewer most enjoys without the necessity of programming a recorder each time, allow live shows to be paused, and make skipping commercials easy. Since the broadcast networks rely on revenues from advertising, they worry about how to reach the audience with messages about products and services. One answer is product placement, in which the cast of a show uses and maybe even discusses a product that a company has paid to include in the program. For example, the judges of *American Idol* display cans of Coke during the contest, and *Extreme Makeover: Home Edition* mentions Sears many times during the hour. So far, the audience seems willing to tolerate these intrusions, but what if they get more numerous and even less subtle?

Networks are cramming more commercials and promotional announcements into the valuable prime-time minutes between shows. To keep the audience from using their remotes to click through the competition, networks now use pop-up inserts in the corner of the picture to encourage the audience to stay tuned to the next program. Soon, advertisements may appear in a similar format. Another technique used to keep the audience glued to the network is to go directly from the end of one show to the beginning of the next with no commercials in between. The credits are squeezed down to an unreadable small size, and promotions fill up the rest of the screen, as one show ends and the other immediately starts.

Television sets have been technically improved as well. New sound systems and bigger, better screens make the experience of television viewing more like watching a film. One trend in housing is to have a dedicated media room with a giant screen, high-quality speakers, and luxuriously comfortable chairs. A high-definition picture could make the investment worthwhile, although the question of whether there's much worth watching remains.

The FCC, at the behest of Congress, has required that all television stations must be capable of broadcasting high-definition signals, perhaps as early as 2006, if the FCC doesn't change its mind as it has in the past. This new technology allows an amazingly clear, sharp picture with small details that can be easily seen. The proportions of the high definition screen are like a movie theatre screen. Some cable and broadcast systems already use high-definition systems.

Stations may choose to broadcast a signal in high definition, or they can choose to "multiplex" the signal and broadcast up to four programs simultaneously. For example, channel one could consist of their regular programs; channel two might be programs delayed by an hour or more; channel three could be a for-pay channel; and channel four could run 24 hours of news. Another possibility is that a station might use all four channels except during prime-time, when one high-definition picture would be sent to homes. The effect on programming should be interesting. Special effects are cheaper and easier with this technology, so will we see more science fiction? Will producers create more visually interesting scenes to take advantage of the technology?

In the other direction, televisions are getting smaller. Walking around with a portable set is easy enough now, but now viewers can get the picture on their iPods. Programs that require minimum attention would suit the audience on the move.

Another potential complication for the broadcast industry is the role of the Internet. It is, first of all, competition for the audience's limited time. Ratings data indicates that young men in the valued 18-to-34 demographic are watching less television than they were a few years ago. One explanation is that they're spending time instead on the Internet. Secondly, there is the concern at the networks that audience members can download programs illegally. Although additional viewers are desired, they're most appreciated when they watch the commercials (and buy the products). Producers, stations, and networks lose the potential for revenue with this kind of electronic competition. However, in the future, more programs may be available via the Internet to paying subscribers, which will add a stream of revenue.

On the plus side, the Internet can be used to promote new shows. ABC identified potential viewers for *Desperate Housewives* and *Lost* and spread the word about them through the Web. Also, fans can become more involved, even build support for a failing program, when they are linked by the Internet. Likewise, audiences can be enticed through short samples of the program available on the Web.

Another influence on the programming of tomorrow may be video games. They're already a source of competition for the young audience's attention, and "gaming" seems to be spreading from its core of teenaged boys into older, more affluent groups of men and women. But are video games training a new generation of active viewers, who are accustomed to interacting with the screen and controlling the image? Will they become couch potatoes like previous generations or will they be a more demanding audience? Or, even worse, will they stay with their video games and ignore television completely?

THE FUTURE OF PRIME-TIME TELEVISION

Technology is not the only influence on programming. When broadcast networks look into the future, some other changes can be predicted. One is the growth in the percentage of the audience that is African-American, Hispanic, and Asian-American, which together comprise about 35 percent of the current population of the United States. More minorities will have to move into producing, writing, and acting to create programming for this growing segment of the audience, and the networks will have to hire staffers with a wider diversity of ethnic backgrounds to develop prime-time content.

Research will remain important in making decisions about which programs to schedule, how to keep them popular, and when to cancel them. The technology of gathering ratings information continues to change, allowing the networks to get more demographic information and to get it more quickly. Many affiliates have been dependent on handwritten diaries for information about the viewing patterns of their shows, but this method is only done four times a year during the important "sweeps" months, when advertising rates for the following quarter are set. But now more affiliates and their networks get instant feedback on the success of their programs through meters. In the future, as more markets get wired, fewer diaries will be used and the sweeps will be less important. Networks and stations will no longer need to throw expensive specials, designed to draw abnormally large audiences, on the screen during November, February, May, and July. Instead, efforts to attract viewers can be spread more evenly throughout the year.

Traditionally, TV viewing has declined in the summer, as most people find outdoor activities to be more attractive than sitting indoors in front of the television set during good weather. But in recent years, Fox has perfected the technique of introducing new series in the summer months when competition from the other networks consists mostly of reruns. The method has worked well when the new show offered something fresh to bored viewers.

And Fox has been reluctant to throw all of its new series into the madness of fall premiere season. The resulting glut of programs means that some programs with potential don't get sampled by the audience at all and are canceled because programmers have no way of telling whether they would be a success or not. The other networks may decide that introducing new series throughout the year is a more logical and less expensive strategy.

CONCLUSION

The last ten years have seen increased competition for the broadcast commercial networks. UPN and WB have enjoyed some success. Pax is struggling to stay alive. Cable networks continue to siphon viewers away from broadcasting. The internet and video games compete for the audience's time.

For the most part, the networks' response to this onslaught has been to continue doing the basics—sitcoms, legal and medical dramas, detective shows, and so forth. New formats have been tried in the area of reality programming. Some have been successful; some attracted attention initially, but never developed a loyal audience. *Desperate Housewives* and *Lost* would seem to point the way to a new kind of TV series, but the programmers have been unable to analyze the reasons for their success and have thus far failed to produce worthy successors. A second strategy has been to form partnerships with rivals in an effort to share programming, expenses, and audiences, but then revenues have to be shared also.

It's difficult to say what lessons have been learned by network executives in the last ten years, but the older audience remains optimistic, checking out the new shows and remaining loyal to their favorites. The younger audience may make other media their primary source of entertainment and go to the networks only when they offer something unique, special, and worthy of their attention.

Conclusion

The factors that have influenced broadcast programming in the past will probably continue to be important: law and regulation, technology, the industry, culture, leaders, advertising, and research; but many predict major changes in television programming may occur within the next decade. Some of the factors driving change for broadcasting are discussed here.

The demographics of the United States are changing as the Baby Boomers get older and as the number of Hispanics, African-Americans, and Asian-Americans increase. How will programmers react to this new audience? And the answer to that question will depend on how advertisers react.

A new generation is growing up surfing the Internet for information, relying more on person-to-person communication with cell phones and instant messaging, and playing for hours on video games. As adults, will they be willing to accept a role as passive couch potatoes or will they demand more interaction with their TV set and more control over its content? The computer is usually used by one person at a time. If that model continues, what will happen to the family gathering around the modern hearth, the TV set?

Networks and production companies, like other businesses, will continue to consolidate and strive for vertical and horizontal integration. One aspect of that movement will be reaching out internationally. Will Americans see more programs from other countries? Will producers strive to make their products more marketable around the world?

Broadcasters have been mandated by Congress and the Federal Communications Commission to have the capacity to deliver high-definition programming to the home. The result can be top quality video, equivalent to a movie seen in a theater. The question is: Will stations use this capacity to give viewers an excellent picture or provide more channels? Perhaps, a more interesting question is: Does the audience want better quality technically? The answer may depend on where they do their viewing—in a well-equipped media room or on a portable, handheld device.

Other people look into the future and ask: Do we still need broadcast networks? Why shouldn't all programming be delivered via cable or satellite without going through the process of network to station to home? Should people pay for each program they see in a system where they would have unlimited choices, where they could view what they wanted when they wanted, as long as they were willing to pay for it? What would be the role of advertising then?

The programming of the past sometimes creates nostalgia in people, as though their memories of characters in TV series are more comforting and more vivid than their memories of friends and relatives, who are, after all, merely mortal and who can be aggravatingly human. Perhaps the best evidence of this phenomenon is the rash of Hollywood movies based on series of the past like *Charlie's Angels*, *The Dukes of Hazard*, and *Bewitched*. Their names are instantly recognized, but their failures at the box office indicate their failure to deliver on the expectations of the audience. This book may have stirred some memories in you. After all, many programs can be seen on cable channels every day. Even teenagers can feel nostalgia for *The Brady Bunch*.

The truth is that there has been no one time when TV programming has been wonderfully superior to all other times. Certain genres have blossomed and others have failed over the decades, but the overall content has remained, with a few exciting exceptions, determinedly mediocre.

There are some justifications for this blandness: the difficulty of pleasing a mass audience of different ages and backgrounds; the desire to avoid regulatory problems; the need to make a proper setting for commercials; the demand for making profits; and the problems involved in creating a series that has to please week after week, year after year. Perhaps the most difficult problem is finding creative people who can work together as a team to produce good programming with the constant, endless pressure of deadlines and budget and the necessity to deal with network functionaries who may have their own conflicting agendas. Ideas that look good on paper can fail in execution without the right alignment of talent in acting, writing, and producing.

The good news of this book is that despite all of the limitations of the medium, some producers, some studios, and some network executives are willing to break the rules occasionally with memorable results. But maybe the readers can also be grateful that certain producers, while not artists, used the formulas of genre and the demands of a commercial environment to create shows that displayed a craftsperson's care and skill. Some programming may break no new ground in themes, in plots, in dialogue, in production values, or in acting—and yet it can bring pleasure to viewers, not just in the present but afterward as they remember the fictional friends and family members they shared time with. The question for the future is: Will the audience continue to be satisfied or will they demand more from the medium?

Notes

CHAPTER 1

1. Lawrence W. Lichty and Malachi C. Topping. *American Broadcasting: A Sourcebook on the History of Radio and Television* (New York: Hastings House Publishers, 1975), 298.

CHAPTER 3

1. Tim Brooks and Earle Marsh, *The Complete Directory to Prime Time Network and Cable TV Shows, 1946–Present*, 8th ed. (New York: Ballantine Books, 2003), 1007–8.
2. Ibid., 197.
3. David Marc and Robert J. Thompson, *Prime Time, Prime Movers* (Boston: Little, Brown and Company, 1992), 20.
4. Brooks and Marsh, 1271.
5. Ibid., 674.
6. Ibid., 1190.
7. Michele Hilmes, *Hollywood and Broadcasting: From Radio to Cable* (Urbana: University of Illinois Press, 1990), 166.
8. Ibid., 157, 165.
9. Christopher H. Sterling and John M. Kittross, *Stay Tuned: A Concise History of American Broadcasting*, 3rd ed. (Mahwah, NJ: Lawrence Erlbaum Associates, Publishers, 2002), 342.
10. Brooks and Marsh, 803.
11. Robert L. Hilliard and Michael C. Keith, *The Broadcast Century and Beyond: A Biography of American Broadcasting* (Boston: Focal Press, 2001), 144, 175.

CHAPTER 4

1. Marc and Thompson, 22.
2. Thomas Schatz, *Hollywood Genres: Formulas, Filmmaking and the Studio System* (New York: Random House, 1981), 35.
3. Gerald Nachman, *Raised on Radio* (Berkeley: University of California Press, 1998), 92.
4. Brooks and Marsh, 685.
5. Brooks and Marsh, 82–83, 102, 929–30.
6. Ibid., 329.
7. Anderson, Kent, *Television Fraud: The History and Implications of the Quiz Show Scandals* (Westport, CT: Greenwood Press, 1978), 73.
8. Ibid., 51.
9. Ibid., 55.
10. Ibid., 55.
11. Will Wright, *Sixguns & Society: A Structural Study of the Western.* (Berkeley, CA: University of California Press, 1997), 5–6.
12. Sterling and Kittross, 345.
13. Schatz, 38.
14. Ibid., 112.
15. Sterling and Kittross, 307.
16. Brooks and Marsh, 346, 811.
17. Ibid., 381.
18. Ibid., 1286.
19. Ibid., 117.
20. Ibid., 1195.

CHAPTER 5

1. Hardy, 244.
2. Ibid., 819.
3. Ibid., 294.
4. Marc and Thompson, 25–26.
5. Schatz, 37–38.
6. Brooks and Marsh, 736.
7. Eric J. Sanow. *Encyclopedia of American Police Cars* (Osceola, WI: MBI Publishing Co., 1999), 93.
8. Brooks and Marsh, 607.
9. Ibid., 171.
10. Hilmes, 166.
11. Ibid., 162.
12. Brooks and Marsh, 55.

CHAPTER 6

1. Janet Staiger, *Blockbuster TV: Must-See Sitcoms in the Network Era* (New York: New York University Press, 2000), 145.

2. Muriel G. Cantor and Joel M. Cantor, *Prime-Time Television: Content and Control* (Newbury Park, CA: Sage Publications, 1992), 109.

3. Nachman, 215.

4. Staiger, 113.

5. Ibid., 138.

6. Brooks and Marsh, 712.

7. Marc and Thompson, 224–25.

8. Cantor and Cantor, 109.

9. Alvin H. Marrill, *Movies Made for Television: The Telefeature and the Mini-Series 1974–1986* (New York: Baseline Books, 1987), 54.

10. Marc and Thompson, 293.

11. Brooks and Marsh, 1094.

CHAPTER 7

1. Alex Ben Block, *Outfoxed: Martin Davis, Barry Diller, Rupert Murdoch, Joan Rivers, and the Inside Story of America's Fourth Television Network* (New York: St. Martin's Press, 1990), 270.

2. Ibid., 202–4.

3. Sterling and Kittross, 502.

4. Robert J. Thompson, *Television's Second Golden Age: From Hill Street Blues to ER* (New York: Continuum, 1996), 15.

5. David Marc, *Bonfires of the Humanities: Television, Subliteracy, and Long-Term Memory Loss* (New York: Syracuse University Press, 1995), 104.

6. Robin Nelson, *TV Drama in Transition: Forms, Values and Cultural Change* (New York: St. Martin's Press, 1997), 32.

7. Steven D. Stark, *Glued to the Set: The 60 Television Shows and Events that Made Us Who We Are Today* (New York: The Free Press, 1997), 237.

8. Thompson, 186.

9. Nelson, 186.

CHAPTER 8

1. Richard Levinson and William Link, *Stay Tuned: An Inside Look at the Making of Prime-Time Television* (New York: St. Martin's Press, 1981), 617.

Bibliography

Anderson, Kent. *Television Fraud: The History and Implications of the Quiz Show Scandals.* Westport, CT: Greenwood Press, 1978.

Auletta, Ken. *The Highwaymen: Warriors of the Information Superhighway.* New York: Harcourt, Brace & Company, 1998.

Bensman, Marvin R. *The Beginning of Broadcast Regulation in the Twentieth Century.* McFarland: Jefferson, NC: 2000.

Blanchard, Margaret, ed. *History of the Mass Media in America: An Encyclopedia.* Chicago: Fitzroy Dearborn, 1998.

Block, Alex Ben. *Outfoxed: Martin Davis, Barry Diller, Rupert Murdoch, Joan Rivers, and the Inside Story of America's Fourth Television Network.* New York: St. Martin's Press, 1990.

Booker, M. Keith. *Strange TV: Innovative Television Series from the Twilight Zone to the X-Files.* Westport, CT: Greenwood Press, 2002.

Brook, Vincent. *Something Ain't Kosher Here: The Rise of the "Jewish" Sitcom.* New Brunswick, NJ: Rutgers University Press, 2003.

Brooks, Tim and Earle Marsh. *The Complete Directory to Prime Time Network and Cable TV Shows, 1946 – Present,* 8th. ed. New York. Ballantine Books, 2003.

Buzzard, Karen S. *Chains of Gold: Marketing the Ratings and Rating the Markets.* Metuchen, NJ: The Scarecrow Press, 1990.

Caldwell, John Thornton. *Televisuality: Style, Crisis, and Authority in American Television.* New Brunswick, NJ: Rutgers University Press, 1995.

Cantor, Muriel G. and Joel M. Cantor. *Prime-Time Television: Content and Control.* Newbury Park, CA: Sage Publications, 1992.

Chunovic, Louis. *One Foot on the Floor: The Curious Evolution of Sex on Television from I Love Lucy to South Park.* New York: TV Books, 2000.

Dunning, John, ed. *The Encyclopedia of Old-Time Radio.* New York: Oxford University Press. 1998.

Einstein, Mara. *Media Diversity: Economics, Ownership, and the FCC.* Mahway, NJ: Lawrence Erlbaum, 2004.

Feuer, Jane. *Seeing through the Eighties: Television and Reaganism.* Durham, NC: Duke University Press, 1995.

Gitlin, Todd. *Inside Prime Time.* New York: Pantheon, 1985.

Godfrey, Donald G., ed. *Historical Dictionary of American Radio.* Westport, CT: Greenwood Press, 1998.

Hardy, Phil, ed. *The Overlook Film Encyclopedia: Science Fiction.* Woodstock, NY: The Overlook Press, 1995.

Head, Sydney W., Christopher H. Sterling, and Lemuel B. Schofield. *Broadcasting in America: A Survey of Electronic Media,* 7th ed. Boston: Houghton Mifflin, 1994.

Hilliard, Robert L. and Michael C. Keith. *The Broadcast Century and Beyond: A Biography of American Broadcasting.* Boston: Focal Press, 2001.

Hilmes, Michele, ed. *Connections: A Broadcast History Reader.* Belmont, CA: Thomson/Wadsworth, 2003.

———. *Hollywood and Broadcasting: From Radio to Cable.* Urbana: University of Illinois Press, 1990.

Inglis, Andrew E. *Behind the Tube: A history of Broadcasting Technology and Business.* Boston: Focal Press, 1990

Lenburg, Jeff. *The Encyclopedia of Animated Cartoons.* New York: Facts on File, 1991.

Levinson, Richard and William Link. *Stay Tuned: An Inside Look at the Making of Prime-Time Television.* New York: St. Martin's Press, 1981.

Lichter, S. Robert, Linda S. Richter, and Stanley Rothman. *Watching America.* New York: Prentice Hall Press, 1991.

Lichty, Lawrence W. and Malachi C. Topping. *American Broadcasting: A Sourcebook on the History of Radio and Television.* New York: Hastings House Publishers, 1975.

Longworth, James L. *TV Creators: Conversations with America's Top Producers of Television Drama.* New York: Syracuse University Press, 2000.

MacDonald, J. Fred. *One Nation under Television: The Rise and Decline of Network TV.* New York: Pantheon Books, 1990.

Marc, David. *Bonfire of the Humanities: Television, Subliteracy, and Long-Term Memory Loss.* New York: Syracuse University Press, 1995.

——— and Robert J. Thompson. *Prime Time, Prime Movers.* Boston: Little, Brown and Company, 1992.

Marrill, Alvin H. *Movies Made for Television: The Telefeature and the Mini-Series 1974–1986.* New York: Baseline Books, 1987.

McCrohan, Donna. *Prime Time, Our Time: America's Life and Times through the Prism of Television.* Rocklin, CA: Prima Publishing and Communications, 1990.

Monroe, Robert B. "101 Years of Television Technology." *SMPTE Journal* 8 (August 1991): 100.

Nachman, Gerald. *Raised on Radio.* Berkeley: University of California Press, 1998.

Nelson, Robin. *TV Drama in Transition: Forms, Values and Cultural Change.* New York: St. Martin's Press, 1997.

Papazian, Ed. *Medium Rare: The Evolution, Workings and Impact of Commercial Television.* New York: Media Dynamics, 1991.

Ritchie, Michael. *Please Stand By: A Prehistory of Television*. Woodstock, NY: Overlook, 1994.

Roman, James. *Love, Light, and a Dream: Television's Past, Present, and Future*. Westport, CT: Praeger, 1996.

Sanow, Eric J. *Encyclopedia of American Police Cars*. Osceola, WI: MBI Publishing Co., 1999.

Schatz, Thomas. *Hollywood Genres: Formulas, Filmmaking and the Studio System*. New York: Random House, 1981.

Spangler, Lynn C. *Television Women from Lucy to Friends: Fifty Years of Sitcoms and Feminism*. Westport, CT: Praeger, 2003.

Staiger, Janet. *Blockbuster TV: Must-See Sitcoms in the Network Era*. New York: New York University Press, 2000.

Stark, Steven D. *Glued to the Set: The 60 Television Shows and Events that Made Us Who We Are Today*. New York: The Free Press, 1997.

Sterling, Christopher H., ed. *Encyclopedia of Radio*. New York: Fitzroy Dearborn, 2004.

Sterling, Christopher H. and John M. Kittross. *Stay Tuned: A Concise History of American Broadcasting*, 3rd ed. Mahwah, NJ: Lawrence Erlbaum Associates, Publishers, 2002.

Sturcken, Frank. *Live Television: The Golden Age of 1946–1958 in New York*. Jefferson, NC: McFarland & Co. 1990.

Tartikoff, Brandon, and Charles Leerhsen. *The Last Great Ride*. New York: Dell Publishing, 1993.

Thompson, Robert J. *Adventures on Prime Time: The Television Progams of Stephen J. Cannell*. New York: Praeger, 1990.

———. *Television's Second Golden Age: From Hill Street Blues to ER*. New York: Continuum, 1996.

Tinker, Grant, and Bud Rukeyser. *Tinker in Television: From General Sarnoff to General Electric*. New York: Simon & Schuster, 1994.

Tropiano, Stephen. *The Prime Time Closet: A History of Gays and Lesbians on TV*. New York: Applause Theatre and Cinema Books, 2002.

Walker, James R., and Douglas A. Ferguson. *The Broadcast Television Industry*. Boston: Allyn and Bacon, 1998.

Wild, David. *The Showrunners*. New York: HarperCollins, 2000.

Wilk, Max. *The Golden Age of Television: Notes from the Survivors*. New York: Dell, 1977.

Wright, Will. *Sixguns & Society: A Structural Study of the Western*. Berkeley: University of California Press, 1997.

Index

About the Authors

BARBARA MOORE is Professor in the College of Communications, University of Tennessee. She co-authored the textbook *Radio, TV, and Cable Programming* (Iowa State University Press, 1994).

MARVIN R. BENSMAN is Professor at the University of Memphis, a member of the board of the Broadcast Education Association, and the author of *The Beginning of Broadcast Regulation in the 20th Century* (MacFarland, 2000).

JIM VAN DYKE teaches at Marian College in Milwaukee, and has published television criticism in various journals.

DATE DUE

DEMCO, INC. 38-2931